WHERE I
COME FROM

Aarón in chef's attire, 1980s, New York City

WHERE I COME FROM

Life Lessons from a

Latino Chef

AARÓN SÁNCHEZ

WITH STEF FERRARI

ABRAMS PRESS, NEW YORK

Library of Congress Control Number: 2018958855

ISBN: 978-1-4197-3802-9
eISBN: 978-1-68335-679-0
B&N Edition ISBN: 978-1-4197-4455-6

Printed and bound in the United States
10 9 8 7 6 5 4 3 2 1

The material contained in this book is presented only for informational and artistic purposes. In the interest of maintaining the privacy of the individuals whose stories are discussed herein, some names and other identifying characteristics have been changed.

Abrams books are available at special discounts when purchased in quantity for premiums and promotions as well as fundraising or educational use. Special editions can also be created to specification. For details, contact specialsales@abramsbooks.com or the address below.

Abrams Press® is a registered trademark of Harry N. Abrams, Inc.

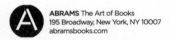

ABRAMS The Art of Books
195 Broadway, New York, NY 10007
abramsbooks.com

TO MY SON, YUMA,

MY LATE FATHER, ADOLFO,

AND MY MOTHER, ZARELA

*Zarela cooking with Aarón and Rodrigo in their first
New York apartment, on the Upper West Side, mid to late 1980s*

CONTENTS

CONTENTS

INTRODUCTION

Cinnamon. Chocolate. Chile. I'd tasted them hundreds, thousands of times. But never had these flavors seemed so profound as they did to me one night long ago in a Oaxacan cemetery. So grounding to the world around me. To the *earth*.

The year was 2000, the start of the new millennium, and I was twenty-four years old. Mexico was in the throes of its annual Day of the Dead celebration—the Día de los Muertos—when I arrived. It was fall, but in Oaxaca the temperature can still climb to nearly 80 degrees during the day, and everywhere you turn are the blindingly vibrant colors of a warmer season. Bold sugar skulls and folks in skeleton costumes were a stark contrast to the somber faces and black shrouds I'd been told, growing up in the States, were more suitable for anything related to death.

But this was Mexico, where color defines the culture—from the characters that populate the city streets and countryside, to building facades and diverse natural landscapes, to the language and choice turns of phrase. And the food. Always the food. Rusty, dried *guajillo* peppers. Verdant sprigs of curled cilantro. Flavors that take days to develop, layered with wildly complex blends of spices and ingredients, techniques that take years to master, so that every dish pops and dances on the palate. There is nothing about the food of Mexico that is dull or muted.

Cinnamon. Chocolate. Chile. *Earth.*

There comes a moment when cultural and personal identity collide. When *who* you are ceases to be exclusive of, or regardless of, *what* you are and where you come from. When you stop trying to rebel against being typecast or stereotyped, and start to feel an ancient homing system seizing at something inside you that you never knew existed. Something in your bones, calling out to the earth or the cosmos, or to other human beings cut from the same cloth. Living or dead. Past or present. Even future.

Food is the purest reflection of the Mexican people. As a bicultural Mexican American kid, I had been exposed to that sensibility, but I was about to find out, in the midst of the chaotic celebration, exactly what being Mexican was really all about.

* * *

We had flown in that fall to film a new show, *Taste of Mexico*, for Food Network. It was a wild experience, a no-holds-barred culinary adventure, just me and a production crew eating our way through the country my ancestors come from, getting a crash course in culture and cuisine. For as much as I saw, cooked, and tasted, though, there was one thing I was really hungry to get my hands on from the minute we landed: traditional *mole*. It's become a sort of unofficial national dish of Mexico, and today versions of it appear on Mexican restaurant menus from San Diego to South Dakota.

But the canon of mole variations is so much more vast than most diners recognize. It can be made from almonds or pumpkin seeds. It can be yellow or green or red or pitch black. There are legends about its invention, one tale including nuns, another involving an Aztec king. Regardless, the constant is the sauce's complexity. Some versions use thirty or more ingredients, the spices and peppers carefully toasted and ground together, most often by hand, in a *molcajete*—a sort of Mesoamerican mortar and pestle. I'd made it before and tasted it in a ton of places, including my mom's kitchen, but I was looking to find the inspiration for all those interpretations. Two regions lay claim to creating mole sauce, one being Puebla. The other was the final destination on our production schedule—Oaxaca.

Mole is a major part of the Día de los Muertos holiday. For the show, we planned to visit a cemetery where, after dark, families congregate around gravesites to eat and dance and commune with the dead. It's an unbelievable scene, and we were going to capture the procession, the people, and the custom in full swing. It was all sounding super exciting, but of course, above all, I couldn't wait for the food.

Before we could begin our own tasting tour of the celebration, we had to actually get there. We were a small crew, and when we arrived in our van,

we were stopped and told no vehicles were allowed. The cemetery was at the top of a massive hill, and now we'd have to park about a mile away and haul our gear up this impossible incline. I'd never shot at night before that trip. The lighting rigs were extensive, and—I was learning—damn heavy. We were rounding out weeks of travel, and everyone was exhausted and frustrated by this new development. In those early days of on-location shoots, I realized enthusiasm can only carry you so far when you're running on fumes, and I was starting to fantasize about my bed back in New York.

But then, as we were scaling the path, alongside families in costume, carrying flowers and candy and bottles of mezcal, the sun set, and from a distance we could see the revelers. Candles encircling the cemetery gave the summit a haloed appearance. It was a beacon, totally aglow against the inky Mexican sky. Maybe it was the cool air that had come along with dusk, or maybe it was the spirits being summoned from their own grueling paths passing through us, but I had chills. If those souls could make the journey from *mictlan*—the Aztec beyond, a sort of spiritual in-between—I could make it through this fucking climb.

When we finally arrived at the peak, the party was well underway. The path was lit with more candles to guide us, but we really didn't need them. We easily could have followed our senses—the aromas of *masa* cooking on the *comal* and warming cinnamon from spiced hot chocolate, caramelized sweet fruits candied in syrups, piquant peppers, and smoke and sizzle—all emanating from about a dozen different food stalls that lined the procession path on either side. Everywhere we turned folks were set up, serving juices and tequila, making tacos, sharing sweets, eating, and drinking.

We were rejuvenated by the otherworldly energy of the place. We set up and began making our way through the scene, documenting as we went along. We were trying a little bit of everything, and I was being handed a glass of tequila when a fifty-gallon drum caught my eye. It was hollowed out and situated over an open fire. Inside, corn cobs were waiting to become *esquites*—a traditional Mexican street food.

I approached and watched as people in front of us were served. The old man at the drum looked like he was about 120 years old, and he was sweating in the night, pulling up ear after ear upon request. With fingers that looked

as if they'd never been clean of the soot that covered them now, he pulled off some ninja move barely visible to the naked eye. He impaled cobs on a convenient stick, slathered each with *crema*, tons of *cotija* cheese, and chile, and passed them off into hungry crowds.

When I finally had mine in hand, at first I made an attempt to be civilized. This was for television, after all. But in evaluating ways to attack the thing, I realized there was no earthly way to be delicate about it. *Fuck it*, I thought, and dove in for a massive bite—and I was rewarded. Smoky, charred kernels detonated with sweetness underneath this rich, creamy, salty, spicy coating. It was transcendent. It was visceral. My nose ran and my face was covered in cream and char. And I couldn't have been happier. As a trained chef, I could tell the camera this had everything a dish needed from a technical perspective—acid, heat, salt, fat, sweetness, texture—even though it wasn't prepared by some hotshot in a New York City kitchen. But as a human being, I knew there was no way to describe its perfection and really do it justice.

Looking around at the celebration, I could see why someone would come back from the dead—and after that corn, I could have died a happy man. But I still had unfinished business: my mole. And it wasn't hard to find. I followed the path until I came to a Zapotec woman, and before her was a big, beautiful ceramic pot with a deeply colored paste percolating within. The Zapotec is a matriarchal society, led by strong women who manage everything from the economy to the cooking. Having been raised by a fierce Mexican mother, I was entirely at home with the archetype. But there was something a little unsettling about the way this particular woman looked at me when I approached her. It was as if she could sense I was searching for something—like she could actually see past the cameras and the lights, straight into my soul.

She had been making tortillas with handfuls of fresh masa she'd pressed into the scorching *comal*. Slowly, ceremonially, she reached for one. Wordlessly, she dipped it directly into the mole and handed it to me, past the other partiers patiently queuing up for their turn. I took the tortilla and waited for a moment, wondering where the rest of it was. Where was the chicken thigh? Where was the substance?

She must have sensed my hesitation. Without speaking, she indicated for me to eat it. As if to say, *No, baby—this is the essence right here. This is Mexico, right in your hands.* What followed when I finally took her silent instruction was nothing less than an epiphany. It was an explosion of flavor. It was chocolatey and bitter, fragrant from a symphony of different spices. There was a little bit of heat, and then it teetered on the edge of sweetness, before pulling back at the last minute. It was the most incredible sensation of flavors. I never knew food could be so balanced and deeply layered. So complex. So *profound.*

When I looked at her, she smiled softly and nodded. I couldn't find the right words—not in English or Spanish—but I tried to communicate. *I get it now,* I nodded in return. *This is it.*

This is Mexico. It is ingenuity and a certain kind of perfection born from resourcefulness, care, and keen awareness. It is a masterful layering—of thousands of years of influences, of ingredients both indigenous and introduced from other cultures—all folded into each bite. Flavor that isn't just about raw materials, but about feeling. It caused a paradigm shift inside me, and cameras be damned, it brought tears to my eyes.

* * *

That trip marked a lot of firsts for me. It was also the first time I filmed on location. Chef Alex García and I had cohosted a series called *Melting Pot* back in Food Network's early days; he was Cuban and I was Mexican, so we had this great thing going with Latin recipes. We had an easy rapport after working together over the years in restaurants, so when we were approached to tag-team a cultural deep dive into Mexico, it seemed like the perfect scenario. The purpose was to highlight the flavors of regional Mexican cooking, so each of us would tackle three separate regions. For the show, designers created fun little animated icons of us traversing our respective territories, and eventually we'd meet up in the middle.

My itinerary started with Mexico City. I'd been to Mexico plenty of times, first as a kid with my dad, and then as a punk teenager who liked to sneak

across the border with my older cousin to find—and cause—a little trouble. But this was new territory. Not only in terms of place (most of my time had been spent in Juárez, a twenty-minute skip from my Texas hometown of El Paso), but personally. I was older. I was more thoughtful. And most importantly, I was on the clock. Food Network was still pretty new, and no one could have dreamed what the power of food TV would become back in those days. I had no idea how important television was going to be for my career, but I still didn't want to fuck it up.

I can't imagine a more chaotic setting for my first on-location shoot than the crush of the city's center. I'd been on TV for a few years, but this was a totally different animal than the so-called stand-and-stir kind of shoot I was used to. When I got the call, my first instinct was to say, absolutely—*yes*. My second was to freak out a little. I was extremely nervous; I had no idea what it was going to be like to be out in the wild. There were so many questions. Will I be reading lines? Is there going to be a script? Am I going to be acting? Who will I be shooting with? And, of course, am I going to be any fucking good at this?

One of the first scenes we wanted to get in the can was to show the street life of one of the most densely populated cities in the world. The idea was to get a long shot of me walking through the city from a distance, so the camera could capture the scope of the crowd. It was an autumn morning, still crisp and temperate, but performance anxiety made me feel like a piece of *pollo* left under a heat lamp. I was mic'd up and sweating my face off. My job was to explain what was happening around me, and also to give some context to viewers about the city with facts and figures and statistics. I was trying to connect with a camera about five hundred yards away, but even without distraction it would have been a challenge to navigate the abundance of shopping and bartering and bustling around me. And I had to do it all while on the move, out of the controlled safety of the studio I was so accustomed to. I'd stayed up late the night before, memorizing my lines, but in the moment I worried I might have sudden amnesia.

We started rolling, and I launched into it, with as much joviality as I could muster.

"Hi, I'm Aarón Sánchez, and we're coming to you from Mexico City! The capital is home to . . ."

People around me stopped to stare at this *loco* dude speaking accented English into the ether, as if to no one. It took everything in me not to address their stares, or to at least give a smile and let them know I wasn't a total whack job. I'd shot hundreds of hours in my career before that moment, but nothing prepared me for how difficult it was.

Holy shit, I thought when we finally cut. *This is what it takes.*

But somehow, I pulled it off. I was thrilled when we wrapped that morning and high on adrenaline, but relief was fleeting. We were just getting started. The itinerary was grueling: we'd spend three or four days in each region, plus a day of travel on both ends. Call times were early and we shot late into the nights. Every morning, I was made up and the producers would roll me through the agenda. We're going to hit this market. We're going to eat at that restaurant. You're going to talk about this dish. Some shots of you walking on the street. Some shots of you coming out of your hotel. It was meticulously planned and scouted for the most authentic experiences, but frankly they could have taken me to a bull castration and I would have been up for it.

Beyond trying to keep up with the task at hand, I had a lot on my mind. My own restaurant back in New York, Paladar, was still very new, and I'd recently signed my first cookbook contract. Outwardly, I was a celebrated chef, a competent business owner and TV personality, and with Food Network beginning to expand its reach, my star was definitely on the rise whether or not I knew or was ready for it.

But on the inside, I was starting to realize maybe I didn't have it all quite so locked up. If that first day of filming was an indication, I had a long way to go before I could call myself a television expert.

For better or worse, I didn't have a whole lot of time to worry. When I wasn't terrified about nailing my on-screen performance or trying to stay in touch with my staff back home, I was totally lost in the excitement of it all. I was learning *so* much. Not only about making television, but about my culture and myself—something that has become a major theme in my life over the

nearly two decades since. TV has been a source of income, of promotion, of branding—a big part of my career, no question. But it has also been an indispensable vehicle for me to learn about the world. In being a conduit to teach viewers, I've had so many of my own mind-expanding experiences. That trip was just the beginning.

We traveled all around Mexico during those weeks, and I soaked it all up. I learned about the food, of course, but also the customs, the people, and the country itself as a deeply textured mosaic of historical influences. I could see the Spanish architecture and the colors of the royal guard—the red and blue everywhere—and I started to understand the Spanish conquest and its impact on the way people prepare their meals today.

Above all, I started to grasp the amazing diversity of Mexican cuisine, and how and why it varied from region to region. I met tons of home cooks, and for the first time, I encountered true experts on food. Before then, a culinary school degree, or a seasoned chef who could execute every technique in the book, was my bar for epicurean authority. But this was a whole new level—people who dedicated themselves to understanding the intricacies and intersection of history, culture, and eating. I decided then that this was what I wanted to do. To become extremely good at my craft, but to also understand food in a deeper way, to know where it comes from and what it means in a broader context. The traditions and customs. The mindset and purpose behind a plate of food.

Día de los Muertos was a major lesson in that relationship between food and cultural philosophy. Growing up, I was aware of the celebration, and we observed it at home and in my mom's restaurant—it was a good reason for her to change things up, bring in some cool dishes and traditions. But to experience it in Mexico is something else entirely, and I understood the idea in a much more profound way. I finally grasped why in Mexican culture, death is not a somber topic. As far back as the Aztec civilization, there was an acceptance of dying as a natural part of the life cycle. You wake up, you make your way through your day, you go to sleep. You are born, you make your way through life, you are laid to rest. It's important not to linger in grief. Some people actually fear their dearly departed would take offense to such

mourning. Others are more concerned that sadness could cause more logistical problems—a river of tears would make a perilous and slippery journey for spirits crossing into unfamiliar territory. (Mexican people are nothing if not pragmatists, even in their mythologies.) But they also believe that death isn't the last time they'll get to interact with their lost loved ones, as long as they remain in their memories. So, each fall, a special three-day ceremony is held to invite them back to the living world and keep that memory alive. This is Día de los Muertos. And since no Mexican is ever okay with missing out on a *fiesta*, rousing the dead from eternal slumber to come party with their people seems perfectly natural.

In homes, altars called *ofrendas* are built to honor the dead. At my restaurant in New Orleans, Johnny Sánchez, we construct a brilliant *ofrenda* every year, in an effort to share a little bit of Mexican culture with our guests along with the food. Traditionally, it's decorated with photos and personal effects, candles, statues, and incense. Corn kernels and gold marigold petals are sprinkled along a path to a family's front door, a breadcrumb trail for souls to follow from *mictlan* back home, where families leave their doors open for easy entry. The first day is for the *angelitos*, or the spirits of children. The second is dedicated to deceased adults. People host huge gatherings and play games. There are parades and processions, prayers and offerings. Loved ones sit around and tell stories and anecdotes about the people who have left their worldly posts. It's about sharing a drink and a laugh, and remembering loved ones as they were in life.

And just as in celebrations among the living, above all, there's food. In Mexico, cooking for someone is the ultimate gesture of love, so what better way to draw your brother back from the dead than with his favorite earthly delights? Each home is a little different, because offerings are tailor-made for the spirit they're trying to attract. But *tamales* and *tortillas* and pillowy, eggy *pan de muerto* are traditional, and there are always tons of confections. Sweet fruits and cookies and candied pumpkin, cups of *atole*—a drink that's a little like hot chocolate, but spiced and thickened with *masa*—and of course, those iconic sugar skulls now so popular even in American culture. To see families gathered around plates of *mole poblano*, on porches decorated with

multicolored *papel picados* (confetti), to hear the sounds of their music and laughter in this celebration of death, is the strongest proof that Mexican culture is so vibrantly full of *life*.

When I was thirteen years old, living in New York City with my mom and my brother, my dad died back in our hometown of El Paso, Texas. Somehow this made Día de los Muertos even more mysterious to me. Losing him was such a crushing blow, so exquisitely painful every day, that I couldn't possibly understand how anyone would want to celebrate such loss. I grew almost resentful of the practice, as if that would be no way to honor the man I so desperately missed and wished were still on earth with me, not on some *ofrenda* or in a grave surrounded by dancing and dining on tacos and corn.

But that day in the Oaxacan cemetery, watching everyone around me remember the people they'd lost, I realized it wasn't at all a disrespect of the dead. On the contrary, these parties were thrown out of respect for the lost souls' memories by celebrating their lives. I considered the funeral traditions of the United States, in which tears and sober silences, and the utmost levels of decorum, are imposed on people at their most vulnerable. In contrast it seemed totally inadequate.

For more than a decade, I was angry every day: that my dad had been taken from me, that he wasn't going to walk through the door, that he was lost and gone forever. But this put my dad's death in perspective in a totally new way. He wasn't gone. He was there with us, in that cemetery. And he was conjured every time I recalled riding around in his car, or got a whiff of his cologne, or imagined serving him a dish I thought he'd have enjoyed. If I looked at his death the way my bereaved Mexican brethren viewed the passing of their loved ones, he was always going to be accessible to me, as long as I kept on calling him to mind. For the first time, I got it. In that cemetery, while we roused the long-since laid to rest with a raucous party, I finally felt a little peace.

The experience also instilled in me a new appreciation for my Mexican heritage. I felt so proud to know that I was a part of this culture, these people who had found a way to keep their spirits up while also keeping the memories of their loved ones alive. It felt like such a healthy, novel way to approach death, which had been such a torturous, taboo subject for so much of my

life. Of course, everyone must find their own way to grapple with grief. But Día de los Muertos resonated with me so much more than the American way of grieving, and it was perhaps one of the first things that made me feel truly Mexican in my heart.

That trip—the food I tasted, the places I saw, the ceremony of Día de los Muertos—taught me a lot about myself, and about ancestors who have endured so much but refuse to be victims of suffering. They cling to family and community. They search for joy even in the face of grief; they bring unimaginable color to the most grim circumstances, create culinary masterpieces from the humblest of ingredients. History has taught them that they have no way of knowing what tomorrow will bring, so for a people who have seen such pain, a celebration isn't just a chance to party. A meal isn't just sustenance. The pursuit of happiness isn't recreational; it's a survival strategy.

* * *

Being on location gave us a chance to capture Mexican life in a way we could never have conveyed in a studio, cooking mole or making *pan dulce*. I realized then that there was something incredible about making television in this way. My shows had always been planned down to the last detail; I knew what I was going to make and had a general idea of how I'd explain it to home cooks. But this was totally authentic. I was on camera, having real experiences and learning about customs in real time. I felt like my limited experience with Día de los Muertos didn't give me anywhere near the base of knowledge I'd have needed to competently host a show on it. Here I was, learning right along with the audience—every reaction genuine, because it was happening in that moment.

It was that trip, and that moment in the cemetery, that set off my formal education in Mexican cuisine. I decided then that if I was diligent and curious and respectful, maybe I could do justice to the food I loved so much. Prior to *Taste of Mexico*, my food was never what you would consider Mexican. I cooked with pan-Latino flavors and preparations, but I never had the confidence to tackle Mexican food. But I realized then that cooking isn't just

about technique and ingredients—it's about an understanding of people, heritage, culture, and connections. That was the added dimension that turned something you could say tasted good into an experience that could speak to the soul. It was a moment when I realized that the individual is stronger as a part of the whole. A spice to a sauce. A person to a people. Maybe everyone has a moment like that. I happened to have mine on television.

Chile. Chocolate. Cinnamon. *Earth*—and a connection to it. To the ingredients. To people and culture.

My entire life has been about searching for connection—through food, TV, and conversations. But being immersed in Mexican culture for that month put me in touch with a part of myself I didn't know existed. It taught me about something deep and inexplicable and ancient and soulful. Something that connected me not only to family, but to a cultural identity. And it taught me that more than anything, I had a whole lot more to learn. Now I understood why my mom wanted to share this food with the world when she opened her restaurant. Why it was so important to her. Why it would become so important to me. I knew the food that I cooked would never be the same. I would never be the same.

When we're young, we take on this obsessive search for individuality, and being categorized feels like a threat to our very soul. It's all about standing alone and standing out, blazing our own trail. Being our own person. But then suddenly, in the right moment, the idea that we might be a part of something so much bigger than ourselves becomes inspiring. Humbling. Comforting. It becomes an asset, not a creative liability. It's a moment that will strip you of ego and replace youthful hubris with worldly awe.

It's no surprise that many people arrive at a moment like this a little later in life, when the arrogance of youth disrupting that instinctual beacon has quieted down a bit. But it requires more than just the suspension of ego; it usually means a change of mindset, setting, or circumstance. It means laying yourself at the mercy of something unfamiliar, and accepting that some exchanges take place on another plane, without words or typical transaction. It can be ethereal. Supernatural. For me, it came almost from beyond the grave.

Twenty years later, I can still taste that Zapotec woman's mole. The sweetness of her still-warm tortilla, the depth of the dark fruit and chocolate,

the warmth of her spices. I wonder about her now—if she's still with us, or if she's a photo on someone's *ofrenda*, called back to the celebration every autumn by her own family. Her legacy may have been a humble one. No food magazines would have commemorated her passing. But in that simple act, she found a permanent foothold in my consciousness. Every batch of mole I have made since then has a little bit of her memory layered in, like so many spices I remember from her sauce. Her presence lives through food for new generations, whether or not the people who come to my restaurant ever visit Oaxaca, whether or not they appreciate the depth of Mexican culture and how it has enriched their own lives. That is the subversiveness, the power, and the beauty of food.

The trip also yielded some more practical results, in establishing me as a chef who could pull off travel television. That changed the course of my career, which would go on to be largely travel-based shows. And it proved to me that there was more to TV than mindless entertainment. After years of telling people how to cook, I realized I could also use the medium as a way to share culture, to teach and reach people. It made me understand that my responsibility as a Latino with a platform was about a lot more than just sharing recipes for *chile rellenos*.

Before we left Oaxaca, we had to shoot a final scene that would give context to the event. My part of the storyline started with a morning in Mexico City, a place where you could go to see every kind of Mexican food, people from all walks of life in a bustling metropolis. It culminated under the Oaxacan moonlight, in a spiritual element.

I knelt before a grave, illuminated by candles and covered with golden marigold petals. I thought of my father. I put my palms in the soil. Then I looked to the camera and explained. "In Mexico," I said, "death is not somber; it's a celebration when people pass. This is a transfer of energy, this is just the next step." I'd later watch the scene, myself on one knee on the earth, with candles lighting up the night. It was both poignant and personal, and it could not have been more real. "This is not the end," I told viewers. "This is only the beginning."

CHAPTER ONE

EL PASO TO NEW YORK CITY

I'll never forget the first time I saw the city.

It was after dark when I opened my eyes, and I had to adjust to the fact that I was waking up to a night sky. I was totally disoriented—not just by the time of day, but by my surroundings. I'd been in the back of my mom's catering van tons of times, but it still took a few minutes for me to remember exactly where I was—and why being there this time was so different from the rest.

It was a rickety, white Econoline with the words "Zarela's Catering" splashed across the side in green and red paint. It had the permanent, piquant aroma of chiles and *guisados*—the super-savory and comforting traditional Mexican braises that my mom served at so many of her catering gigs. I loved those smells, and I loved that piece-of-shit van. When she first bought it, it might as well have been a stretch limo. To me as a kid, it seemed gigantic—even luxurious. But most importantly, it was always packed full of my mom's most delicious food. *Gorditas* filled with her signature *salpicón de huachinango*—a red snapper hash made with fresh jalapeños and tomatoes, perfumed with a blend of cinnamon, cloves, and cumin. Spicy *macarrones con salsa poblana*—a buttery, cheesy pasta dish that was about as close to Italian food as I had ever seen in those days—and grilled meats of all kinds, served with rich and classic *rajas con crema*—roasted poblanos. It was a wonderland of her greatest culinary hits.

I loved to tag along to her different jobs and help out with whatever I could. My sister, Marissa—my father's daughter from his first marriage—would come and help with the serving. I couldn't carry much in those days, but I thought I was being a big help, carting jars of chile-spiked *salsa de cilantro* or hotel pans layered down with fresh tortillas for her guests to

1

enjoy. I also always had the privilege and super-critical task of packing the cookies. They were good times, and I always tried my best. I did a lot of work in that van—and I stole a *lot* of snacks. But one thing I hadn't done up until that point was sleep in it. And it definitely never had the couch in the back that I was sitting on when I woke up that night.

The passenger side of the front seat was papered with Rand McNally maps, a few days earlier set open to southeastern US routes and now creased to display northern states so she could follow along (there was no Google Maps back then). My twin brother, Rodrigo, was passed out next to me. I figured I must've fallen asleep somewhere in Virginia—a state that felt never-ending. We were pretty tuckered out from singing along to endless rounds of Johnny Cash and Hank Williams, and all the other classic country tunes Mom was blasting and belting out through the first few states of our journey. Her favorite was Rockin' Sydney's "Don't Mess with My Toot Toot," which she played on repeat, tapping the steering wheel, just because it cracked us up to hear her sing it. She knew she had two pretty terrified six-year-old boys in the back seat—two boys who had only ever seen their Texas hometown and had absolutely no concept of the faraway land of New York City she told them they were moving to. She made it her mission not only to deliver us safely, but in good spirits.

Before we left El Paso, and our tiny apartment on the west side of town, she tried to prepare us for the road ahead. "Boys, this is going to be a *big* adventure," she said. "I have an amazing opportunity, and the three of us are going to start something totally new." She promised we would love it. In the weeks leading up to the trip, she told us all sorts of stories about how magical the city was, and how lucky we'd be to live there.

I wasn't so sure about this New York place, but while she was busy packing up the last of our things the morning we left, I stole a peek at the *really* important stuff. It was clear this was a special trip, because inside the cooler she'd filled for the road were all my brother's and my favorite snacks. *Flautas* and *picadillo dulce* tacos, *albóndigas*, and her homemade tortilla chips with tomatillo salsa. I didn't know where we were going, but I was sure as hell that I was going to enjoy getting there.

But then the time came to actually take off. At that age, it was nearly impossible for me to really grasp what was happening. We'd spent the weekend with my dad, and the morning we were to leave town, we had to say our good-byes to him and the rest of our relatives. We had a big, tight family, and it wasn't out of the ordinary for all of us to spend time together, but I could tell by the sober faces that this was something different.

"Don't worry, I'll see you in just a few months," my dad said, squatting to meet me and looking from beneath his worn cowboy hat in the springtime Texas sun. My parents had already worked out an arrangement: Rodrigo and I would fly down and spend summers with him. I idolized my father, and even though my folks had already been split up for a few years and we weren't living together, the idea of not being able to see him on a regular basis was a concept I couldn't quite wrap my head around—and I didn't want to.

He told me to take care of myself. He told me he loved us and would see us soon. "This is going to be a good thing for you boys and your mom—don't think of it as something scary," he tried to reassure us.

Looking back now as a father myself, I can't imagine how he managed words of support, when I'm sure my dad—who absolutely adored his kids—didn't want to let us go. But he tried to impress on us that this was important to the family, and he knew I always wanted to be a man like him. He hugged Rodrigo and me, and a few minutes later we were dropped off at my mom's. We climbed into the van, which was fixed up with a trailer on the back, got settled on the couch, and watched the only home we'd ever known disappear in the rear window of the old Ford.

The distress of leaving was quickly replaced by the excitement of the unknown. Maybe it was adrenaline—or maybe just that I was a six-year-old without the foresight to be too concerned about where we'd been or where we were going—but I thought it was amazing to see the country from the road. My mom had done the research ahead of time so we would find iconic regional foods along the way. First, we trucked through our own massive state, sampling slabs of Texas toast the size of my head, slathered with butter, rubbed with sweet roasted garlic, and broiled to golden, crispy perfection. We stopped in St. Louis, where I ripped into my first rack of baby-back

barbecue ribs—the leathery, smoky bark so black it was almost blue. In the Carolinas, it was chowchow and pralines. When we got up north and passed through Amish Country, Rodrigo and I filled up on fresh apple butter while my mom browsed antique shops and promised us that someday, when we had the cash, we'd come back for that furniture. It was my first real taste of the world, not to mention its many foods, and my first time traveling. I was totally enamored by it. In fact, I loved the road so much, I almost forgot where we were headed.

Making our way along those interstates, I also witnessed for the first time the power of food, sheer kindness, and a genuinely hospitable spirit to connect with people. Mom was the kind of woman who was a hit no matter where she went—even in the middle of nowhere. All along the journey, we'd run into these big, tough-looking trucker dudes at gas stations and rest stops. I thought they were scary as hell, but not my mom. She made fast friends every time. "You want to know how to make *enchiladas*?" she'd ask them. These people were from all over the country; a lot of them had probably never had a real enchilada or anything even close to it, and they certainly weren't used to having a square meal. So she shared her recipes, and in giving them the ins and outs of a simple Mexican dish, she gave each of them a little of herself. It was always a sight, to see my little Mexican mother talking to some big, bearded Southerner about the finer points of broiling chile rellenos, but most of these guys were family men far from home, and they were deeply appreciative. A lot of times, knowing she was a single mother, they took it upon themselves to look after us, sort of our truck stop guardian angels.

The trip took four days. Rodrigo and I were restless kids—and these were the times before TV screens were mounted into headrests. There were no iPads to keep us occupied or babysit us for my mom's relief. But when we weren't eating or bickering or generally driving her bonkers, we tried to make our own fun. We played little travel-sized board games and magnetic checkers. We read. We slept a lot. We made a sport out of ticking off license plates from different states, counting potholes, that sort of thing. I spent a lot of time looking out the window, imagining where the other cars were

coming from or where they were going, how long their journeys were, and whether they'd been to this magical land of New York City. And my mom told tons of stories. She made us feel warm and secure, at a time when she was probably pretty terrified herself.

The journey was a total eye opener for me, and while we were still crossing through, living in between worlds, it felt a little like a daydream. But what I saw when I woke up—crossing the George Washington Bridge and seeing those big-city lights—it was like a smelling salt snapped everything back into focus. I could finally put a visual to what my mom had been talking about all that time. It was so big and foreign, and all I could think was, "Wow. This is *real*." I felt like an explorer at the start of an exhilarating adventure. It was exciting and new. And it was really, really scary.

* * *

I don't know what was going through my mom's head at the time that we made the trip, but I know she had to be scared, too. She was taking a major leap of faith—leaving the safety and comfort of our home in Texas where she was surrounded by family—to set up shop in one of the biggest, most hectic and intimidating cities in the world, with two kids in tow and nothing but a gut feeling that she was somehow guiding us to a better life.

Things had been tough for us back home since my parents split a few years before. Mom was a social worker for the Texas Department of Human Resources in El Paso. She had emigrated from Chihuahua in 1971 and married my father after she lost her own dad in 1974. Her dad really influenced her in the kitchen—they experimented together a lot. She would say that after my grandpa was gone, the memories of their time together were a big part of what kept her inspired all those years.

I'll always remember how hard Mom worked. When she came home at the end of the day to cook for my brother and me, she looked like she'd run a marathon (being a single mom to twin boys and keeping up with a full-time job was probably not far off). The day job helped pay the bills, but it definitely wasn't a passion. She was running a catering business on the side

just to supplement her income, mostly doing gigs servicing medical offices in town for their lunch breaks or meetings. But little by little, she began to build up her clientele, and started to find herself really falling in love with the food business.

In her spare time, she looked for recipes everywhere, and she got them from everyone who would give them up. She cooked from stacks of *Gourmet* magazine that I flipped through when she wasn't poring over them and dog-earing pages to revisit. She read and reread all the cookbooks she could get her hands on. She didn't limit her education to strictly Mexican food, either. I remember some wild Middle Eastern experiments with pomegranates and eggplant, unheard-of Chinese foods and exotic Indian dishes; she also tinkered with techniques, like corning beef. Looking back, it was pretty advanced stuff for the time. These weren't cuisines one just found on any street corner in rural Texas—or really anywhere in the 1970s and '80s, for that matter.

She knew traveling would help build up her repertoire, so she started journeying to new places whenever time and budget allowed. She wanted to get serious about cooking, and to find a way to get ahead, not just get by. In 1981, when I was five years old, she and my grandma—an incredible and dedicated cook in her own right—planned a pilgrimage to New Orleans. The trip was structured around a lineup of cooking classes, but the itinerary ended up falling through at the last minute. They felt defeated, but still wanted to make the most of the trip. My grandmother suggested they eat their way around town and take notes, so they decided to splurge on a meal at a restaurant that had become legend—K-Paul's.

Mom still talks about that dinner—the sticky chicken she had, the smells of simmering gumbo and powerful creole seasonings, the sound of andouille sausage and blackened swordfish sizzling in cast-iron skillets. It had such soul, and the flavors were unlike any food she'd tasted before. My grandma encouraged her to introduce herself to the chef, a man who had become a culinary kingpin at a time when such a thing didn't really exist yet—Chef Paul Prudhomme.

She'd only intended to say hello, thank him for the wonderful meal, and maybe ask for a tip or two. But, as I would come to know very personally

in my own life and experiences with him, Chef Paul was such a warm and caring human being, it was in his nature to want to know more about this young woman who'd approached him. Chef Paul was as generous and genuine as the New Orleans summer days were sweltering—and so after that very meal, a young Zarela Martinez found herself sharing her story with one of the world's most famous culinary figures. She was a young, single mom—bonkers about food, ambitious, and full of fire for her craft.

Chef Paul hadn't known my mom more than a few minutes when he made an offer that would change her life forever. He asked her to stay in town for a few days and work with him—he'd teach her some of his secrets, and in exchange, he asked that she share a few Mexican recipes. At the time, the only people eating Mexican food were Mexicans—and there were definitely no go-to cookbooks or tools for someone who might've been interested in the cuisine. To Chef Paul, who had the foresight to understand the food of Mexico had serious potential on the global culinary stage, my mom was an invaluable source of knowledge and information. They had a deal.

After she came home, Mom kept in touch with Chef Paul. A month later, a major food event was being planned in New York City—the *Maîtres Cuisiniers de France* at Tavern on the Green. It was to be an introduction to American food, attended by more than two hundred French chefs. Cooks from all over the country were coming to represent their regional cuisines and show off our collective national palate. The New York food elite looked to Chef Paul for an opinion on who might be able to cook up the Mexican food they felt would best represent Southern states. He had just the cook in mind.

"Listen, Zarela," Chef Paul said when he called my mom. "I need help pulling this thing off." He invited her to come with him to New York City. To say she was intimidated by the offer was an understatement; other than those couple of days at K-Paul's, she hadn't cooked for any critics tougher than her own kids and the few doctors that ordered her *frijoles* for their Friday office lunches. But Mom's philosophy was always that if she worked hard, studied, and prepared diligently, she could figure anything out. She would never, ever let a little something like fear meddle with opportunity.

A few days later, she packed her bags and headed for the city—and she was never sorry she did. The event was like a culinary coming-out party. Mom

cooked for an elite crowd, was interviewed by top food writers, and instantly became a fixture in the city's dining scene (and by extension, the national one). In an article published that year, the famous *New York Times* food critic Craig Claiborne explained, "We also wanted to have Mexican-style food from Texas. When we canvassed our contacts for the best cook of the region, we were told that person was, hands down, Zarela Martinez-Gabilondo." He went on to rave about her cooking and later made a referral that would lead to her cooking for President Reagan. Suddenly, food was opening up more than just the doors to the old Econoline.

She started traveling to New York regularly, leaving Rodrigo and me back in Texas. We had enough family around to keep us busy and looked after when she was away—all that really mattered to us—but we could never have imagined the importance of the work she was doing. Our mother was setting an example for working, creative women that in hindsight was truly trailblazing. She was out there, refining her own cooking and defining Mexican food, demonstrating how dynamic it could actually be to hungry new audiences. Because there was so little understanding of the cuisine, my mom realized she possessed something powerful that she could share with the world. She also knew that in El Paso, the community wouldn't find Mexican food particularly compelling—it was too commonplace, too available. Everyone in town was bicultural. They all had their own secret family recipe for tomatillo salsa or *carne asada* (and were all ready to have a throw-down over whose was best). So she believed branching out would be key to her success.

After a number of trips to New York for various events, Mom saw the city as the perfect place to test her theory. She'd been busy building a name for herself, and people were responding in a big way. Now she knew the restaurant scene. She knew the right people. She knew that no one in New York was giving Mexican cuisine the treatment it deserved, and that no one was meeting the demand for it that people were demonstrating when she cooked for them. She knew what she needed to do, and not long after her first fateful meeting with Chef Paul, we were bouncing along the interstate on that couch, en route to the Upper West Side.

* * *

We moved into a duplex on Eighty-Fourth Street. Our unit was an airy apartment on the second floor. It had a long dining room and a staircase that emptied into a backyard. The kitchen was typical 1980s decor—a study in pastels—and my favorite part was downstairs, where a bunk bed waited for Rodrigo and me. The city was like nowhere I'd ever been, but even though we'd arrived, we were far from settled. In El Paso, we had tons of family around at all times. In New York, my mom was so busy hustling that we didn't see a lot of her. It would be a full year before she had steady work, which stressed her enormously. I figured out later on that there were financial issues, but she managed to keep us from seeing the dire straits we were in. She was working tirelessly with odd catering jobs to make sure food was on the table.

And that, there most certainly was. There were flautas and enchiladas and tamales and all the Mexican staples we craved—dishes that weren't so easy to come by in New York during those days. She had to scour markets and improvise when ingredients weren't available, all so she could keep cooking the dishes we'd been growing up on. It took some adjusting and adapting to our new surroundings.

I can't imagine my mother could possibly have wanted to cook after all the hours she spent on her feet at work day after day, but she knew food was the only tangible, familiar link between our Upper West Side existence and our memories in El Paso. Beans, rice, and tortillas were the tin can telephone lines back to Texas, and she wanted to make sure we stayed in touch with those roots.

I was just a kid; I wasn't thinking too much of chowing down on my mom's *chili con queso* and *chimichangas* as if nothing had changed. I didn't exactly understand at the time what my mom was giving us by putting those dishes on the dinner table, but I knew it felt good. Although I was still a long way from understanding how critical food would be to my future and career, I was beginning to see exactly how important it was for my sense of self.

CHAPTER TWO

MI CASA ES SU CASA

Today, I'm lucky enough to call some of the most celebrated chefs in the world my closest friends. I've gotten to cook beside and break bread with the best in the business over the last few decades. Some of them took me under their wings, teaching me a technique or a knife or life skill (and in a lot of cases, all of the above). Others gave me a job. And almost every one of them gave me at least one solid piece of advice I've carried with me, from how to keep my whites whiter to the way to treat a woman on a first date.

I've always been the baby in my peer group. The upside is that I get to tease the hell out of my friends for getting old. I point out graying temples. I give them shit for slowing down the line—or abandoning the kitchen altogether, on account of bad knees or early arthritis. Of course, that stuff is catching up with me now, too. I notice the difference when I'm on the concrete floor for more than a couple of hours, and when my metabolism after a night out and one too many glasses of rosé doesn't quite crank the way it once did. Cooks are kind of like football players; ours is a young gun's game. But over the years, I skipped some average life steps, which meant I started even younger than most, and maybe clocked a few more years as a result. By the time I turned forty, I'd been professionally cooking for more than two decades. A lot of cooks today don't even get started until they finish culinary school, which these days can put them well into their twenties before their careers begin.

I think it all made me gravitate toward folks who have *lived* a few more years than me, too, and that's been true ever since I was a kid. Long before I picked up my first knife, I was forced to get a little older, a little quicker than other kids my age. My mom loved my brother and me, and she always

worked super hard to make sure we never went without. But that also meant she *worked*. A lot. And she had some unconventional methods of making her name. So in the process, some of what my brother and I were exposed to was pretty grown-up stuff.

When we landed in New York, one thing became clear fast: *We ain't in El Paso anymore.* New York City in the early 1980s was an eclectic place. Reagan was in the White House. Studio 54 had been exposed as a breeding ground for scandal. There were heartbreaking headlines: AIDS was claiming lives, confusing and terrifying an entire population. We grappled with the loss of John Lennon on the Upper West Side, while *Rolling Stone* called Forty-Second Street the sleaziest block in America. But there were bright spots, too—indications of a changing world. Graffiti became appreciated as an art form. Hip-hop was exploding from clunky boom boxes on every corner, minds were blown when RuPaul debuted in the East Village, and breakdancing took over dance floors all over the country. Thanks to MTV invading homes everywhere, music wasn't just a soundtrack anymore; it was setting the tone for pop culture and style on a much bigger stage. There were promising strides by powerful women: We had our first female Supreme Court justice, and of course, Madonna took her first steps toward world domination. That was all good news for my mom—a single, young mother poised to become a prominent woman in her own field. In 1983, the food world watched as the sushi spot Hatsuhana got a four-star review in the *Times*—a sign of evolving palates and a curiosity about other cultures that helped prop open the door for efforts like my mom's.

It was a glamorous and gritty and colorful and wildly creative era. And on Eighty-Fourth Street, in a duplex where a young Mexican mother was raising her twin boys, another new scene was starting to take shape.

My mom had done a lot of legwork networking and meeting the right people before we even left El Paso—stuff that paved the way for our move. Now that we were in the city, she had to get creative putting those connections to work. Zarela Martinez wasn't just a phenomenal cook; she was a savvy, perceptive businesswoman right from the start of her career. She understood the power of talent and hard work, but also appearance and prestige. And she knew how to exploit what was most special about and unique to her; she

knew what she could offer people that they couldn't get anywhere else. That was her food, for sure, but it was also good old-fashioned Mexican hospitality. When my mom pulled that Econoline into the Big Apple, those gringos had no idea what they were in for.

She had ten grand in her pocket when we unloaded that van. Subway fare was 75 cents in those days, so maybe she could have stretched her pennies a little further with some shitty downtown apartment. But instead, she took her cash and doubled down. Our last apartment in West El Paso was a fucking dump. Toward the end of our living there, burglars broke in while Rodrigo and I were home alone. I don't think I realized how poor we were until I was sitting there telling these dudes to help themselves to the last of the food in the fridge—an old, crusty package of bologna and not much else. So although I do believe she wanted my brother and me to have a sense of stability and safety after that life, she also had ulterior motives.

"We may be poor, but we're sure as hell not going to look like it," she said when we got to New York. My mom was awesome at using her creativity to make sure of that. She was ultra-stylish and always ahead of her time. Over and over again, I'd seen her take something secondhand—something humble that could have been a sad-looking ensemble—and make it look like a million bucks. She embroidered her own jean jackets, glued glitter on shoes or shirts. She could create a look and an aesthetic, something eye catching, something other people wanted, and wanted a part of.

Her business strategy was no different. She was prepared to pound the pavement, to discover and be discovered by the New York restaurant scene, but she also knew how to work smarter than that. She wanted to *create* a scene. She trusted her skills and her food, and she knew that if she could just get the right people to taste her cooking, the work would come. Like appealing to those burly truckers with family recipes, she'd offer of herself, give people something they couldn't get anywhere else and that they wouldn't forget. Before ever dreaming of financing or running a restaurant, she'd promote herself by providing hospitality—but this time, instead of operating tractor-trailers, the audience would be driving the social and food scenes in New York City. Forget following trends—she was going to set them.

Almost immediately, my mom kicked off her campaign to become a

fixture in New York society. Like most Mexican women from a big family, my mother knew how to pull off a damn fine fiesta, so once a month in the beginning, she started throwing these epic, lavish parties, inviting only the coolest people in town. During the time she'd traveled back and forth to New York from El Paso for events and parties, Zarela had met and impressed a lot of the big names in the business. She always told me, "I had exquisite manners and I wrote everyone thank-you notes," impressing on me the importance of gratitude and courtesy early on. By the time she arrived in New York, she'd developed a reputation for hospitality before she ever invited a single person into her home. And when the time came to finally do just that, people would ask her what they could bring as a contribution. "Bring someone who could help with my career," she told them.

And they obliged. Jazz musicians and artists. Chefs and writers and critics. It was such a cross section of the city's coolest people—all bohemian, all wild and interesting. It was the first time I realized that creative people, no matter their art, attract other creative people. These were people who loved to party. People who had connections. And people she knew would talk. Our apartment wasn't just an investment in a comfortable lifestyle; it was a business expense.

She would fill giant tin tanks with powerful margaritas, and, this being the '80s, she also handed out some other goodies: a little weed, the occasional magic mushroom. She made sure no glass went dry, and no one *ever* went hungry. She was cooking traditional northern Mexican food, stuff I had grown up on. For us it was nothing special; we took for granted how good we had it. For her guests, though, that food was foreign, exotic, and *exciting*. Maybe people were getting hooked on other things in those days, but one thing was for sure—these folks all left bent on my mom's food.

My brother and I were witness to it all. My mom was too busy to baby us, not that she would have tried. That was never her style. It probably sounds ludicrous to parents today, who keep their kids on a tight leash and would throw themselves on a beetle that dared to step in front of their precious child. But we were always expected to participate and behave like grown-ups. There was never talk of sending us to a babysitter during her soirées or anything like that. It's also a cultural thing, I think. When you're part of a Mexican

family, you're always at grown-up parties. Kids are accepted and expected, usually running around, cutting up with some cousins and causing a little trouble, so this was nothing out of the ordinary.

I think my mom was also trying to get us accustomed to having people around. She wanted us to know *these* people were important, that we needed them for us to make it in this new place. And on the flip side, she wanted them to see her hustle, as a single mom doing it on her own, depending on nobody but herself to provide for her family. And she was pulling it off with fucking *style*.

I was on my best behavior when she threw her parties. I loved being a part of the crowd, and I never wanted to put my standing invitation in jeopardy. Maybe it was an unintended consequence, but my mom was giving us more than a free pass to hang out with the cool adults; she was giving us an education. And maybe a little more than she bargained for in some cases. I'll never forget my first introduction to same-sex love; I was about nine or ten years old when a lesbian couple wandered down to my bedroom and, whether they were too wrapped up in each other to notice me, or they just didn't give a shit, started making out. I was so stunned. Before that moment, I had no idea two girls could *kiss*. My eyes were bugging out of my head like a cartoon character.

In fact, most nights I couldn't believe my eyes. There was just so much *happening*. My home was frequently packed with people, anchored by aromas and flavors that were a part of my DNA—and a connection to my past life—in the face of all this unfamiliarity. I watched guests fawn over my mom, complimenting her food and house, talking about how cute her kids were. It was a few years before I started trying to pinch some of the booze for myself, but I was totally drunk on the attention, and the attention my mom was getting. I couldn't believe all these people were going wild for her just because she was cooking for them. Who knew those plates of chile rellenos and enchiladas, which were so commonplace for me, actually worked like some kind of potion, spellbinding all these new, cool-looking folks.

Even with all that happening in my home, I never felt neglected or like I was in any kind of danger. I loved it, because I felt included. I felt helpful, too, passing hors d'oeuvres or giving my mom a hand in the kitchen with

little tasks. It gave me a sense of purpose and relevance, like I was an important part of what my mom was trying to achieve. I had to be the man of the house, after all.

I also thought these parties were for me in some way, and I learned a lot about myself during those days. Rodrigo spent most of the time in our room, doing his own thing; he wasn't really interested in what was going on. But I was a totally different story. This was the first time I found myself with a captive audience. And I liked it. A *lot*.

Those parties were a way for me to get in front of people, an early sort of audition for a life I could never have known would include so much stage time. I always wanted to dress the part, to be cool like my mom and her new friends, so I showed up in little suits and ties and wearing flip-up glasses. I wanted to see and meet everybody and let them know who I was, and I had no filter whatsoever. I was always chatting everyone up, telling jokes and flirting with the ladies. Maybe they thought I was an annoying kid, but I couldn't tell you. I was too busy eating it all up. There were beautiful women everywhere, and as always, I thought I was a lot older than I was, so I spent a lot of time wondering why they weren't coming on to me.

I may not have been closing deals during those days, but my mom was definitely getting shit done. It wasn't long before word about her parties and her food started to spread, and within a year she was approached about opening Café Marimba as executive chef. By 1987, she had gained enough traction and confidence to open her own restaurant, which she called Zarela.

Watching my mom's hustle was life changing for me. It showed me that being successful meant being not only meticulous and constantly curious about your craft, but also savvy and adaptable, socially and professionally. I didn't watch from the sidelines—I was right there on the court. I saw her response to pressure and how she didn't shy from the challenge of carving out a name in one of the world's most competitive cities. I saw the creative ways she found to cut her own path, and above all, I got the real message: Work hard, connect with people, and you'll get noticed.

Later, long after my dad was gone, I'd find out that he told my mom that she'd never amount to anything outside of El Paso. That it wouldn't be long before she'd be doing an about-face, crawling back to Texas. Maybe that was

16

the fuel she needed to turn up the fire on her cooking career. But honestly, I'm not sure Zarela Martinez needed any more motivation than her own will. I was mesmerized by her talent, her ability to turn raw ambition into Tina Turner–style success. Her kids and her name—that's all she took with her from Texas. And what she turned her name into would become legend in the food world in no time at all.

Sure, she could have done it the old-school way—a slow climb up the kitchen ladder, one agonizing rung at a time. My mom was always willing to do the work, but she knew how to work smarter. To cook for someone in a restaurant—where they come and pay for the meal, where they might hear your name but never see your face—was no match for the kind of connection you could make by inviting them into your own home. Zarela was going to feed people, give them an intimate experience she could control, where they could see her and talk with her, watch her work a room, and get a sense of what her cooking and her life were all about.

Today, young cooks ask me about success. This business has changed so much that sometimes it's hard to know the best advice. But there is one thing I always tell them: Ask around. Find the movers and shakers near you (today, they call 'em "influencers"), and ingratiate yourself to them. Be humble, be insightful. Be generous with your time and talent, and most importantly, be kind. "Come into my home." That was the invitation my mom extended to all these people. It's no surprise that Mexicans coined the phrase "Mi casa, su casa." My mom gave her time, her style, her attention, and her cooking (not to mention what it actually cost her to feed people), and she gave them a window into her culture.

She also created a community, providing a place to gather, to meet new people, to exchange ideas and information and inspiration. It was a place warmed by friendships and, of course, her fantastic cooking. Even today, in a city of nine million people, New Yorkers will tell you it can be a lonely, isolating place. It's easy to get lost, to become invisible, even for the most recognizable residents. So to invite them into her home—people who had come from all over the world, often leaving their own behind—was a special thing.

There were a lot of unforgettable experiences in those days, but I never

forgot the look of gratitude when she handed her guests a warm flauta or refilled their drink. It's a powerful thing, to take care of another human being. My mom knew that. Sure, she had a motive, and a mission, but the reason it all worked so well is that it was *real*. I think it brought her a lot of personal satisfaction to give so much of herself; I know doing for others does the same for me today.

It was still a few years before I really understood her calling would be mine, too. I was just a kid, on the verge of becoming a self-centered teenager. As my mom's star started to rise, her schedule became busier and more intense. For me, growing up wasn't a matter of time or natural progress. It was a matter of necessity, accelerated by circumstance. Like a warp zone in one of my '80s video games, I had to skip a few levels. But as much as my mom's parties gave me an early taste of some adult experience, they couldn't prepare me emotionally for what was coming my way in the years ahead. And while she was providing so many others with a sense of home, I was still struggling to understand where mine was.

CHAPTER THREE

TWO STATES OF MIND

"Bicultural" is a word that gets thrown around all the time today. It's in the news and on the covers of books. It's in conversations about everything from border control to fashion to whatever Hollywood's cooking up for the box office. Now, it's a major part of my identity and my career. But when I was a kid, it wasn't something I understood right away.

Right off the bat in New York, I had a really diverse group of friends. Dominicans and African Americans and Puerto Ricans—I was just one color in the city's big box of crayons. I knew I was Mexican, and along with that came a certain set of values and traits. A language, a look, obviously a type of food. I did feel torn, but it wasn't between being Mexican and being American. That was a struggle I'd grapple with later down the line. What I really wrestled with in those days was reconciling two *other* cultures—not being a Mexican American kid living in America, but being a Texan living in New York.

Don't get me wrong—the Upper West Side of Manhattan was a pretty magical place to live, even then, before it was sterilized and started getting name-dropped in newspapers as one of the safest and most desirable neighborhoods in the city. This was when it still had rough edges and avenues you wouldn't dare venture down at night if you didn't want to get your Nikes ripped off your feet—or much worse. But still, that part of the city was a destination for millions of tourists, and it was our very own playground.

Rodrigo and I didn't even know how good we had it, living half a block from Central Park and five blocks from the Museum of Natural History. When she had time, my mom made sure we weren't just residing in the city, but really *living* in it. Marinating in the culture, taking advantage of all those things that

weren't available to her growing up. She introduced us to the arts. She took us to museums and shows. She strolled with us through Central Park. If she had any spare time, we took trips around the city, always doing something cultural, educational. She wanted us to be well rounded; she always pushed for us to broaden our horizons. "Aarón, you need to read," she always told me. She emphasized that being interest*ed* would make us more interest*ing*.

Zarela never took for granted that we were in the best city in the world, with opportunities to learn and become cultured on literally every corner. So for ten months a year, we attended class on Columbus Avenue during the week, and when the weekend came, we got schooled on the world at large.

No surprise that a big part of that education involved food. My mom loved to eat and explore as much as she loved to cook, and she took us along on her journeys around town. We approached every block with the fresh eyes of newcomers. She took us to have tea with high society at the Plaza. We slurped briny, slippery oysters at Grand Central. Eating was an introduction to so many cultures outside our own. I was very adventurous even then; I ate whatever my mom put down in front of us, whether that meant making my way through the Taiwanese menu at Pig Heaven, going down to try dim sum in Chinatown, or sampling Russian food in Brighton Beach. The cool thing was, my mom was being exposed to it all at the same time, so it was something we got to share together.

In El Paso, pretty much everyone was Mexican, but I recognized then that New York is a city of immigrants. People were from all over the place, all with their own parts of town and their own flavors. They were preserving their heritage through food, and it started to really open my palate and my mind. I never felt like an outsider as a bicultural kid; I felt accepted because there was so much of everything else. Seeing how much was out there, by way of pickled herring or Peruvian soups, made me start to appreciate my own uniqueness in a way I hadn't before.

But in those days, even though we were totally immersed in the city, we were still very much between worlds. I was getting accustomed to New York and learning to appreciate it, but what I lived for most was summertime. Every June, Rodrigo and I boarded a plane to make the pilgrimage back to El Paso, where we got to spend time with our old man and our family there.

During the school year, I got to talk to my dad occasionally—maybe once a week or so by phone. I knew he wouldn't forget me, but being so far away, I was actually a little afraid I might forget him, and forget my life there. Memories fade so fast when you're young, but while I sat in the classroom on Columbus Avenue, my mind was back in Texas, on a little patch of grass where I knew my dad was spending his days off, drinking beer with Mr. Estrada and chowing down on my Tia's cooking. New York was fun, a departure, a change of scenery. It was a massive maze of things to see and do and eat. But El Paso still felt like home.

So as soon as the late spring heat was starting to set in and the city began to empty, almost instinctively I knew it was just about time to go. I couldn't wait. Today, my New York friends make jokes that I've gone soft, choosing New Orleans over more happening scenes in Manhattan or Brooklyn, LA, or even Chicago. But the truth is that even as a kid, full of energy and attitude, I appreciated a life that was a little slower. A little sweeter. I remember telling my mom I preferred Texas to the city, and she straight up told me I was nuts. Now I can see why. For her, New York was about opportunity, a place that offered her a future. She was also a woman who always sought culture; she was way too worldly for El Paso, which, for all its Texas-sized wide-open spaces, couldn't have been a smaller town.

But honestly, I still didn't understand why we had to move to such a big place. I was adjusting to our little corner of the big city, but it was a separation from more than our roots and routines—it was a split from our father and our big, warm (and, truth be told, totally unruly) extended family. I missed my Tio Mario and Tia *Gringa* (we called her that because she had the lightest skin of all of us), my half-brother Spanky and half-sister Marissa, my cousins and neighbors. It was a community totally unlike anything we had in New York. I know now that what makes a place feel like home isn't just location, but the people and the love in it, and the memories created there. El Paso had that trifecta for me, and then some.

So those summer trips meant everything. I remember boarding the plane in New York with Rodrigo, two little knuckleheads, young and unaccompanied. I could barely sit still on the trip. I was always cutting up, trying to be cute with the flight attendants and asking for extra snacks, craning my neck

to look out the window at the clouds below. I fidgeted the whole way, willing the plane to go faster. When we finally hit the ground in Texas, my dad was always waiting for us, right there at the gate. He wore cowboy boots and a big, thick mustache; he smelled like tobacco and leather and aftershave. He looked massive to me.

We had a tradition of going to this old-school barbecue place called Smitty's for lunch on the way home. It was right near the airport and was surrounded by auto dealerships. I remember watching all the sales guys in their suits come in and place their orders, talking about cars that had come in while they collected their trays. I learned then that Texas barbecue was all about the beef. We'd get this huge spread: pickles and white bread—always untoasted—and then the beef brisket and massive fucking *Flintstones*–style, dinosaur-sized racks of ribs. It was always super hot outside, so we had huge red cups of Coca-Cola packed with ice to wash it all down. I always left with sticky fingers and a smile on my face, full and satisfied, knowing I had a whole El Paso summer ahead to spend with my father. Even now, the flavor of smoke and brown-sugar-sweet, vinegar-spiked sauce is enough to take me right back in time, to that little Texas joint, and bring back those feelings of excitement and anticipation, love and hope. Sharing a side of slaw with my dad and talking about how we were going to spend the season.

Adolfo Sánchez was a man's man. My mom always described him as being very "dynamic." That was her word. It's what made her fall in love with him in the first place. In those early years after their divorce, if she spoke about him, she generously omitted stories about his darker side that I would come to know existed years later, the side that drove her to divorce him and to drive the three of us two thousand miles to the northeast. But as a kid, I only knew that he was larger than life—and he was everything I wanted to be as a man. He was my idol.

My dad was born in Valentine, Texas, a town that currently has a population of 125 people. No, that's not a typo. The place has fewer residents than the number of covers most restaurants I've worked in do in a slow lunch service. But he was a very astute dude—a great student, a man of few words but great intelligence. His own parents couldn't read or write, and they

impressed on him early on that education was a ticket out of town. It wasn't long before he found his place in the big city of El Paso.

Once there, the handsome, always well-dressed Adolfo took a job in a clothing store to put himself through school. As a Mexican American in the 1950s and '60s, my dad did something totally unheard of—he earned a master's degree. He put his schooling to use as an English teacher, and like a true Texan, he coached football on the side. But in El Paso, there are only so many ways to make more money, and academia had a ceiling. By the time I knew my father, he'd left that world and taken a gig as a probation officer for the state, in charge of pissing guys at the border for purposes of drug testing.

I don't know if my dad had any big dreams. I mean, he bothered to go through the trouble of getting some pretty impressive educational credits, so he must've had something in mind. But he had been married before my mom, and had three kids before Rodrigo and me. His first wife, Helen, was actually my grandma Aida's hairdresser. Aida was fond of her, and after Helen had become ill and passed away, she suggested to my mom that she reach out to the widower, Adolfo. My mom was new in town, and my grandma thought maybe he could help her find work.

At the time, Zarela was working at a finance company, which was her first job in El Paso. Adolfo told her he just so happened to have an opening for a secretary, but my mom didn't feel qualified for the position. "That's okay," he said, "I'd rather go out with you. We'll find you another job." They dated for four years before they got married, so by the time we came along, my mom had already been stepmom to my half-siblings, Spanky, Marissa, and Henry, for some time.

I thought it was cool, having a big family. I didn't understand how complicated that was for my parents, for my mom. I didn't consider the heartbreak my dad must've experienced, losing his first wife, or how challenging it would have been to guide his three kids through that grief. Looking back, I think, in a way, by the time Rodrigo and I came along, he was kind of done, and by the time we started our El Paso summer trips, he was a tired man. If he'd had any big ambition, it had evaporated.

The way I remember it, my dad worked hard for one thing—his week-

23

ends. Few people appreciated down time like my dad. I watched him closely for cues on what being relaxed really meant. He had these funny, shitty old corduroy shorts, and he'd put on his white T-shirt and slippers, and that was how he liked to chill. When I saw my dad in that getup, when I heard him scuffing around, I just knew—he was home.

In Mexico, your BFF is your *compadre*, and my dad's main compadre was Mr. Estrada. The scorching El Paso sun did no favors for lawn care, and water was expensive. But on Saturdays my dad would get up and mow the one little patch of green under the palm tree where there was shade, and the two of them would set up a cooler of Miller Lite and just sit on the porch, talking for hours. I remember wondering, *What the fuck are they talking about all this time?* All day, they didn't move, until later in the night, when the cooler was emptied of cans and they'd bring the whiskey out—my dad liked to drink Chivas Regal. Mr. Estrada was a nice enough dude, but he scared the hell out of me. He was like Hercules, except he had only one arm. He wore Wrangler shirts with the sleeve taped up over his stump, and by the end of the night, he'd start in on me. "Hey, *mijo*! Want me to tell you the story about how I lost my arm in the saw mill?" I wonder what I must've looked like, staring back at him with big, wide, *Are you kidding me?* eyes. I was freaked the fuck out, this big one-armed drunk dude trying to tell me his horror story.

But while those two did their thing on the homestead, I had my own socializing to do in the neighborhood. When you're a Mexican kid, you've got your friends, and then you've got your cousins who are also, by default, your other friends. Sarah and Amanda and Liz lived up the street; when I was younger they were my buddies and we all kicked it, but once I hit puberty and started really thinking about chicks, it seemed weird to be hanging out with girls all the time. So I started spending time mostly with the guys; my best buddy was Patrick, this wickedly funny white boy. We hung out with his older brother, and our other buddy Roy, whose dad was an assistant principal at a school: mostly playing games, swimming a lot, just trying to keep ourselves entertained. We all raised a little hell, trying to steal booze from my dad and smoke cigarettes when we could get our hands on them, and just trying to act like we were cool. Rodrigo and I were always very different, and other than

family stuff, we didn't really spend much time together. He kept on hanging out with the girls, but otherwise holing up and reading, keeping to himself. I always felt like he was this nerdy bookworm. I just didn't get the appeal.

But by the time I was twelve or so, my life was all about talking to girls again, this time just with different motives. I met this adorable girl named Maribel. Her family lived in Albuquerque but came to El Paso for the summers. When she was in town, we carried on this passionate little puppy love. I tried to be so romantic with her, testing out all those ideas of what a grown-up relationship should be like.

My dad had ladies, too. His last girlfriend was a woman named Vera. She had three kids, all older than us, living on the east side of El Paso. My dad went to work during the week and on Fridays we all went over to Miss Vera's house for sleepovers and had these unbelievable weekends there. We spent afternoons swimming and playing outside, stopping only to chow down on some ice cream or dry off long enough to go inside for lunch or a bathroom break, bare feet slapping on the tile floors and still seeing spots from the bright Texas sun. On Saturday, the adults would put together these big cookouts and make mountains of *carne asada*, and then at night we'd watch scary movies and pass out, thoroughly spent from the sun and with bellies still full from the feasts. The next morning, I would wake up to the smell of tripe simmering on the stovetop; Sundays meant spicy, chile-spiked *menudo*, a hangover remedy. We had a big meal together at the end of the weekend, and we went back home to my dad's very happy.

Occasionally, he took us on little trips across the border. I remember it being just like El Paso in a lot of ways, which made sense given the scant twenty-minute separation by car. Driving down I-10, I could see the fences and the red, green, and white flag, which was there in all its glory, as a constant reminder that *it* was right there. Mexico. When we got to the other side, I felt like I had to switch my Mexican hat on. My dad always spoke English at the house, but as soon as we crossed that imaginary line, he spoke only Spanish.

He took us to the markets, which were vibrant and overwhelming in the best possible way. I loved the colors, I loved watching people barter and buy produce—fresh and dried chiles, tomatoes and tomatillos, onions and

avocados by the basketful—and I'd wonder about what they were going home to cook. On Saturday my dad loved to get *pan dulce*, the Mexican sweet bread. We'd pick up groceries, which were exponentially cheaper there, and then go eat tacos. It was such a treat for us. After the markets, we made the rounds. Dad always had little visits to make; he had his set of homies that he'd stop by to see. And then we'd make our way to see my grandmother's sisters—who we referred to as "the *signoras*."

Adolfo was beloved on both sides of the border. During the week, he'd try to get out of work early to spend a little extra time with us. He took us to this hamburger joint, and it felt like everyone in the place would stop to say, "Hey, Al," with a tip of a ten-gallon hat. And women *loved* him, which was something I desperately hoped would be hereditary. He had all his hair but was totally gray by his thirties; they called him the silver fox. My dad was reliable; he liked to drink and socialize, and he liked the ladies, but no matter what, he was up early every day. He could get fucked up and party at night, but he never, *ever* called in sick. Every day, like clockwork at six in the morning, the coffee was on and he was in the bathroom shaving, ready to roll. Now I realize he was a highly functioning alcoholic. It's something I came to better understand later in life. But back then I thought he was superhuman.

We had a lot of fun adventures in El Paso, but in between, there were a lot of laid-back, lazy summer afternoons. On weekends, we'd come together as a family and have big fiestas. It was barbacoa on the grill with homemade salsas and tortillas, braised meats and homemade chorizo, big pieces of goat or beef that we'd slow-cook and serve with pickled vegetables, and Tia Nini's famous chili con queso. And everyone, everywhere, was laughing, talking loud, kicking back with a cold beer. They were sweet times, and watching my grandmother make these unbelievable tacos and enchiladas—that's when I really started to take an interest in the kitchen. It was hard not to imagine that what she was doing with those sauces simmering away on the stovetop was anything less than magic. I watched her work and absorbed the aromas, asked a million questions, and sampled everything.

While we were in El Paso, my mom traveled. She would go to Europe or to Mexico with other chefs, learn about the food, and appreciate some

much-needed alone time. My mom was never the type to dote on her kids constantly, or to feel totally lost without us. *Mother* was just one small part of her ever-expanding multi-hyphenated job description, and more than anything, she loved to learn and live. She's always been very social, and being tethered to restaurant work and her family most of the year left her with an itch for those interactions.

Later on, it was pretty clear to me why my mom made the choices she did. My dad was more than happy to live a very small, simple life in El Paso for all of his days. He didn't see the need to leave—he had everything he could possibly want right in his own front yard, or a stone's throw across the border. But my mom could never have sat still in that environment; she needed a much bigger world. She needed the city's stage.

It wasn't just ambition that drove her away from Adolfo, though. He was a hero to me—a docile, soft-spoken, Mexican Casanova; an attentive father; and a laid-back and loyal friend to everyone in town. But behind closed doors, he was also an alcoholic and a womanizer. While my parents were together, he cheated and lied. And I learned later in life that he was also abusive to my mom—both physically and emotionally. When she wanted to strike out on her own with a cooking career, he made sure to tell her she couldn't possibly succeed. He let her know that he had zero confidence in her, and when we moved to New York, he said it wouldn't be long before she was back in Texas, broke and broken.

"What are you doing? You're going to wind up right back here," he told her. "You'll never make it on your own."

I wasn't there to see it, but I can only imagine the fire in my mother's eyes when she responded. "I'll sell burritos in Central Park," she told him. "But I'm never coming back."

We all know now that she never had to resort to those measures (though visitors to the park would have been pretty lucky if she had). Maybe my father's biggest mistake in life was underestimating my mother. One thing I'm sure about my family is that once you count us out, we're going to work that much harder. I have always excelled when people thought I couldn't do something; I become very single-minded. It's pride, very Latin. But that's

one of the big things I've gotten from my mom—that need to be great. I wonder how much of her motivation came from my dad's open doubt and his flagrant abuse.

Of course, I knew none of that at the time; we were very protected and sheltered from those darker truths. I'm not sure what it was like for my mom to watch her sons idolize a man who'd caused her so much personal pain, but it couldn't have been easy. Sometimes, I was angry with her for taking us so far away. Maybe there was an element of selfishness to her decision—a desire to prove herself, to have some level of fame and glory, to see her name in lights. That was the side of it that had my attention at the time. It wasn't until later in life, when I became an adult and then a father myself, that I realized it was most importantly about self-preservation. She needed to get as far from El Paso as she could. If she had stayed, I'm sure she could have continued catering parties, maybe even opened a little restaurant someday—one more Mexican place in an ocean of Tex-Mex joints, serving people who couldn't possibly have appreciated the level she was cooking at. But in order to be the best mother she could, she had to be the best version of herself. And that could only be achieved in a place that would give her that freedom and a platform for her talent.

So for five years, we were a different kind of bicultural. Texans. New Yorkers. For all the instability in my childhood, we actually had a routine for a while there. Fast-paced school years spent in the city, slow summers in El Paso. There was a rhythm to life I could rely on, and I carried on my days knowing what to expect and when, blissfully ignorant that we were at the center of a storm's eye.

CHAPTER FOUR

PUSHING BOUNDARIES

Back in the city, my mom was crushing it, finally enjoying the success she'd been building since our days in Texas. By the time we were eleven, her eponymous restaurant was in full swing, her work in full view of the food media. She'd become a critical darling long before we set foot in the city, and by '87 her own restaurant was a hotly anticipated opening, one that was highly praised by New York's diners and writers alike. *New York* magazine wrote that "her fierce pride in her country's maligned cuisine is backed up by her fiery bravado in the kitchen." And Zagat focused as much on her personality as it did her food, saying "Zarela conveys the utter charm and ageless vivacity of its owner, Zarela Martinez."

It was the culmination of her years of work—a lifetime of struggle and ambition—and it was a total triumph. It was packed constantly, and my mom was in her element like never before. The food was a revelation. The perception of Mexican food in those days was limited to some pretty sad little burrito spots, outer-borough ethnic enclaves, and of course, the neon lights and sounding chimes of the illustrious Taco Bell locations. Her cooking was a celebration of regional Mexican, based on meticulous research and experimentation, and a re-creation of dishes found all over the country, from Oaxaca to Puebla to Veracruz. In today's foodie culture it may not seem revolutionary, but at the time dishes like Oaxacan lamb, *huitlacoche* crepes, snapper hash, chiles poblanos bursting with chicken and picadillo, and *costillas con longaniza*—sausage and ribs made with garlic, lime, and herbs—were revolutionary. My mom was a consummate host, and the restaurant felt like a natural extension of her parties back home. The scene was vibrant, the margaritas were powerful, and the tables were taken, taken, taken.

That left Rodrigo and me to our own devices—a lot. My mom didn't neglect us. She always made sure we had exactly what we needed. But she couldn't be with us much, either, so instead she kept a beautiful tradition going of cooking something for us in the morning that we could reheat when we got home from school. Most kids were ripping open bags of Doritos or pasting together squishy peanut butter sandwiches from white packages of whiter Wonder Bread. A lot of times, I rolled home with a group of friends, excited to show off whatever it was she had made—my mom always made sure there was so much food it could feed everyone.

My mom made us culinary masterpieces, even if they seemed simple on the surface—and they weren't all Mexican. She stuck to regional specialties at the restaurant, but at home, my mom experimented with all kinds of cuisines. My personal favorite, a dish I have spent decades trying to duplicate perfectly, were these unbelievably delicious chicken wings. Not some bottled hot sauce and clarified-butter bullshit, either. Hers were these epically tasty, sticky drumsticks made with a marinade of soy, freshly shaved ginger, citrus and pineapple juice, garlic, and scallion.

She also created these amazing pasta salads. She'd take anything we'd had left over and toss it into a salad with a homemade pesto, which was a pretty avant-garde kind of thing in the '80s. It was savory and herbaceous, and though I wasn't sophisticated enough yet to pick out individual flavors and elements, I knew the sum of its parts was nothing like any other pasta salad I'd had before, and there was a good reason for that.

The food was so stripped down; I couldn't see anything in there that looked like a magical ingredient, and this introduced me to the power of simplicity. Honest stuff made with a few quality ingredients, the kind of cooking that reminded me of watching my grandmother during those slow weekends in El Paso, wondering what kind of alchemy was going on behind the scenes. The food and the settings couldn't have been more different, but they both gave me the same feeling: a warmth, and a curiosity. I was so transfixed by cooking, how this act could transform basic ingredients into something exploding with flavor, and how it could make a house into a home.

Of course, mom made some Mexican staples for us, too. A few years after we arrived in New York, she decided to do something special and make

a mole sauce. True to form, she wasn't about to cut corners just because of a little thing like the limitations of urban ventilation. She started toasting the chiles in our tiny kitchen, and pretty soon she'd damn near smoked out half the building. People ran outside, certain there was a fire. And when I went to look for her, there she was at the stove, tongs in hand, happy as could be. The smoky, spicy aroma floated in the hall for a week. The neighbors may not have appreciated that, but it sure helped me feel at home.

When she couldn't cook for us herself, we had an amazing nanny who took over. Adella was a Salvadoran woman, and I'll always remember her big, strong hands, rough and worn and weathered from years of washing clothes and dishes, plus whatever struggles she must've encountered coming to the United States. That was all beyond my comprehension then, but when I was young, I held onto those hands when she'd walk us to school in the morning, and afterward when she'd come to get us. She was a woman with presence. Strong women were always around me growing up—my mother made sure of it. Adella was so good at pulling off my mom's cooking in her absence that eventually, when we were old enough to take care of ourselves, she started working at Zarela, too.

So, I can't sit here and say I started pushing boundaries because I had a rough home life. Some kids have that as an excuse, or at least a starting point for parents or teachers looking to find the source of a cry for help. I had divorced parents, sure, but lots of my classmates did. We were in good company among latchkey kids in our neighborhood. In the end, I was always loved and cared for. And my brother certainly didn't feel the need to act out. He did exactly what he was supposed to: buried his nose in books and behaved according to the rules. My mom always said I was more like my dad: Optimistically, I guess I thought she was referring to his charm and good looks. But it could be that in some ways, she was talking more about that reckless side he covered up so well.

I didn't have so much of a rebellious streak as a full-blown racing stripe. I figured if I was going to have an accelerated childhood, I ought to be living in the fast lane. Maybe it was because Rodrigo was always such a goodie-goodie, never causing so much as a ripple in the calm waters of my mom's world. Maybe it was because I was the more brown one of the two of us, and

I started to notice a difference in how the world responded to us because of it. I had dark hair and darker skin, and I looked and identified a lot more as Mexican. I remember him being called *whero* by the kids at school, which means "white boy." Later, I really began wanting to understand my roots and get more in touch with my heritage. I don't think I ever considered how hard that might've been for Rodrigo as a kid. In a lot of ways, I believed he was going to have an advantage. We may be twins, but our lives diverged dramatically from an early age. I think he never quite felt Mexican enough; I faced more adversity in being American, and he had a hard time being accepted as Mexican.

Regardless, at the time, Rodrigo was getting good grades, coming home and going to sleep and getting up for school when he was supposed to. I knew my mom wanted me to be more like him, and I started to feel like she loved him more than me. I always felt an inherent resistance to authority, but I was going into my teenage years, and I was becoming an angry kid.

I began to have questions. Why did we have to leave Texas? Why didn't my dad fight harder for us? Why did my mom have to work so much? We loved the summers, and my mom's time off in the city with us when we were younger, but there was still a lot of time in between when we were expected to take care of ourselves. It left me wide open to start wondering these things. I had a tendency to get caught up in my own head, analyzing my situation and wondering if maybe I was being cheated a little. After always feeling like I had to act like a man, I resented whenever someone treated me like a kid. It only compounded that natural rebelliousness that starts to set in when puberty comes along, and it was definitely not my best recipe.

Growing up without regularly seeing my dad started to take its toll, and I was living in a city that never quite felt like it fit my spirit. I had a revolving door of authority figures: Adella and Tio Mario, my dad's girlfriends and my mom's boyfriends, the guys at mom's restaurant, my *tias* in Texas, the teachers at school. It was hard to know who to listen to sometimes, so I sort of chose to stop listening altogether. My brother was the golden child, and I was trouble. And I had a lot of time on my hands to cause it.

In New York, that meant cutting up with the kids on my block, ignoring the rules, and skipping out on curfew. We lived in a two-story duplex that

required two keys—one for the building door, which I had the key to, and the other to our apartment, which my mom left unlocked for us. If I missed my curfew, which I started doing on the regular, she'd bolt the top lock. I'd come home late, knowing full well I was breaking the rules, only to find a pillow and a little blanket on the landing. I slept on those stairs many nights, waking up the in the morning to my mom tossing my book bag out the door and telling me to get my ass up and go to school. I'd sit through morning classes, eyes drooping, exhausted and a fucking mess, and then sleep away my lunch period. I was consumed with trying to be an adult, trying to be cool, and I was especially busy with my friends trying to show off what I picked up during my Texas summers, where I had started hanging out with my cousin Luis.

Luis was two years older than me. His mom was Tia Gringa, and he had two sisters: Larisa, who was around my sister Marissa's age, and Sophia, who was a few years younger than me. After my parents split, my dad and Tia Gringa, my mother's sister, stayed close friends, and I loved getting to kick it with my cousins whenever I came to town.

On the border where I'm from, the big joke is that half your family is in law enforcement and the other half is in the drug business. That's how I grew up. A lot of my cousins and uncles were involved in the latter world on the Juárez side, but when we'd all get together on the weekends, it just wasn't discussed. My dad was a federal marshal, and he was friends with some characters who may or may not have been moving drugs across the border. But they were family, and in Mexican culture, when it comes to family, we do *not* ask questions, so we'll never really know.

As I got a little older, Luis started to take my dad's title as the dude I wanted to hang out with most. He was my eldest cousin, fair-skinned with green eyes, a super-good-looking kid. People used to say he looked a little like a young Sylvester Stallone. He was tall, maybe six-two or six-three, and had this unbelievably infectious laugh. Luis was the kind of kid who was full of personality, always up for anything, and wanting to have a good time. And girls *loved* him.

Luis seemed to know his way down every block on both sides of the border, from El Paso to Juárez, and around just about every rule in the book.

He had a penchant for getting into trouble, whether that meant breaking into a pool after dark at a local apartment complex or ripping off cigarettes from the 7-Eleven. I thought everything he did was cool. I ate up every scrap of attention he paid to me, and I scrutinized his every move, taking notes for my return to New York. I copied his swagger and his style. It was monkey see, monkey do. I was smoking pot and disregarding the rules, trying to pull off the same kind of bravado and perfect that playboy look—swapping my old wardrobe out for Z Cavariccis like Luis would wear, and the collarless shirts that were so cool at the time. When he let me hang around, I felt so *in*. For this guy to take me under his wing and invite me out with his friends—it made me feel like the man I wanted to be. And for him, as the middle child between two girls, I think he liked having a little-brother type who looked up to him. I got to hang out with him and his buddies; they taught me how to bend the rules and how to talk to girls, and it was with Luis and his friends that I smoked my first bone when I was twelve years old.

Of course, nothing seemed all that serious in those days. I just figured we were having harmless fun. It's not like we were robbing banks or doing anything a lot of my peers weren't getting up to when their parents weren't looking. That wasn't the case for Luis, though. I saw him and his friends doing some harder stuff sometimes, but I was too young to recognize real red flags. I still wonder if I maybe should have been more aware, and if that might have made a difference. Because within ten years, we would lose Luis to a drug overdose, shattering my Tia Gringa's heart when he died in her arms.

Tio Mario had done his best to be a good stepdad when he married Tia Gringa, but Luis always had a tenuous relationship with his own father. Over the years, I noticed how hard certain things would hit him. He was very sensitive; if he had girlfriends, which he often did, breakups devastated him. When we got a little older, he struggled with the fact that he didn't really have a calling, professionally, and without that grounding force, he always seemed to feel a little lost. It took me a long time to recognize that my cousin was profoundly depressed. I figured it out only later, when I accepted and recognized the diagnosis personally, after I became educated on my own mental health and began to see that depression was prevalent in so much of my family. For Luis, it manifested differently than it would for me throughout my life. He

relied on drugs to help him get through his lowest points, and in the end, the drugs he turned to as medicine for his pain poisoned him one last time.

Twenty years later, I think about him every day. I sometimes wonder why it was him when it so easily could have been me. We had such similar starts in life. Both Mexican kids from El Paso. Both from broken homes. Both coming from more or less the same means. It was a crushing wake-up call, and by the time that happened, I really was a man, at least by society's standards. I guess that means I should have been able to make some sense of it all, but I can't say that I did. I learned a lot from Luis in the years he was alive, but that was the last lesson he taught me in his heartbreakingly abbreviated life: Age doesn't make you a man, and whether you're twelve or twenty-two, you always need someone to lean on.

* * *

Luis's tragic destiny was set in motion in those younger days. I guess I was already banking hard off course on my path, too, and in the distance, a fork in the road was starting to reveal itself. Soon, I was going to be faced with a decision of my own: straight and narrow, or wild and winding. It was a hair's-breadth turn between following my cousin to self-destruction or finding my way.

With Luis, or with my buddies in New York, I felt bold and confident. I felt like I was already grown. All that insecurity coupled with my simmering resentment—at my situation, at my parents for what I perceived to be selfish decisions, at my brother just for being himself—were the makings of a powder keg for me. What happened when I was thirteen was the spark that lit the fuse.

ZARELA'S PINEAPPLE-GINGER CHICKEN WINGS WITH SOY-PINEAPPLE GLAZE

This is one of the first things I remember my mom cooking. She worked at night, so she always made a dish that could easily be reheated for us in her absence. I remember having all my friends from elementary school come over to the house, and she'd have these chicken wings ready, always enough for all of us. The flavors were unique—that little bit of sweetness from the pineapple and spice from the ginger balanced by a salty element from the soy. I didn't appreciate it at the time, but as I got older I realized how sophisticated and cool this recipe is. It's kind of a riff on Hawaiian huli-huli *chicken, but instead of orange, we use pineapple. When you cook this recipe at home, it helps cleanup immensely if you line the baking sheet with foil, as it can become extremely sticky and tough to scrub!*

½ cup (120 ml) pineapple juice

¼ cup (60 ml) orange juice

¼ cup (60 ml) lime juice

¼ cup (60 ml) soy sauce

¼ cup (50 ml) grapeseed or vegetable oil

1 teaspoon kosher salt

1 teaspoon ground coriander

½ cup (15 g) chopped fresh cilantro, plus more for serving

4 cloves garlic

1 serrano pepper

2-inch (5 cm) piece peeled fresh ginger

Ground black pepper

4 pounds (1.8 kg) chicken wings (24 wings), tips discarded

3 green onions, thinly sliced on a bias

2 tablespoons (20 g) white sesame seeds, toasted

1. Preheat the oven to 225°F (110°C). Set an oven-safe wire rack on top of a baking sheet, or line the sheet with cooking parchment.
2. In a large bowl, whisk together the juices, soy sauce, oil, salt, and coriander until thoroughly incorporated. Fold in the ½ cup (20 g) of cilantro and, with a Microplane, grate in the garlic, serrano, and ginger. Season with pepper.
3. In a small saucepan, reserve half the sauce. Toss the wings in the remaining sauce to coat and marinate for 15 to 20 minutes (any longer and the pineapple will start to "cook" the meat).
4. Arrange the wings in a single layer on the rack or parchment, cover with foil, and bake for 30 minutes. Meanwhile, set the saucepan with the reserved sauce over medium-low heat and cook, stirring occasionally, until it's reduced by about half.
5. Remove the foil and adjust the heat to 425°F (220°C). With a brush or spoon, glaze the wings with the reduced sauce, then bake for another 20 to 25 minutes, until an instant thermometer registers 155 to 160°F (69 to 71°C). Glaze the wings once more as soon as they're out of the oven.
6. Sprinkle the green onions, sesame seeds, and remaining cilantro over the chicken. Serve warm.

CHAPTER FIVE

A LESSON IN LOSS

My parents were taking notice, and it wasn't long before my behavior strained my relationships with them. One day, one of my mom's boyfriends—this douchenozzle named *Michele*—found a dime bag of smoke in my jeans when he was doing his laundry. When my mom found out, she did something she almost never did—something that meant she meant business. She called my dad.

Adolfo Sánchez loved to have a good time, and the man loved to drink. But he made no fucking bones about how he felt about drugs. He ran urinalysis at the border, so the idea of drugs was completely taboo. When he found out his youngest kid was smoking grass, he fucking *flipped*.

My mom handed me the phone. "Your father would like a word with you." I looked at the receiver like it was a grenade with the pin pulled.

My dad was old school; he sharpened his own razors and made his own shaving soap. Honestly, I think he really went through all the trouble just to scare the shit out of us, and you know what? It worked.

His voice was as steady as always when he said, "Look, boy," and I could tell I was about to get it. "I'm going to put a photo of you next to my mirror," he said, slow as molasses and chillingly calm. "So I'm reminded every morning when I pick up my razor, that I'm gonna kick the shit out of you the next time I see you."

I handed the receiver back to my mom and cried my eyes out.

Getting reprimanded like that always straightened me out for a little while, but it was a palliative, temporary fix that wasn't addressing the real root of the headache I was causing them. And when the dust settled, I went right back to my old tricks. Had I known the days I had left with my dad were numbered, maybe I would have behaved differently.

* * *

If stable ground felt elusive to me before, the earth beneath me was about to erode entirely. As transient and in flux as my life to that point seemed to be, I still had a few things I could count on: The sun would rise and set, the subway would always show up (if I waited long enough), the tortillas would always find their way to the dinner table. And every summer, I would see my dad.

But the year I turned thirteen, another layer of certainty was peeled away, turning my entire world upside down and changing every part of my life forever.

For all his discipline and attention to taking care of himself outwardly, my dad wasn't a man all that concerned about health. He was of a generation that didn't put much stock in staying fit, and if that wasn't clear from weekends spent draining six-packs of Miller Lite and bottles of Chivas, then it would be from his pack-a-day smoking habit. In those days, that was pretty par for the course. The idea of balance for my dad and his buddies in Texas meant a beer in one hand and a burrito in the other, and there were definitely no dudes talking about "wellness" or hitting the CrossFit gym after work.

By that summer, a lifetime of blissful ignorance was catching up to him, and my dad had already survived a few strokes, either by luck or divine intervention. His health complications extended to his heart, and so in July, he was scheduled for double bypass surgery. The procedure sounded serious, but I was as excited as ever to see him. Even though he appeared to be moving a bit slower to me, I wasn't too worried; that summer was hot as hell, and it seemed like we were all a little lazier. Besides, I was of the belief that the man was made of steel—or at least of some combination of gunmetal and Mexican guts.

At thirteen, I also didn't completely understand the complexity and gravity of the operation he was about to have. I worried about the things a kid would be most concerned with: How long until he was back on his feet? Would we still be having the cousins to the house over the weekend? My questions were more about *when* than *if.* It wasn't until one night, when I

could hear him wheezing and coughing from my bedroom next to his, that for the first time I realized something might really be wrong.

* * *

"Mr. Sánchez, do you have a will?"

I was in the exam room, sitting in a white plastic chair beside one of those hospital-issue scale towers, letting my mind wander around the room and taking note of the implements and impressive-looking plaques on the wall. It was the day before the procedure, and I wasn't paying too much attention to the conversation between my dad and his doctor until that moment. *Will* was a word I understood, and it caught my ear when the doctor asked the question.

I looked to see how he'd react. My dad was on the exam table in a hospital gown, which already made me feel a little uncomfortable, like I was seeing Batman without his cowl and cape. Before that moment, I'd never seen the dude actually look fearful of anything. I didn't even know that was something he felt. But sitting there, he suddenly seemed so small to me. So mortal. And even though I knew that word was associated with the worst of outcomes, I always believed in the triumphant ending.

Which is why I felt so blindsided when on July 24, the scheduled day of the surgery, we arrived at the hospital to find my aunts and uncles crying in the waiting room. These people I knew so well were almost unrecognizable in their grief. Their eyes, red and puffy from their own tears, were trained on me and Rodrigo, and told me what I needed to know long before anyone said a word.

I had lost my hero.

* * *

I was thirteen years old; I understood the concept of death. It had just never applied to my world. It was something they talked about in the news and that happened in movies. Maybe it touched the life of an unlucky classmate. But

death had never come close to me, not yet. It was such a foreign presence, and I was totally unequipped to process it.

Tio Mario quietly took a place by my side that day in the hospital, and he hasn't left since. We were always close before, but it was that day, under the flickering fluorescent lights, among the aroma of burnt coffee and rubbing alcohol, that he went from favorite uncle to de facto dad. Today, he still lives with me in New Orleans, and I've always done my best to return the favor, to be there for him. We've been through so much together, and in the three decades since that day I've learned a great deal from Mario on what it means to take care of someone, to have a sense of responsibility to family.

But on that day, I was concerned only about taking care of myself. I was confused and numb. I'm not sure denial was so much my first emotion as just disbelief. For a while there, it was like my senses shut down. My body's form of self-preservation, I guess. I couldn't understand the words people were directing at me. I couldn't feel a thing. And quite frankly, I got a little lost in the shuffle and commotion of a big family dealing with crushing, unexpected news.

Maybe he was taking a cue from his dad, but Luis wanted to help me in his own way. His intentions were good, though his execution was probably a little misguided. After all, he was fifteen years old, and really just a kid himself. He pulled me aside and just said, "Let's go." I didn't ask where. I didn't ask permission. I didn't tell anyone we were leaving. I just took off with him, slipping away when we knew no one would notice. I understand now that we caused quite a ruckus, but at the time, I wasn't thinking that my family would be worried about us. I wasn't thinking anything, actually. I was drained and empty, and so for the next two days, Luis and I filled the time by getting loaded, making sure I could continue to stay numb.

Luis put me in his truck and we just drove. It was four hours from El Paso to Tucson, where he had an older cousin named Larry. From the passenger seat, through the occasional bout of silent tears, I watched the landscape change as we barreled down I-10, the burnt plains of Texan cattle country giving way to dusty, cactus-studded roadside scenery across the state line. When we arrived, I followed Luis's lead. We hooked up with his family there and spent the time hiding out from life—drinking beer and listening to

mariachi music, crying and telling old stories. It was Mexican-style therapy. I could never thank Luis enough for giving me that escape. It may not have been the most mature decision, but his heart was in the right place, and it helped me feel like a man in charge of my own emotions at a time when I felt totally out of control.

When we got back to El Paso, the family was not happy, needless to say. But we got a bit of a free pass, given the circumstances. There was a shuffle, trying to figure out exactly who was responsible for Rodrigo and me, and what was going to come next, but we didn't stay much longer that summer. We stuck around another week, for the services and to lay my father to rest, and then we packed up and returned to New York, knowing our lives would never be the same.

* * *

When we got back to the city, it seemed bigger and more chaotic, yet somehow emptier than ever. My mom consoled us the best she could, but her life couldn't stop just because we were in pain. She still had to earn a living and provide for us. After a while, the shock started to wear off and things settled down. Today, I find that I'm very sensitive to other people when they lose a loved one, especially a few months in, or a year later. Condolences always come in the beginning, but a few months down the line, that's when I think things get the hardest. It's when visitors stop coming around with casseroles. When people stop checking on you, ready to catch you should you fall apart at any minute. When you're sort of expected to start getting back to "normal," whatever that means.

I think anyone who has experienced profound loss would agree, there is no such thing ever again. You may find strategies to cope, ways to get through the days, then the months, then the years, but grief isn't a temporary thing. It is a tattoo on your back. You may not see it every minute, but when you catch a glimpse in the mirror, you're reminded of the pain you experienced when it was placed there. It's in those later days, when the attention dries up, when the swelling goes down and the initial sting fades, that you start to make out what that lingering pattern will look like for the rest of your life.

My mom was tied up with the restaurant, and Rodrigo and I retreated into our own routines. People always assume twins are the same person, that they share a brain or at least some kind of telepathic connection, but we couldn't have been more different. He loved to read and study. I loved to party and flirt. He appreciated solitude. I craved the spotlight. But as different as we always had been, it was never more pronounced than after my dad died. We didn't share the burden—we experienced it in entirely individual ways. My brother became even more solitary than ever. He looked for solace in books and school, keeping busy with his studies. I acted out. He was withdrawn and melancholy. And I was straight-up pissed.

The isolation I'd felt since we moved to New York was always tempered by that big Texas sunlight at the end of the tunnel. Those trips to El Paso weren't just fun in the moment; they were a motivator that got me through the entire year. The time with my dad, being with my Mexican family, it was grounding. It was central to my identity. Whenever I floundered in New York, whenever I felt disconnected or invisible, whenever I felt lost, the promise of those southwest trips were my due north.

I was also hitting a point in my life when it felt super important to have a dad. The guys around me were getting the birds-and-bees talks, advice on how to act around girls, lessons on shaving—all that shit you need to make you into a man. But now I was left to figure it out on my own. I thank god I was raised by such strong women—that's something I'd spend the rest of my life feeling grateful for. I am the man I am today because of my mom, Adella, my grandmother, my aunts, and my sister. I learned to be sensitive, thoughtful, empathetic, and aware. I avoided becoming the clichéd macho Latino. I think I'm a more level-headed, considerate man because I was raised by women. But I still felt cheated, and the chrysalis of my youthful sadness and angst transformed into adolescent anger, a response to the depression I would not identify for years to come.

CHAPTER SIX

ON THE ROAD AND IN THE STREET

Eventually, we did go back to El Paso. There was still family there, and Mario saw it as his responsibility to take up the fatherly mantle when I was in town. In those days, he had a business selling imported rugs. He loaded up his van a few times a year and took trips around the Southwest during the summer, selling and delivering his goods. Given Rodrigo and my very different reactions to our father's death, Mario thought it might be good for me to tag along. I was basically his lackey, giving him a hand with hauling, helping him navigate. I could learn a little about the business, plus he threw me a few bucks here and there, but it was more about getting me out of the house and away from my own thoughts.

The coolest part was getting to travel. Since the drive from El Paso to New York, my mom had taken us on some trips, but with her work schedule and the restaurant, it was tough for her to get away for anything resembling a family vacation. Getting to see the different parts of the country—the rusty mountains of Arizona, the roadhouses in Santa Fe, the snowcaps in Colorado—it was electrifying. To think, all of that existed right in my own country. Most of the kids I knew spent their summer breaks in Central Park, or if they were lucky, Disney World. But I was on the open road, just me and Mario.

Naturally, I found ways to test the limits on those journeys, too. Mario wasn't actually my father, and his rules were a lot less rigid than my old man's. As much fun as it was to have him hand me a beer at the end of the workday, though, I had really only one thing on my mind: women. Fortunately, there were an awful lot of them out there under those beautiful, spacious skies, and I was working on that Sánchez charm hard. I turned it on blast for cute girls

who worked at gas stations, or ones who served us pie at truck-stop diners. But I was about to learn a lesson that applied to so many life circumstances: Your best chance of getting lucky comes when you least expect it.

Mario had a buddy named Dan who lived out in Woodland Park, Colorado. It's a tiny town just outside Colorado Springs. Dan was this free-spirited dude—totally the type of guy Mario loved hanging around with. He was Navajo and really tall, and definitely a product of the '60s. He'd skipped out on the Vietnam draft and spent his days off the grid in the mountains, smoking pot and taking quaaludes with his wife, who came from Texas oil money. We stopped to visit them one summer for a night while we were passing through, and as amusing as it was to watch these three adults get stoned and crush cans of beer, I was distracted by something else entirely. While they were yukking it up about god knows what, telling old stories and reminiscing, I was busy falling in love with their daughter, Naomi.

She was older by a few years, and so damn cute, man. She was slender and small with a long nose, chestnut-colored shoulder-length hair, and beautiful brown eyes. She had a distinctly Native American look and was just wildly hip, rocking a pair of Vans sneakers. Her dad had a jewelry store, so she was wearing these beautiful turquoise pieces. She spoke with a sweet little voice, and I was completely smitten.

At some point, Dan stopped puffing a bone long enough to share his brilliant idea with the room: "Let's take the kids out for a steak dinner!"

An hour later, the five of us were sitting at one of those kitschy, middle-of-the-country roadhouses that were all the rage in the '90s. The wood-paneled walls surrounded a big salad bar that I imagine was really only there for show, since the real star was a hulking side of meat that came cooked to order with a piping-hot baked potato, skin split open, steam vaporizing the golf-ball-sized scoop of butter sinking into fluffy white flesh.

Normally, I had a healthy appetite for a meal like that, especially one on someone else's dime. Mario and I didn't exactly live high on the hog when we were out on the road, so this was a pretty special occasion.

But I could feel my palms sweating, and I honestly couldn't care less about the T-bone on the table in front of me, or whether it was medium-rare or well-done to shoe leather. Naomi and I were the only sober ones at

the table, but I was drunk with my desire to kiss her, touch her, smell her. We kept shooting glances at each other, and in the middle of the ruckus caused by the punchline of one of Dan's legendary stories, she leaned over and whispered to me. "Tell your uncle you want to stay the night." I almost did a spit take with my Coca-Cola.

When they finally piped down a second, I saw the opportunity. "Um, Tio, can I spend the night at Naomi's?" The man knew me well enough to know what was on my mind.

He laughed a little and gave a quick answer. "Fuck no, boy!"

But Dan came to my rescue, apparently too trusting of his teenage daughter to be concerned about having this horny kid in his house. "Don't worry, dude," he said to Tio, patting him on the back. "They're just kids, man!"

Mario eyed him a little sideways. "Don't worry," Dan laughed. "We'll keep an eye on them."

Tio figured he put up the fight expected of him and gave in, and all I could think was, *oh my god, I'm gonna get away with this shit!*

In the parking lot after the meal, we went our separate ways, Mario toward our van and me following Naomi and her family. Before he took off, Tio pulled me aside. He raised a finger and lowered his chin, bloodshot eyes looking right into mine, "Don't do anything stupid," he said, as stern a warning as I'd ever seen him muster. "I'm going to be back at eight o'clock tomorrow morning to get you."

Fully loaded with booze, pills, and baked potatoes, Naomi's parents hit the hay almost immediately when we got back to the house. She led me into her room and locked the door. She put on a little mood music—some song by the Cure—but I couldn't hear much of anything over the sound of my heart thudding in my ears. She was really creative, and her bedroom was a temple to everything cool at the time: posters of Depeche Mode and Billy Idol, and a ceiling decorated with tinfoil stars.

I took it all in; I had a feeling I was going to want to remember this room for a very long time. But I didn't have too much time to take mental notes—we started making out pretty quickly. I'd kissed girls before, but she was incredible at it, and as soon as we started fooling around something told me Naomi was not the virgin that I was.

What came next was very quick and emotional. I knew I loved sex long before I'd ever lost my virginity, but I also loved the idea of love. As corny as it may have sounded had I told something like this to my buddies at the time, that moment meant something to me. I was—and always have been—a romantic at heart. Afterward, I spent the night next to her, exhausted, exhilarated, and enamored. I just couldn't believe it. And in the quiet afterglow, I was suddenly very concerned about whether or not I'd done a good job.

The next morning, I woke up and looked in the bathroom mirror. I was half surprised to see the same face looking back at me. I *felt* totally different. Tio showed up right on schedule, but before we even said our good-byes, I was already missing my new *amor*. I told Naomi I would write to her, and that I would think about her all the time. And I made good on both promises, but I knew enough about my life already to know that there was very little chance I'd see her again. Things were too ambiguous for me; nothing was ever certain or stable or concrete. I knew I didn't have that kind of control over my future—and by then I was already wondering if I ever would.

Walking out to the car that morning in the cool Colorado air, I was half heartbroken at the idea of leaving her, and half too elated to care. Tio took one look at me and started shaking his head. "Fucking hell," he said. "Get in the van." We had a fifteen-hour drive back to El Paso, and I kept quiet, lost in the loop I was replaying in my mind. Tio kept looking over at me, and I could tell what he was thinking: *I'm gonna get it out of this motherfucker.*

"Talk to me about last night, bro," he started in on me. "How was it, bro? How was it?"

"Leave me alone, Tio," I wasn't about to spill that easily, but I could barely control the shit-eating grin. I knew he would never let up.

"We got fifteen hours left, bro," he reminded me. "I'm gonna get this shit out of you." He kept fucking with me, elbowing and nudging and needling.

"All right, man, be cool!" I said finally, just to get him off my back. And maybe a little because I was bursting to talk about it. "It was the best thirty seconds of my life!"

He nearly lost control of the wheel, he was cracking up so hard. I was outraged. "Tio, this is not funny!" I said, but I had a hard time controlling

my own laughter, too. It was a release after being so in my head about the whole thing since the night before.

After a little while, we got a hold of ourselves and the cab of the van was quiet again. Just when I thought he was ready to quit and change the subject, he leaned over.

"Okay, *mijo*, okay. But the important part is, did you go again?"

I sat up a little straighter. "Wait, was I supposed to?"

* * *

That was how things went with Tio. He took a fatherly role, but he was no disciplinarian. It's also part of the culture that Mexicans are sort of blasé about raising kids; in a lot of ways, they're allowed to do their own thing. It wasn't unusual for me to go to a family party where my cousins and I were slipped a little tequila or a sip of beer. Sex was not as taboo as today's parents would imagine it to be, and adults rarely delineated between the grown-up and adolescent. Rules were rules, and better to start learning the ropes as soon as possible. Maybe it comes from a culture of insecurity, of never knowing what might happen next. Live in the moment, whether you're thirteen or thirty-two. Mario was the same way with his stepson, Luis, who came along on some of the trips, too.

One night, the three of us were out in Albuquerque, and Mario had a stop to make.

"Listen, stay in the van," he told us. "Just hang tight, and I'll be back soon." To keep us occupied, he picked up a twelve-pack of beer, which may as well have been filled with bricks of solid gold for the reaction it got out of us. When we reached for the case, he held it back, "I'm going to give it to you. But just be cool, okay?" He warned us before handing it over.

Mario didn't specify what "be cool" meant, but I'm guessing he probably wasn't suggesting that we crack a few windows and toss our crushed cans out onto the asphalt. Which is precisely what we proceeded to do.

When he came back for us, Mario was approached by a security guard in the parking lot.

"Is that your van, sir?" the guard asked him. I'm not sure exactly what the conversation was that followed, but I assume it was something like, "Sir, are you aware that you have some asshole kids in the back of your vehicle, drinking beer and throwing empty cans out the window?"

Mario rarely got pissed. But when he whipped open the driver's-side door, we knew we were fucked. Luckily, were too blitzed to think it was anything but hilarious. "What the fuck are you knuckleheads doing? You were supposed to be cool!"

* * *

On the road with Mario, there was at least some semblance of authority. But there were also times when I'd visit El Paso, and my aunt and uncle would go on their road trips alone, leaving Luis and me by ourselves. They made sure there was food in the cupboard, but otherwise, it was totally up to us. I can't imagine leaving a fourteen- and sixteen-year-old to fend for themselves. We would score some pot in a parking lot down the road from our apartment complex on the west side of El Paso, and then hang around most of the day getting stoned. At night we might scrounge up some cash and head to the Circle K up the street where construction workers hung out. We could stand outside and ask them to buy us a six-pack of beer and take us to the border, and in those days they'd actually do it. Imagine complete strangers shuttling teenagers down to the border to go party all night—I would absolutely kill my son if he ever tried some shit like that. But they were different times, and honestly, I can't decide if it was safer then or now.

At the border, it wasn't hard to get your hands on just about anything you wanted. We had our little bit of booze and smoke, but there was heavier shit going around, too. Some kids were doing blow. I remember watching them get completely out of their minds. Maybe my saving grace from real self-destruction was my sex drive. I watched those dudes getting themselves totally fucked up, and all I could think was, *man, how are you going to get chicks like that?* My primary interests were in getting to Juárez so we could go to the clubs and I could try to get laid. The needle in my brain was stuck

in a groove, playing the same lyric over and over: *girls, girls, girls*. For what it was worth, that objective kept me pretty straight.

Back in New York, I got back to a group of buddies who had similar interests. For high school, my mom sent me and Rodrigo to different schools; she didn't want us competing with each other. I went to Dwight High, and it was all really cool, snazzy kids. A lot of my friends were artists, musicians, and actors who came from eclectic backgrounds. My best friend in those years was a guy named Gideon. He was a tall biracial guy whose dad was a blaxploitation actor in the '70s and starred in *Live and Let Die*, and his mom was an Upper West Side Jew. I was surrounded by all these artistic souls, and I wanted that for myself, but I felt like I wasn't good at any of those disciplines.

Luckily, I *was* good at basketball. Aside from girls, it was the only other thing that kept me (mostly) out of trouble for a while. I hung out with a lot of African American and Latino kids, and we all played. One of my close buddies, Jay, lived in Bed-Stuy—back before the hipsters discovered it and sent the rent through the ceiling. That neighborhood was a shithole back in the day. I would take the C train all the way down from the Upper West Side around noon, get off at Clinton–Washington, and we would have these epic Saturdays, playing ball, scoring smoke. Jay's mom worked nights, so when she left around two, we'd head to his house, roll a blunt, and watch *Video Music Box* on Channel Five with Ralph McDaniels and Lionel C, who aired all the new hip-hop joints. We'd eat Chinese food, check out the new LL Cool J and all the rap groups that we loved, and afterward we'd catch kung fu movies dubbed in English. It was a perfect teenage weekend in '90s New York.

The city was the coolest place to grow up, because you didn't just watch hip-hop on TV; you lived down the street from the biggest names in the genre. Gang Starr was a rap group that was totally blowing up at the time, and they hung out right around the corner from Jay. These dudes were our idols. We saw them outside all the time, and one day, we were listening to their record and somebody got the bright idea that maybe, just maybe, if we stood outside smoking a blunt, they'd see us and think we were cool. We daydreamed about them inviting us over, and how we'd all become boys for life. So we rolled a fat one and went ahead with the plan, trying to hang

somewhere in view of where they were kicking it across the street. I don't know if they even noticed us, but I probably don't have to tell you, we never did become best friends with Gang Starr. We still had a pretty good time on our own, though.

Smoking pot wasn't exactly landing me any famous friends, but for me, it was just about being social, creative, being able to roll with a crew. Some days, we'd go to Sheep Meadow in Central Park to score. If we felt like pooling our money at night, there were a few clubs we could get into, like Palladium and Limelight. Those were the days when the whole house music thing was huge, and I *loved* to dance, so we'd go kick it at the clubs. I spent hours cutting up on the floor, turning on the charm for the ladies in the room, then head home in the middle of the night after a long day of doing not much of anything. What struck me sometimes was that for all their vast differences, my lifestyle probably wasn't too far from what it might have been had I stayed in El Paso. Different dudes, different scenes in which to score and chase women, but the general slate of activities would have been more or less the same.

I was able to finance my habits better than most of my friends. When I was fifteen, I started working coat check at Zarela, and I was making bank compared to my other friends. I'd pull home a hundred or a hundred and fifty a night on the weekends, not to mention a few phone numbers here and there. While most of the kids I knew were working as grocery store clerks or ripping tickets at movie theaters, I was greeting some of the city's most famous people, who were especially generous after a few of my mom's margaritas. It might as well have made me a billionaire as a teenager—I could buy me and my buddies an awful lot of dime bags with what I was making.

The money gave me a little freedom, and being a working man made me feel entitled to it. I figured I could do what I wanted with it, which was usually nothing good. It wasn't murder, but somehow I did usually get away with a lot. Of course, there were bound to be some snags. Going to a private school, I hooked up with a more affluent group of kids, too, so I also had a set of friends from the Upper West Side, this cool Albanian and Latin crowd who were older than me by a few years.

When I got together with them, it was at the other end of the city; we

went to Harlem to score, then to Central Park to hang out and smoke. Those guys always took turns rapping when they weren't making out with their girlfriends in the bushes and on benches. No one seemed all that worried about keeping a low profile. One weekend, we were jamming out with this old, piece-of-shit boom box, making way too much noise. The NYPD showed up and realized we were smoking, and in retrospect, they were actually very cool with us. They just told us we needed to get our shit and get moving. But one of the guys decided he was going to be a big man and started mouthing off. There's this phenomenon that I can't really explain, a kind of juvenile groupthink, that when one idiot starts popping off, the object of the group is to see who can be the biggest bonehead, so we all followed suit. In the end, one guy finally told the cops to fuck off, and we all started sprinting in all directions. I can tell you with confidence now, that's not a brilliant idea after a bunch of beers and some grass. The cops chased us down, and the next thing I knew, I was being tackled and tucked into the backseat of a cruiser.

At the local precinct, they sweated us a little, mostly to scare some sense into us (a losing battle), and ultimately they let us go with a warning. Maybe they figured it'd be a wakeup call. But the police and my mom and teachers could send all the messages they wanted, and they wouldn't have been able to get through to me; I tuned them out and never heard a thing.

TIO MARIO'S FAMOUS CHILI CON CARNE COLORADO-STYLE BURRITOS

SERVES 6

Eventually, Tio Mario moved to New York with me, and since I was traveling often, I was usually pretty run down, Tio took it upon himself to do some of the cooking, and when I'd come home, he always had this dish ready for me. He made everything entirely from scratch, toasting the chiles and grinding them by hand. Over the course of my life, it didn't matter if we were staying in a small Brooklyn apartment or a five-thousand-square-foot house in Louisiana, he cooked this chili no matter what. The comfort of returning to a home-cooked meal after being on the road was so meaningful to me.

Chili is always better after a day or two, so this is a great make-ahead recipe. Sometimes, Tio and I would have it stewed for dinner, and then if I was leaving town the next day, he'd make burritos out of the leftovers so I could take them on the plane (yes, I was that guy).

6¾ cups (1.6 L) chicken stock

4 dried guajillo chiles, stemmed

4 dried árbol chiles, stemmed and seeded

3 dried ancho or pasilla chiles, stemmed and seeded

3 pounds (1.4 kg) beef chuck or brisket

Kosher salt

Ground black pepper

¼ cup (60 ml) grapeseed or vegetable oil

1 large white onion, chopped

1 red bell pepper, chopped

1 carrot, peeled and chopped

6 cloves garlic, finely chopped

2 teaspoons ground cumin

1 teaspoon dried Mexican oregano

1 teaspoon ground cinnamon

3 bay leaves

1 medium ripe tomato (4 to 6 ounces/110 to 170 g), finely chopped

¾ cup (140 g) long-grain white rice

6 large (12-inch/30 cm) flour tortillas

1 cup (115 g) shredded sharp Cheddar or Monterey Jack cheese

½ cup (60 g) crumbled cotija cheese

4 radishes, thinly sliced

1. In a small saucepan, bring 2 cups (480 ml) of the stock to a simmer. Meanwhile, set a skillet over medium-high heat and toast the peppers (in batches, if need be) until they're fragrant, slightly charred, and a little more pliable. Transfer them to a heatproof bowl, pour the simmering stock over them (weight them down with a small bowl if they won't stay submerged), and set aside to steep for 30 minutes. When they're soft, cut them open and scrape out some or all of the seeds (leave them in for spicier chili), then, in a blender, puree them with the steeping liquid until smooth.

2. Trim the fat from the beef and cut it into approximately 1-inch (2.5 cm) cubes; season with salt and black pepper.

3. In a large heavy-bottomed pot, warm 2 tablespoons of the oil over medium-high heat until it starts to shimmer. Line a baking sheet with paper towels or a metal rack.

4. Working in batches, sear pieces of beef on one side, leaving space between them so you don't crowd the pan; cook undisturbed for 2 to 3 minutes, until nicely browned. Transfer immediately to the lined sheet, leaving the other sides raw (this helps it stay tender when it braises).

5. Adjust the heat to medium. Reserve 2 tablespoons of the onion for the rice; add the rest to the pot along with the bell pepper, carrot, and 1½ teaspoons salt. Sauté until the onion is soft, with a little color, 5 to 10 minutes. Stir in two-thirds of the garlic and the cumin, oregano, and cinnamon, and toast for a minute or two, until fragrant.

6. Return the beef to the pot along with the bay leaves, chili sauce, and 3 cups (720 ml) of the stock. Adjust the heat to high just until the sauce

comes to a simmer, then adjust the heat to medium-low, partially cover, and cook, stirring occasionally, until the meat is falling-apart tender, 2½ to 3 hours.

7. Meanwhile, make the rice: In a bowl, combine the tomato and the reserved 2 tablespoons of onion and the remaining garlic with 1 teaspoon salt. Set aside.

8. Rinse the rice until the water runs clear, shaking the sieve to get rid of excess water. In a large saucepan over medium-high heat, warm 2 tablespoons of the oil until it shimmers. Stir in the rice to coat it evenly in the oil, then adjust the heat to medium and keep cooking, stirring regularly, for 5 to 8 minutes, or until the rice is fragrant and lightly golden.

9. Stir in the chopped tomato mixture and cook for a couple of minutes, until the tomatoes have melted into the rice. Pour in the remaining 1¾ cups (420 ml) stock and adjust the heat to medium-high until the liquid is simmering. Cover, adjust the heat to medium-low, and cook until the liquid has been absorbed and the rice is tender, 15 to 20 minutes. If the rice finishes cooking but there is still more liquid, uncover the pot and keep cooking until the steam evaporates.

10. Remove the saucepan from the heat and sandwich a clean dishtowel between the lid and the pot; this helps absorb extra steam. After 15 minutes or so, fluff with a fork.

11. To make the burritos, preheat the oven to 400°F (205°C). Over the bottom of a 9 by 13-inch (23 x 33 cm) baking dish, spread a ladleful of the sauce from the cooked chili. Using a slotted spoon, scoop some beef into the center of each tortilla; add some rice. Wrap burrito-style and arrange the burritos snugly, seam side down, in the dish. Ladle more sauce over all the burritos to cover, then sprinkle with the shredded Cheddar and bake for 10 to 15 minutes, until the sauce is bubbling and the cheese lightly browned. Garnish with cotija and radishes; serve with a knife and fork (and napkin).

CHAPTER SEVEN

INTO THE WILD

My mom never did find out about that incident with the cops, thankfully (oops—sorry, Mom), but she was too smart not to know I was up to no good. And she absolutely hated the crowd I was hanging around with. She thought we looked like hoodlums and had no problem telling me so. I'd come home, spinning some outraged story for her about a group of grown-up white folks who crossed the street when they saw us walking their way. I was so self-righteous and full of angst, but my mom had no patience for it. "I'd walk in the other direction too if I saw you kids," she told me. That just fueled my indignation. I was looking for any little reason to be pissed off or justify fucking around.

As it was, my grades were shit and my attitude sucked. My mom wasn't about to let me get away with that kind of disrespect, but she was also running a restaurant and had a whole staff to worry about. She must've figured there had to be another way to get me to straighten out, so the summer I was fifteen, she found the closest thing to an intervention—three thousand miles away.

She sat me down and said, "You're going to camp." Honestly, at first I was pretty excited. I wanted to see the world, and a few weeks in California sounded more like a reward than a punishment. I'd watched *Meatballs* and *Caddyshack*; I figured it was going to be just like that. I was already daydreaming about the girls I'd be romancing in the great wide open when I had my bubble burst. "This is serious, Aarón," my mom told me before I flew out to Fresno to meet up with the ten or so guys I was going to spend my summer with. "There are consequences for your behavior."

When I arrived, the group leaders gave me and my fellow campers a similar pep talk. "The reason you're all here is that you have disciplinary

issues," the lead guide, a kid named Michael who looked barely older than we were, told us. He laid out the ground rules. This was no campfire-singing, "Kumbaya" sleepaway type of situation. The mission of the Outward Bound program is "development of character, leadership, and a sense of service with intellectual studies." That all sounds great, but let's be real: This was fucking reform school in the middle of nowhere. It was Scared Straight, but with snakes and tents and a bunch of gangbangers from all over the country. There was not a s'more in sight, and not a single girl for miles around.

Our group leaders were all hippie, crunchy-granola kids with socks up to their knees, getting their degrees in psychology and similar disciplines from schools like UC Davis. And we were all about to spend twenty-six days together, under the most grueling, backbreaking, will-testing circumstances imaginable.

We had eighty-pound packs, and we hiked ten or fifteen miles a day. We woke up with the sun, built fires at night out of necessity, and passed out from exhaustion when we could barely see straight anymore. There were no magazines, no Walkmans, no books, and not much camaraderie (in the beginning). My initial worries about warding off predatory animals were replaced by greater concerns, primarily protecting myself from the other kids on the trip. The mix of dudes was a recipe for trouble. We had gang members and true menaces to society who had already committed serious crimes, alongside some yuppie stoners with trust funds and too much time on their hands. It was like a prison that had no bars between the murdering lunatics and the crooked politicians. That kind of commingling made for some dramatic scenes.

One afternoon, a few days in, we were hiking along quietly, when one of the gringos lost his shit. "Fuck this!" he shouted, spitting and throwing his pack on the ground. It was hot, and we were all irritable. It was a matter of time before someone cracked. "And fuck you guys! I'm getting out of here." He threw up his middle fingers and ran crying into the woods.

The rest of us looked to our group leaders, wondering what the punishment was for going AWOL. We knew they were going to have to find this kid. They had to be responsible for making sure we went back with all kids accounted for . . . right? That meant slowing down the whole group, which

caused a lot of grumbling for some tired, frustrated, and scared teenagers. But our guides barely flinched. "He'll be back," Michael told us casually. If he was at all concerned about having lost one of his charges, he didn't let on.

Sure as shit, there he was, barely an hour later, trailing right behind us without a word.

But even the tougher dudes came close to cracking—their demonstrations were just different. There was this one hardcore kid named Miguel, a gangbanger from East Los Angeles with teardrop tattoos, and when we were about ten or twelve days in I noticed he was carrying a stick that he'd sharpened to a point on a rock. When we stopped for a water break, he stepped up to Michael.

"I don't like it here, homes." He got right up in our guide's face, twirling the stick in his hand menacingly. "I wanna get out of here." Everyone had been talking a lot of shit, but I remember thinking, *this dude—he's the real deal.* He might actually do something terrible. He held this makeshift shank up to Michael's neck.

"Do it," Michael baited him. We all stood with our jaws dropped, not sure what to do. "But let me ask you a question. Do you know where north is?"

Miguel said nothing, and we were all silent. It seemed like all the oxygen had been sucked out of the group.

"Just remember," Michael said, when Miguel didn't answer. "I'm the only one with the map."

"Fuck you," was all Miguel could muster, before he started crying. I had never seen a bigger demonstration of power in my life. Later on, we all turned on Miguel—it was some serious *Lord of the Flies* kind of shit.

I watched a lot of kids have similar episodes throughout the course of our time there. I guess maybe my stubborn pride gave me a strange advantage, watching them cry or break down. It's not that I took pleasure in their pain, but I decided early on that I just wasn't going to take part in it. I was petrified, but I promised myself never to show it. I couldn't have known it, but as I learned later on, that is how a chef handles business—a chef cries in the walk-in, not in front of the staff.

Toward the end of the twenty-six days, we were well into our daily hike, and there was a definite difference in how we carried ourselves. The mood

was much more relaxed; we could all sense the light at the end of the tunnel. But just when we were all feeling safe and comfortable, counting the hours until we could go home to our cozy beds, Michael stopped us.

"Miguel," he said, calling him to the front of the group. "Right here," he said, pointing to a small clearing on the side of the trail. We all watched, wondering what was going on. For more than three weeks, we'd operated according to more or less the same routine, and this was a definite departure from our usual itinerary. Michael turned to Miguel. "We'll see you in two-and-a-half days." At first, we wondered if it wasn't some kind of punishment, like solitary confinement. Then Michael explained to everyone that starting that afternoon, we were all going to be expected to go solo. "You're each going to be in an area by yourself. You're to make your own structure. You're going to handle your own food, and take care of yourselves—and *only* yourselves. We'll see each of you in two and a half days."

They started dropping us off at about one-mile intervals. After all that time, coming to rely on each other, finding some comfort in the pack, we were getting thrown to the wolves—literally. I was the last one to be assigned a spot. They gave each of us a tarp, which a lot of kids tented over a few tree stumps or stretched between boulders they found to sleep beneath. But seeing as how we had nothing but time on our hands, I figured I'd put it to use.

I spent that first afternoon collecting the biggest stones and rocks I could carry, and started building little walls. I made spackle with hay and muddy water. It took a few tries, but I figured out how to craft a thatched roof from fallen branches and leaves. It began as a way to kill the time, but then I found myself getting super into it. It's not like we had shit-else to do—it was either that or watch ants having sex. By the time I was through, I had a fucking outdoor condominium that rivaled some of the New York apartments I'd seen.

I hadn't ever really built anything with my hands before, and I was pretty proud of my little abode. But when night fell, sitting alone listening to coyotes and wolves cry was enough to scare the shit out of anyone. So the next day, I made an alarm, too. Using some of the twine we each carried with us, I rigged it so that if anything got close, the system would trip, and a branch would snap to wake me up. When they came back for us, even the guides thought that part was an especially cool touch.

A few days after they collected us, the tour of duty ended. To my own surprise, I had mixed feelings about leaving. Once we'd all accepted our fate, I think we all began to appreciate the scenario we were in. We fell into a routine and structure. When kids are acting out like we all had been back home, it's so often because there's some feeling of fear, of being unsafe in some way. Maybe that means absent or abusive parents, or poverty, wondering whether there will be food on the table at night or heat when the cold weather comes. Maybe it means just trying to get through the day without being bullied. For all our fears about being in the wilderness, and the uncertainty of things like weather or terrain, Outward Bound stripped away all those other worries. For three and a half weeks, we may have had a trying schedule of trekking, being physically put through the ringer, but we knew that we were always going to get up in the morning and make that journey, that there was someone guiding us in the right direction. We were going to breathe fresh air every day and see the landscape of a world so much larger than our usual ones. When you take away all those societal demands and variables, even the most hardened kid kind of gets to be himself for a little while, and figure out who that is.

Eventually, we began to rely on one another, regardless of our differences. The every-man-for-himself attitude we came in with softened into a sort of team spirit. There was a sense of camaraderie, that we could get through this thing, but we needed each other. We also learned we could rely on ourselves, which helped insecurities slowly transform into self-confidence, knowing we were all capable of carrying on.

When we'd first set out into the wilderness, I started a mental tally of the days, and every minute felt like an eternity. But by the time we were headed back to the bottom of the mountain, where we'd get our transfers to trains and airplanes and whatever modes of transportation were scheduled to carry us back to where we came from, I found myself a little sad. I saw the most beautiful country that summer, traversing the Sierra Nevada mountains, watching sunrises and sunsets, without distraction. I felt liberated in a way that made me realize for the first time, maybe I'd never felt truly free before. To find a space to just *be*, to see and feel things, to stand in awe of something—that's the space where creativity can thrive and introspection can occur. I learned

how to self-soothe, and the power of having a big, unchecked imagination to keep me company. Loneliness and isolation weren't new to me at that point, but I walked away knowing that when I had to, I could find a peaceful place, even if it was only in my mind.

It also taught me for the first time the benefit of counseling. At certain points throughout the trip, we spent our nights having one-on-one talks with counselors. We primarily discussed our experiences at Outward Bound, but those conversations inevitably brought up feelings from back home, and many nights I found myself lying awake afterward, thinking about my dad or El Paso, considering my mom's or my brother's struggles, hashing out ideas about the person I wanted to become.

It also solidified my love for the outdoors. I was born in such wide-open spaces, and while New York would continue to be my home for a few more decades, something about being in the wilderness agreed with me on a fundamental level. For so long growing up, I wasn't sure which parts of me were Mexican and which were American. When I became anxious or claustrophobic in the city, I worried there was something wrong with me. Being outdoors that summer, building from and living off the earth, breathing mountain air, my restlessness melted away, and I remembered my mother always telling us that the best days of her life were the ones she spent on my grandfather's ranch in northern Mexico. Her father was an artist, and he painted these beautifully moving, evocative scenes of their land that still hang in my mom's home today. I looked at them when I was a kid and felt a sort of longing that I couldn't identify. Later in life, after traveling more extensively, I would reflect on how important it is to Mexican people, despite their vibrant, bustling, metropolitan cities, to commune with the earth, to appreciate where food comes from, and to respect the land from which they draw inspiration and ingredients.

Maybe that's why spending three weeks surrounded by nature in the middle of nowhere made me feel so at home. After that summer, my heart was far from healed, but I was starting to have a sense of what my soul was really craving.

CHAPTER EIGHT

THE BIG (AND NOT SO) EASY

There was no last straw that did it, as far as I could tell. I think that's why I was a little blindsided. But they say the definition of "crazy" is doing something the same way over and over and expecting different results. My mom never lacked for inventiveness when it came to discipline, and she was totally at the end of her rope when, after Outward Bound, I fell back into my old habits. It's not that I didn't take away valuable lessons from the experience, but I didn't know what to do with them yet. Hell, maybe I just enjoyed the whole thing a little too much.

I did begin seeing a therapist back in New York. My mom really believed in strategies like that, which now I can see was pretty forward thinking in that era, especially for a Mexican woman. Even though I'd had positive experiences talking with my counselors in California, I resisted the idea. I didn't want to spend my time sitting down with some stranger and talking about my deep, dark secrets and feelings.

My first therapist's name was Mario Vasquez, a Latino guy who specialized in at-risk teenagers. With a chip on my shoulder, I walked myself to his office. When I sat with him the first time, I think he could sense my frustration. He tried to talk to me about depression, hoping, I guess, to figure out the source of my issues.

"Hey, man," he said to me, "You know, you're not the only one dealing with stuff." I did find some temporary comfort in that regard, but I still didn't want anything to do with ongoing therapy. I kept telling myself and everyone around me that I was fine. In retrospect, I think I was probably fearful of actually having to face those things that I was feeling, to articulate them and say them out loud. Even though he was telling me there were others out

there having similar issues, I didn't want to feel stigmatized or admit there was something "wrong" with me. I kept asking my mom, why do I have to do this? Haven't I been punished enough? Mario was a cool enough guy, but honestly I was too closed off, and there wasn't a thing he could have done to reach me.

It was quickly clear that if I wasn't going to be open to doing the work, there wasn't much point in putting me through it. So for my mom, it was on to the next strategy. I guess she figured if a month in the wilderness surrounded by a bunch of juvenile delinquents, or sessions with a professional therapist didn't set me right, a professional kitchen would get the job done.

She called up her own mentor, Chef Paul Prudhomme, down in New Orleans. I don't know what she told the man about me, but before I knew it, the next three months of my life had all been planned out.

"You're going to work with Chef Paul," she told me one day—in a conversation reminiscent of the one we'd had just one summer before—and just like that, I had a one-way ticket. When I was done with school for the year, I was off to Louisiana.

* * *

I stepped off the plane on a steamy Saturday afternoon. In those days, the restaurant was closed on Sunday and Monday, and Chef Paul was out of town, traveling on a book tour. The plan was for me to move into his guest house, but he wouldn't be back until Monday to get me set up, so that left me to my own devices for a few days.

I wandered New Orleans on my own for a while, and at first, I was totally entranced by it all. The colorful carriage houses, the friendly people, the music. Every single corner had the nutty, burnt-caramel aroma of fresh pralines. Women were dressed in their finery and men paid them the kind of grand deference you almost never saw anymore in New York.

I took myself for a meal at Lucky Dog's and splurged on a bag of pecans because it is physically impossible to pass them up—seriously, if you're ever in town, just try it, I dare you. I stopped in front of the door to a jazz club to listen to the meandering chords coming from within. The whole town smelled

like smoke and sugar. The heat in New York was notorious for baking bags of trash left on the sidewalk—it's not pleasant. But here, it amplified the already intoxicating aromas, allowing them to bloom and be carried through the city streets. The place was like nowhere I'd been. It had elements of El Paso in size, pace, and weather, but with a generous dash of New York's diversity.

Still, I was a stranger in a strange land. What originally seemed like another great adventure soon felt like a terrible mess I'd gotten myself into. With my host and benefactor not returning for two days, I had to check into the local YMCA for a few nights. The place was a shithole. The novelty wore off quick when I realized this summer was going to be nothing like those years in El Paso, with familiar faces and a cozy bed in a warm, familiar house. An afternoon was fun. Maybe even a weekend. But the whole summer? This was going to get old fast.

All I wanted to do was get to work. I didn't know what else to do with myself. But I'd also seen my share of kitchen life, and I knew at least a little of what I was in for. It was fucking grueling. I always loved being a visitor in my mom's restaurant, helping out but never being tied to a serious commitment. Now I questioned whether I was cut out for this kind of work on a full-time basis, especially in a foreign place, with totally unfamiliar cuisine.

When I was by myself in that room without the distraction of the street, I sat on the thin, tattered cot realizing that here I was, banished again. Twice in the span of a year. *Take a hint*, I thought, feeling like an exile. My mom didn't want me around, and I wondered if she worried I'd be a bad influence on my brother, too, who was plodding down his path to a bright, untarnished future. I saw some kids playing basketball from my window and thought about my buddies back in the city, who must've been wrapping up their own game and rolling a blunt. That's what normal kids were doing with their summertime. I looked at my watch and thought about Rodrigo, probably getting ready to tuck into some of my mom's cooking. I wondered what was on the table back in New York. There was no way I was going to sit in that room all night, so I grabbed some change and took a walk down Poydras Street. I found a pay phone, and I stared at it for a long while, trying to decide if making the call was a good idea. I knew it wasn't going to be well received, and that's if she picked up the receiver at all, but in the end I caved.

"I don't know if I can do this," I said, after I finally punched in the New York exchange. I was surprised at the sound of my own voice. Self-doubt was not a style I tried on very often, and it made me sound small and callow.

"Boy, you need to man the fuck up," my mom said. I mean, I knew she wasn't going to be thrilled, but I was still a little surprised to hear such disdain in her voice. She told me she'd already heard from Chef Paul, who called her to make sure I'd made the trip safe and sound. "Trust me, he has your best interest at heart." It hadn't occurred to me that this guy—this stranger—might actually give a damn about me. I felt so alone and isolated, it hadn't registered that there was all this planning around my visit. Other people who cared about me, who were organizing my trip, making certain I got to where I was going. Who were thinking about me.

Then she reminded me that she had her own reputation to protect. "I asked this man to do me a favor, Aarón. To get you right." Here I was, a walking, talking representation of Zarela Martinez.

"He'll take care of you," she assured me one last time, and then hung up the phone.

So that was that. Failure was not an option. By the time I returned the scuffed black receiver to its cradle and heard the quarter drop, I knew I'd cashed in my one lifeline call.

* * *

By the time Tuesday morning rolled around, I had found new resolve. If anything motivates me to do something, it's the idea of not being able to do it. I reached back for the way I'd felt during Outward Bound. I needed to summon that same kind of strength and self-confidence, and prove that I had what it was going to take no matter what the circumstances. I was sixteen years old, but once again, I had to be a man, and I knew I was going to be working among men for the next few months.

K-Paul's was a restaurant like none I'd ever seen. New York had some of the classiest restaurants on the planet, but the scope and style and grandeur of this place blew me away. When K-Paul's opened up for dinner service every night, it was a fucking *party*. Upward of 80 percent of our business

was tourists and travelers who had heard of Chef Paul. This was before food television; the number of chefs who could be referred to as "celebrities" was pretty limited, but Chef Paul, thanks to his mega-successful cookbooks and line of seasonings, was one of them. We closed during the lull between lunch and dinner, and by the time we opened up again at 5 P.M., there was always a line of people already outside, waiting to claim their reservations or clamor for whatever walk-in tables might be available. There were always these really cool doo-wop musicians playing for the crowd and keeping them entertained and in good spirits.

The restaurant was a perfect representation of New Orleans personality. In New York, the most in-demand restaurants usually had a little touch of pretension, intentionally. Diners were made to feel fortunate just to be walking through the doors, and everyone behaved with a level of seriousness that befit that exclusivity. K-Paul's was the polar opposite. When the doors opened to let those folks in, they were treated like true guests, like royalty. The whole staff erupted in applause to greet them. There was more live music inside as tables started filling up. It was so festive and energetic, even a little dramatic. It was something very particular to K-Paul's, and I've still never seen another restaurant like it.

But I wasn't there as a guest—I was there to cook. The plan was for me to present myself at K-Paul's that Tuesday morning, and once I passed through the swinging doors, all that Southern hospitality seemed to dry up quick. A surly crew of cooks grunted a welcome at me, and I could suddenly get a glimpse of myself in their eyes.

This was the era of Bourdain's *Kitchen Confidential*. This was a pirate crew, misfits and miscreants whose only currency was their honor and integrity. No one was in it for the money. There wasn't much to go around anyway. No one was in it for fame, because that wasn't something cooks even knew they could dream of yet. The only glory you could walk away with at the end of the night was the personal satisfaction of knowing the number of covers you pulled off, or wearing some triaged wound like a battle scar, its not having put you out of commission a badge of honor.

From the moment I walked into the kitchen, I could feel I was being sized up. I had been amping myself up as some great asset to the team—a

pair of strong young hands to help out with the work, like I was at Zarela. But now I saw that to them, I was just some punk kid who was going to need training and attention, who was going to suck up time and take up precious space and energy. I was a nuisance. Despite the New Orleans humidity, my welcome was pretty icy.

I introduced myself to the executive chef, a guy named Paul Miller. He said they were expecting me, and put me to work right away. The ladder was pretty old school at Chef Paul's, which meant starting at the bottom. It's a two-story restaurant, and they've since renovated the place, but in those days, there was a small kitchen downstairs and a much bigger one on the second floor. That's where we did all the baking and the majority of the prep. That was going to be my first department.

Within an hour, I was upstairs working with a guy named Mark, who we called Boogie. Don't ask me why—I wasn't about to ask any fucking questions, that's for sure. Boogie tossed me a bar towel and a bus tub and put me to work, peeling what I could only guess was about a metric ton of fresh New Orleans shrimp. These fuckers were *still moving*. I had a quick, quiet freak-out moment—I'd seen shrimp plenty of times, but not writhing around like this while I was trying to strip them of their shells.

From there on out, I was a grunt worker, ready to go at 6 A.M. every day, doing the same things over and over (and over and over) for a twelve-hour shift. The days started running into one another while I was busy cutting mushrooms and eggplant or peeling endless piles of shrimp. The restaurant's food relied heavily on what we call "the trinity": celery, bell pepper, and onion. To make ten gallons of Chef Paul's famous gumbo, we needed about fifty pounds of that stuff. No amount of scrubbing at the end of the day could rid the smell of onions on my hands after I peeled them all day long, or of briny seafood after I spent an afternoon cleaning crabs until my fingers were shriveled and calloused.

We had an interesting way of doing things at Chef Paul's. The chefs made a list so that everyone had a duty or chore that affected another part of the restaurant, all based on tenure and skill level. It created a kind of excitement to come into work and see the assignment. It was like this culinary grab bag— some days you could score something cool, like boning rabbits or breaking

down some whole animal. Other days, you got stuck boiling potatoes. But it was a really good way of cross-training everybody, and making clear that everyone's actions affected the rest of the kitchen.

So cleaning those soft-shell crabs was a gig I came to really appreciate later, when I was tasked with working the fryer station. When those suckers aren't done properly, pockets of water can accumulate inside, and when you drop them into the sputtering oil, those pockets pop. If the prep cook on the job that day was lazy about cleaning them, I'd wind up with hot oil bursting in my face. We had a cook named Bundy who was basically a walking tree trunk: this huge, African American dude, who would scream at me, "Boy, you better come up with those crabs, or I'm gonna *kick* your ass!"

Honestly, I still wonder if the guys in that kitchen weren't a little prompted to give me shit and break me in, put me through the ringer. After a while they started being a little sweeter with me—when I began to prove I could pull off the basics, and do it without complaint. I was seeing how I might come to feel at home at K-Paul's. It was the first time in my life that I realized something that would be important so many times in my future: that no matter where in the world I'd travel, what circumstances I found myself presented with, I possessed something that would help me survive. The people in kitchens spoke a universal language, regardless of culture or place. I may have been green, but I already had a working vocabulary of that dialect thanks to my mom. I would spend the rest of my life honing it, becoming more fluent, which meant that wherever I might venture, I would always find my countrymen.

Those first few days, though, it was all Greek to me. Or, to be more precise, all Cajun and Creole. And a whole slew of other things that were totally foreign. But I paid close attention to everything I was given to do. I didn't just peel the shrimp, I watched to see how they were prepared after I finished that part, what plates they ended up on and how they were cooked. I hated looking stupid, and the only way to avoid that was to get myself educated. After about a month of prep, I got a little bit of a promotion to stocks and sauces. I was really stoked to be getting recognized, and I was definitely ready to turn over the prep duties. But then I realized I was going to be in the back by myself, roasting bones and moving around brimming

twenty-gallon pots. I got strong quick, tipping them into the sink to strain them out without spilling a single precious drop. It was hot as hell, but that's when I got exposed to the stove and ovens, and I felt good knowing that my work was a critical part of the process.

Somewhere in the crush of it all, I became totally transfixed by the food. It was no wonder my mom wanted to meet Chef Paul after her first meal there. The man was a magician. I remember tasting his gumbo and feeling for the first time what all those people at my mom's parties must've experienced, being introduced to that broad palette of Mexican flavors. It's a powerful thing to taste food associated with a personal memory, and it's eye-opening when it comes from someone else's past. Eating a cook's food is like reading their memoir. It's a window into another world, another culture, another history, another soul. I felt like I understood Chef Paul on a whole new level after eating at his restaurant.

Like my dad, he was a soft-spoken man; he let his food do a lot of the talking. Every bite was like one of his winding stories—tales from his upbringing in rural Louisiana, something he was trying to tell people about his home state. I could close my eyes and be transported to his family's farm in Opelousas, only to reopen them right back in the New Orleans kitchen. It made me wonder where people traveled when they tasted my mom's food.

I got to know Chef Paul a little more personally than the other guys, because he wasn't just my boss, he was kind of my guardian. After those first few nights, I got settled into my place at Chef Paul's. Behind his family's home, there was a separate building with little apartment that was all mine, and man, was it an upgrade from that cell in the YMCA. It was this cool loft situation with a kitchenette where I could practice cooking for myself when I came home after a long shift. For a sixteen-year-old kid, it was exciting. It felt like living in my own place, and I was living *right*.

My days at the restaurant were spent picking up the basics, but in between, when there were moments to breathe, Chef Paul was also teaching me culinary lessons I've carried with me to this day. The man had the most amazing palate. A lot of today's cooks come out with a culinary degree and think they've got it all down pat. But Chef Paul came from an era when it was all about practice, repetition, paying intensely close attention to every

nuance, and dialing in every recipe. He had decades of experience in cooking to taste. In addition to the restaurants and his cookbooks, Chef Paul had a line he called Magic Seasonings. He developed these meticulously formulated spice blends that were super specific. Vegetable Magic. Blackened Steak Magic. Seafood Magic. Poultry. Pork & Veal. He made a Magic for just about anything you could possibly want to eat.

I couldn't imagine at the time why you'd need this whole line of different flavors. I asked him one day when we had one of those moments of calm, "Chef, what's the deal with the Magics? Why are there so many?"

"Boy, let me tell you," he said. Chef Paul's answers always came in the form of anecdotes. He had this thick Louisiana accent that I had trouble understanding in the beginning, but it came to be like picking up a dialect. He told me, "When I was growing up in Opelousas, food was *truly* free range and organic. We didn't have our animals closed in, so when the sassafras tree fell, or the leaves or lemons dropped from the branches, or when the wild oregano started to dry out, chickens would run around and eat that all up." I was so rapt by the way he painted a picture, I almost forgot what I'd asked him. "That meant all those flavors would make their way into the meat. Those chickens tasted like the earth; they had what you'd call *terroir.*" He almost took personal offense to the types of factory-raised chicken most people were purchasing. He was determined to make them see what they were missing out on when they came to his restaurants, and Magics were his way of extending that education to home cooks. "Nowadays, the chicken don't taste like nothing. I wanted to reintroduce nature—*flavor*—with those seasonings." He explained why each one was specific, and what it highlighted. Chef Paul was the first one to make me think about where food and flavor really came from.

I learned to cook at K-Paul's, but he also taught me how to *taste*. Not just to get seduced by the first thing to hit your palate, but the second and third, and even the fourth. To take time to savor food and not rush it. It was a lesson in slowing down and studying, appreciating, and understanding food, not just eating it. Such a lesson had to be learned in a place like New Orleans. It's a slower way of life that allows for observation, rather than the constant crank of New York City. It was a pace that agreed with me.

We also cooked a lot of stuff in the test kitchen next to his house. I went there to watch him cook up perfectly seasoned pork chops, or make a roux for étouffée. I learned the word *étouffée* meant "smothered" or "suffocated" in French. You could have drowned me with anything that smelled that good. My mouth watered when he plated up that rice and shellfish. Other times he fried rabbit tenderloin and paired it with this creole mustard sauce that had a punchy vinegar bite to balance out horseradish heat. It was addictive. I learned to make really classic New Orleans stuff, like oysters Bienville and stuffed soft shells with sauce Choron. I got to see the influence of French culture in Louisiana food, which gave me the first hints that world history was so important to understanding food.

I picked up knife skills and accumulated some of my first cuts and burns during my days at K-Paul's, but I also developed some personal interests from spending time with those guys. There was a gentleman named Canon Weiss, who I really admired. He had this scruffy voice and smoked like a chimney. He rode motorcycles, which I thought was so cool. Chef Bundy, this huge dude with a gold tooth, had a tattoo sleeve. He caught me looking at it one day, and put down his knife. I wasn't sure if he was going to tell me to get lost or put me through a wall. But then he smiled with that gold tooth glinting at me, "That's a tattoo sleeve, son. You ever see something like that?"

"No, Mr. Bundy," I stuttered.

"All right," he said. "When you're older, maybe we'll get you a tattoo. We'll see what kind of man you are then." He had no idea that by the time I was thirty, I'd be covered from neck to toe.

I listened to the stories of Chef Paul's crew while I learned the commandments of the kitchen. Outside the restaurant, I was learning a few things from them, too, and chief among them was this: Thou shalt not be an asshole. It took a little time for them to get that part through to me.

Since I didn't have a car, Bundy was kind enough to give me a lift home at night. Once I was over being utterly petrified of him, I got pretty comfortable, even bold enough to crack a few jokes. One night, I started making some stupid comments about his car, just being a wiseass.

"Bundy, man, you need to get these cushions reupholstered," I said to him one night on the way back to Chef Paul's.

"Boy, stop messing with my car," Bundy warned.

The next day, I finished work and hopped into the passenger seat. "Bundy, I like your music, man, but your speakers in this car suck."

"Boy, stop messing with my car," was all he said.

On the third day, in all my fucking infinite, sixteen-year-old wisdom, we were driving and I made a comment about the air conditioning. "It's hotter than shit in here, Bundy, can't you get the air conditioning fixed?"

Errrrr!! Thank god there was no one else on the road, because he slammed on the brakes so fast and violently that we left tire tracks for twenty feet. We were on Rampart Street, by Louis Armstrong Park, which was a notoriously dangerous part of town.

"Get the fuck out of my car," was all he said.

I was in shock. I looked around at the dicey neighborhood and gestured out the window. "You're joking, right?" I asked him.

"I'm not joking. Get out," he said again, barely looking at me. "Run your ass to that house now, and let's see if you make it." After I shut the door behind me, he rolled down the window to say, "*Maybe* I'll see you at work tomorrow," before he put the car back in gear and drove that thing—shitty speakers, broken air conditioning, and battered upholstery—all the way out of sight. I was terrified, and just stood staring for a minute before hauling ass like some Kurt Russell *Escape from New York* kind of shit.

Somehow, I survived in one piece, but man, was my confidence a different story. All that bravado went right out the window. The next day, when I showed up for work, I was quiet for once. When Bundy arrived, he looked at me with this sadistic smile and that gold tooth gleaming. "Oh, shit, boy. I didn't know if I was going to see you today. You get your mind right?"

"Yes, Chef Bundy," I said.

"Ya ain't gon' mess with my car anymore, are you, boy?"

"No, Chef Bundy. I ain't gonna say shit about your car anymore." He didn't say anything else, but he did go on driving me home from work every night.

Stuff like that suddenly made my mom look like a softy. But as tough as they were, and as much as I was a thorn in their sides, those guys still extended themselves to me. I only wish now that I had been more gracious and appreciative. Another cook—a guy named David Volion—was a big dude

who lived out in the Louisiana backwoods, about an hour from the city center. We called him Volio. He came to me one day while I was busy boiling chicken bones and said, "I'm inviting you to my house for a cookout on Sunday." I told him thanks, politely, and then went on with my afternoon. Of course, Sunday came and I had some other shit that I deemed more important. I didn't show up to Volio's cookout, and I didn't think much of it again.

That is until Tuesday, when I got to work.

"Aarón," Volio called to me when he got into work.

"Hey, Volio!" I was totally tone deaf to what was coming.

"Let me tell you something, boy," he said, with a seriousness that caught me off guard. "I don't know about where you come from, but down here, when people invite you to their house, it's a big deal. I told people you were coming. I spent *cash* to make sure I enough had food for you," he said. "Do you think I have extra money to buy meat for someone who doesn't show up?" I knew the answer to that question. None of these guys had that kind of money. It never even occurred to me that I'd be putting him out. "Don't do that again," he said. That really hit me. I thought about all the work and time and energy and money my mom put into those parties she had. I should have known better, and I felt like a shit.

Those guys never held back when they had something to teach me, and those lessons slowly started forming the man I am now. Being consistent, following through, being a person of your word. Those were things that my mom could have told me till she was blue in the face. But at Chef Paul's, I was in the real world, and I was never babied, not on the job or out of the restaurant. I never liked when my mom was disappointed in me, but I really wanted the respect of these gentlemen.

But nothing felt worse than letting Chef Paul down. One weekend after about a month and a half, when I'd gotten settled, I had plans to head home to New York for a visit. Before I packed my things to head home, though, I decided to take advantage of my new digs. Chef Paul parked his truck right next to my little space out back behind the house, so most of the time, I couldn't really mess around too much without fear that he'd pull up and catch me in the act.

That weekend, he was out of town. I'd made a few friends and figured it was a good time to invite them over for a little soiree. We trashed the place, like the knucklehead teenagers we were, but when I woke up the next morning and was running late for my flight, I figured I'd clean it up when I got back.

Fuck, was that a mistake. Chef Paul called me up while I was back in New York, and it was really the only time I ever heard him sound truly pissed. "You think I'm here to take care of your mess? Boy, you're going to clean this up when you get back here, and don't *ever* let me catch you pulling this shit again."

I got the message, but for some reason, I still thought I could get away with anything. No surprise, my next boneheaded move was because I was after a woman. On one of my days off, I met this gorgeous girl over on Canal Street. I think being able to cut it in one of the best restaurants in town gave me a cockiness outside of the kitchen, too, so I walked straight up and asked if she wanted to go out with me. In those days, we didn't have cell phones. Kids don't know how good they've got it now when it comes to dating. I mean, I would have made smoke signals to communicate with this girl. I was working the six-to-six shift the next day, so we made a plan to meet in the same place when I got through with work.

I floated into work the next day on a cloud of anticipation. I had a laundry list of prep to do, but I decided I was going to hustle like hell and get out of there a few minutes early so I could get myself right before my big date. At around four o'clock every day before service, we lined up and our chefs would sample all the sauces for the night. They tasted whatever you made that day, and gave it a pass or fail. I was tasked with was making the jalapeño vinegar that day. It was just three ingredients: sugar, jalapeño, and vinegar. You brought the mixture up to a boil, let it simmer slowly, then strained and covered it. That's it. It was one of those really simple things that added so much depth to Chef Paul's dishes.

It should have been a piece of cake to pull off, but I wasn't paying enough attention because I was rushing through my list. I boiled it too hard. All the jalapeños blistered, the sugar dissolved too fast, and it was a total mess. I knew it would never pass, but I didn't want to spend the time to do it again.

I figured, shit, I'm going to just bring this out there, and maybe he'll never know the difference. Forty-five minutes later, I brought the stuff to the tasting.

Chef Paul took one taste and put down his spoon. He was quiet, and for just a split second, I thought I might get away with it. Then he turned to me.

"You think I'm stupid, don't you?" The entire kitchen staff was standing there, watching this play out. They all started stepping back like I had the plague. One of the guys looked at me, shaking his head like, *Mexican, you fucked up big time, bro.*

"What's her name?" Chef Paul asked.

"What do you mean, Chef?"

"What's her name?" he asked again.

I was silent for a second, before I finally meekly admitted, "It's Chrissy, Chef."

"Kiss Chrissy good-bye, boy. You're working late tonight." The man had a sixth sense for bullshit. "I've been making this vinegar all my life," he said, a finger raised. "And you think you can put this past me? Let me tell you something, there will be women all the time, but we're not always going to have customers." He handed the vinegar back to me, and I went straight back to my station to start again. I never took a shortcut again after that.

* * *

I wasn't ready to leave when the time came to go back to the city, back to a regular life. The food bug had sunk its teeth in hard. By the time I left, I recognized that I'd just spent a season getting a culinary crash course in one of the most prestigious kitchens in the country, under the personal mentorship of one of the industry's most celebrated leaders. Nowadays, cooks pack their bags for Copenhagen, they follow around the René Redzepis of the world for a chance to stage at places like Noma. Back then, K-Paul's was high on the list of restaurants that could make or break a résumé. People came from all over the world to study his food. It was training no money could buy, and a gift that I'd be grateful for so many times in my career. My time at K-Paul's gave me an edge long before most of my contemporaries were even peeling carrots.

Something clicked in me that summer. Rather than being indignant

or rebellious, or feeling like the victim, for the first time in my life I started to fall in line. Not because I was being forced to, but because I felt like my contribution was important to the team. I knew that if I weren't there, my work would have fallen on someone else, and we couldn't afford that kind of thing. *We.*

I learned the things a kitchen can provide, in discipline, structure, and mentoring. To have consistency and be held accountable doesn't just keep you out of trouble; it gives you a sense of self-worth. Strong mentoring, finding somebody who can nurture you, see the best elements in you, have faith in your ability and believe in you, can be life changing.

Having to show up and hunker down was also a way out of my own head. For the first time in a very long time I didn't feel that same ache and apathy that had been so intense since my dad died. I was a part of a family, and I belonged somewhere, and though I would return to traditional therapy later on, food, cooking, and learning the ropes of the kitchen were exactly the remedy I needed at that moment.

I left New York pissed off at my mom for putting me out, but now I know that sending me to Chef Paul's was also a vote of confidence on her part. She wanted me to get my shit straightened out, but I carried her name, and Zarela Martinez would never have risked my compromising something so important if she didn't believe I was up to the challenge. She worked too damn hard to earn that respect. I like to think I did her proud during those days, and by the time I got back on the plane and watched the Gulf Coast shrink below me, I knew I'd spend my life following in her footsteps.

A QUICK NEW ORLEANS SHELLFISH ÉTOUFFÉE

SERVES 4 TO 6

This is the first dish I cooked for my mom at a dinner party after I finished training in New Orleans. It's a rite of passage in a cook's life to really get to show off for the people they love, and I couldn't wait to make this for everyone when I came back. I must've been seventeen at the time, and seeing my whole family take such pleasure in eating my food was a defining moment.

Later, when we had a challenge to celebrate New Orleans culture and food heritage, I cooked this on MasterChef. Everyone, Gordon Ramsay and Joe Bastianich included, ate it up.

¼ cup (½ stick/55 g) unsalted butter

¼ cup (30 g) all-purpose flour

½ yellow onion, finely chopped

1 green bell pepper, finely chopped

2 stalks celery, finely chopped

2 teaspoons kosher salt

4 cloves garlic, finely chopped

¼ cup (60 g) tomato paste

1 tablespoon fresh thyme leaves, minced

1 teaspoon sweet paprika

½ teaspoon celery seed

¼ teaspoon ground black pepper

¼ teaspoon ground white pepper

1 bay leaf

2 cups (480 ml) seafood stock

1½ to 2 pounds (680 to 900 g) shelled and deveined shrimp (21 to 25 medium to large shrimp), crawfish tails, lump crabmeat, or a combination

2 cups (240 g) cooked white rice

4 green onions, thinly sliced

Hot sauce for serving (I like to use Crystal, from Louisiana)

1. In a Dutch oven or large cast-iron skillet, melt the butter over medium heat. When it stops bubbling, adjust the heat to medium-low and stir in the flour. Cook, stirring regularly, until it's smoothed out a bit and is a dark blond color.

2. Stir in the onion, bell pepper, celery, and salt. Adjust the heat to medium and sauté until the onion is translucent and the vegetables begin to soften, 5 to 8 minutes. Stir in the garlic, tomato paste, thyme, spices, and bay leaf and toast them for a minute or two.

3. When the tomato paste no longer smells raw, pour in the stock and bring to a simmer. Cook for 5 to 10 minutes, until the stock has thickened slightly but is still actively, rapidly simmering, then fold in the seafood. Be careful not to overcook—it'll only need 3 to 5 minutes—and remove the Dutch oven from the heat when the meat is opaque but still tender.

4. Ladle the étouffée over scoops of warm or room-temperature white rice and top with fresh green onions and hot sauce.

CHAPTER NINE

A LESSON IN HIGHER LEARNING

After Chef Paul's I was on a mission. I can get through almost anything if I know it's only temporary, especially if there's something on the horizon I can train my eyes on. For me, that meant getting through high school on the promise of being a cook—a real, working one. I felt disconnected from my old friends in New York when I got back; they suddenly seemed so young, telling me the stories of their summer antics. By senior year, the distance only got wider when they started talking college scouting and applications processes. I knew I wasn't going to college. First of all, I didn't have the grades. Second, I was a future chef—there was no point spending that kind of money and time on a traditional four-year school.

Today, culinary school is treated a lot like other colleges and higher-learning institutions. It's an admirable career path with a whole lot of doors for opportunity to go knocking on. Graduates have their pick of disciplines: not just cooking, but marketing and food styling, writing and photography—the possibilities are limited only by what the right entrepreneur can dream up. Now, an education in food is a respectable, even enviable choice; in those days, it was basically one step up from boot camp, where kids went when they didn't have the grades or the gumption for a university but weren't total lost causes yet.

Being a cook never really required a degree—there was always the option to get a job in a kitchen and work your way up. Plenty of cooks did that, and still do. But I wanted that college experience, too. I wanted to live in a dorm and meet new people. I wanted to see a new city, and the idea of all the *mamacitas* I could meet had me more than a little excited.

Rodrigo was, not surprisingly, destined for higher education. It was never about whether he'd go to a university, just where. My brother is such a smart dude, and he applied himself like I only ever had in the heat of Chef Paul's kitchen. He probably could have had his pick of any school on the East Coast, but we were still dealing with my father's death in our own ways. For me, Tio Mario had been an acting father figure in El Paso, and then I found another patriarch in Chef Paul. For Rodrigo, it was always our older brother. So instead of Tufts or Brown or Yale, he packed his bags and headed straight back to the Lone Star State where he could be close to Spanky.

My mom didn't love the idea of him being so far away, but she was thrilled when he got his acceptance letter from Texas A&M. I wanted to make my mom proud, too. I hoped my chosen path would earn me a little of her approval. It was more complicated than just making decision to have a life in cooking, though. Because she had worked so hard to get where she was in her career, my mom knew firsthand how serious I was going to have to get if I wanted to make it in her world, especially as a Latino. That insight made her pretty tough on me, but she always led by example.

My mom never stopped pursuing her own continuing education; she was still taking regular trips to Mexico and elsewhere to stay sharp and ahead of the game, especially now that more Mexican restaurants and chefs were showing up on her turf. I sometimes wondered why she bothered with those trips. Her story was already a culinary and business model for success. For all my resistance to authority and lack of appreciation for traditional education, though, that was something that stuck with me. She never stopped trying to get better, to evolve and further her understanding of her craft. To this day, it's something that I consider a personal philosophy—not just in cooking, but in life. You know nothing unless you know there's always more to learn.

So I guess it's not surprising that even though my mom never went to cooking school, she was adamant about her kids getting an education one way or another. I think I also knew somewhere in my mind that it would have been a big deal to my old man, too. He always took school so seriously, and to that point, I really never had.

Around the time that I needed to really hunker down on my college scavenger hunt, my mom had one of her trips planned. Most of the kids I

was in high school with were doing their college scouting on the weekends with their parents. They'd all pack up in their family station wagon or a train, and go tour schools up and down the Eastern Seaboard. Those kids didn't have a mom who was an entrepreneur and a free spirit. My mom left the task in my hands before she took off. I was seventeen, I should have been able to handle the responsibility of choosing my own future.

"When I get back, let me know what you decide," she told me as she was packing her bags, and left me enough cash to travel and tour a few schools.

I did what any red-blooded American teenager would do. I spent the cash on weed and took my high school sweetheart, Annie, out on a few dates. By the time my mom came home, I'd visited exactly zero institutions of higher learning. I looked at the stack of brochures that had come in the mail: International Culinary Center (ICC), Culinary Institute of America (CIA), a few community college programs. Then the Johnson & Wales pamphlet caught my eye. I thought Providence sounded cool. It was far enough away that I'd be on my own, plus Annie was going to school at Clark University in Worcester, Massachusetts, and being romantic types, we'd both promised we would take trips to see each other. Those all seemed like good enough reasons to go ahead with it. Mission accomplished.

When my mom got home, I was ready with my answer: "Johnson & Wales."

* * *

Today, JWU (or *J-woo*, for the cool kids out there), has earned a level of prestige. Some of today's top-tier culinary talents have degrees hanging on their walls from the school. But in the mid-'90s, we had a saying: "When all else fails, Johnson & Wales." For every kid who went to its hallowed halls with some daydream of global food-industry glory and Michelin stars, there were fifty like me who had to pull a name out of a stack just to confirm for their parents they could be a contributing member of society. Those days, chefs weren't revered—they were barely given the respect of the cockroaches they shooed out of their kitchen. And they were *definitely* not celebrities, so no one was going to those institutions with stars in their eyes like they do today.

When I went to culinary school, we understood it meant signing up for a lifetime of painfully long shifts in punishingly hot kitchens, notoriously pathetic pay, poor health insurance (if any at all), and entering into a business where the percentage of failure both professionally and personally (I couldn't name a chef who wasn't divorced—and that's if they had ever been functional enough to get married in the first place) was matched only by the probability that physical burnout, or some kind of mental breakdown, would force you out the door by age thirty-five.

There were only three reasons you went to cooking school. One: You had no other options. Two: You were totally, unequivocally in love with the craft, and nothing else could possibly make you happy. Three: You were insane.

I was a little of all three.

* * *

When the big day came, I packed my duffel bag with a few necessities, plus the school's required supplies. I thought it was the coolest thing that while my friends were out buying those mechanical pencils and dropping a thousand bucks on computers, I was picking out knives in all shapes and sizes. My sister, Marissa, had moved to New York from El Paso, and she and her boyfriend, an Italian jeweler named Joey Germano who I always really liked, were going to help me get moved in.

When the day came in August, we drove up I-95 through New York into Connecticut, and I watched the city give way to the shores of the Long Island Sound. When we got into downtown Providence and passed through Federal Hill, kids from Rhode Island School of Design and Brown were all outside, playing Frisbee and volleyball, and there might as well have been choirs of angels singing, because it felt like there were hot chicks everywhere.

But then we crossed the train tracks into Cranston, where I was going to be living. The streets were beat up, potholed, and dilapidated, and when we turned down Narragansett Boulevard, my sister started crying. Joey, the loving boyfriend that he was, looked shocked.

"What's wrong, baby?" he asked her.

She turned to him and I could see her tears from the backseat. "I can't leave my baby brother here!"

When we pulled up to the address, I didn't know it could get any worse, but it did. The dorm was called *Hospitality*, but the place looked barely habitable. It was actually an old Howard Johnson's that the school took over and converted into dorms. We unloaded the car while Marissa got a hold of herself, and as we walked down the hallway, scanning the rooms to find the number that matched the piece of paper in my hand, I started to smell something ultra-gnarly. I sniffed the air dramatically and looked at Joey. He raised his eyebrows as if to say, *Don't look at me, dude.*

It only intensified as we got closer to our destination. *Fuck*, I thought. And of course, *of course* it led us directly to my dorm room. The door was already wide open, and the stench was overpowering. Inside, this big, hairy dude was lounging on one of the beds, stinking to high heaven. I'd worked in sweltering kitchens, in the humidity of New York City and the height of a Louisiana summer. I had a pretty high tolerance for funkiness. But for fuck's sake, this school was educating the future of the food service industry—homeboy needed to clean himself up before he could start cooking someone's food.

"Hey, bro," was as much of a greeting as he could muster without sitting up, which seemed out of the question, and before I knew it, Marissa was crying again.

Without missing a beat, Joey took her arm and led her back the way we came, all three of us trying not to breathe through our noses. "Okay, let's go for a ride," he told her. "We gotta go get the kid some beer."

Fortunately, there were some other spots available, so I suffered in silence, holding my breath for a night, and the next day arranged a room transfer. I spent the next night getting familiar with the laundry situation; I was afraid I might never be able to deodorize my stuff enough to interact with other human beings again.

After that first nightmare, I got hooked up with a cool group of guys—some Puerto Ricans who played basketball and reminded me of my friends back home—and things started looking up. Being in the Northeast, I also got

introduced to the kinds of people I'd never met in the city or in the South. I became good friends with a guy named Schuyler Mast. When he introduced himself, I legitimately thought his name was a joke, and I half expected him to tell me he grew up on a yacht. Schuyler was this tall, hip-hop white boy from Wellfleet, Massachusetts, who played basketball and loved to smoke pot. His girlfriend was a super-fine Olympic figure skater. He and I would kick it all the time, but he was really dedicated to his girlfriend. I appreciated and respected that about him. I, on the other hand, was having doubts about my own relationship.

I loved Annie, and I'd been really devoted toward the end of high school, but I also wondered what else was out there. After a few months of making those bus trips back and forth on the weekends, we both realized we might have made a mistake. We'd violated the number one law of higher-education living: Never go to college in a relationship. It's like bringing sand to the beach. It's not that we didn't care about each other, but neither of us were really getting the full experience of living away. We were watching our single friends and envying their freedom, and I think we both just understood our young love had run its course. We ended things amicably, and after a few months, I was a free man.

I realized there *was* something pretty great about my building—it was co-ed. We had some very hot girls, and I made up for lost time after Annie. I'm not sure I slept a single full night while I was there; I was ready to rock at all times. I spent time between classes hanging out with friends, drinking some beers, talking up the ladies, smoking a little grass, and always having elaborate, nerdy discussions about food and cooking. I was excited to find some like-minded kids.

Courses were pretty intense, and classes were either in the morning or evening, when they lasted until 9:30 or 10 P.M. As much as I was enjoying the social part of my education, in the classroom I was disappointed to find myself uninspired. By then, I'd worked in some of the best kitchens in the country, under renowned chefs. Spending three hours learning to brunoise carrots felt like torture to me.

I liked a handful of classes, though, and all the instructors were characters. Baking was taught by this old Bavarian dude, who must've been breathing

unrefined flour for thirty years. Between his thick German accent and the fact that he spent most of the class time wheezing so hard I was thought he might keel over any minute, it was nearly impossible to understand him and tougher to retain any real information. But there were some great perks to that class; on days we'd make croissants or scones, we were sent back to our rooms with a few boxes, which was a pretty good way to barter for smoke.

Meat class was a good time, too, and I loved learning from the old butcher who absolutely refused to be referred to as "Chef."

"I'm a butcher!" He always told us. "Stop calling me 'Chef!'" During one lesson, I got a good laugh out of everyone by running around, slapping pieces of meat that all the students were supposed to be breaking down while the butcher was out of the room. From then on, I was known as "The Loin Man." I never really did stop being a ham.

We had a service class, where we dressed up in little bow-tied tuxedo shirts and learned to take orders, drop food, and interact with customers. I'd never worked front of house before, so I enjoyed the contrast. Garde manger, on the other hand, where we were making aspic and tomato flowers, left me wondering when the hell I was going to use that stuff in the real world. And absolutely no one liked the food service course, which was a sort of on-the-job training, cooking for the students in the mess hall. It meant getting up to go make scrambled eggs and toast for five hundred kids at four in the morning, and it was such a grind.

My favorite class, and the only one I passed, was American Regional Cuisine. The chef instructor really took to me. I wasn't the only kid who had some real-world experience, but between my mom's influence and my time at K-Paul's, I had a lot of diversity in what I could cook by then. I managed to impress him when an assignment called for a special regional dish, and I made gumbo with shrimp and andouille sausage. I made a roux in class, dark and deep and aromatic, with tons of French butter and layers of seasoning. It was pretty advanced stuff for that stage in the game. The dish had to be accompanied by a write-up, so I recounted its history, and my own experience in Louisiana. I was genuinely proud of the project, and I couldn't wait to show my mom that I'd finally done something right. I think she still has the paper to prove it.

Outside the classroom, I started to realize the value of my heritage, too. There were some other Latino students, and other kids of color, and a lot of us got connected on the basketball court. But there weren't a lot of Mexicans, and I still felt like an outlier. Sometimes, I'd take trips to the city and my mom or my sister would send me back with food, a lot of which was foreign to my classmates. It was spicier and bolder than what many of them had been exposed to, and I found myself giving lessons in Latin food (long before I was really qualified to do so). I taught them about enchiladas and they taught me about whatever it was they brought back from their homes. There was an exchange of food and culture, and I think I learned more in those experiences than in the classroom, where the formal education was primarily European.

We made béarnaise sauce and fondant and whipped potatoes, all that old-school French technique. I honestly didn't really care for the food we were cooking, which was part of my problem. That was totally different than my experience at Zarela or K-Paul's, where I was always in awe of every ingredient and flavor. I later learned to really appreciate those dishes, but at the time I still had so much to learn about subtlety and nuance that I couldn't detect any of that yet.

There was also a general feeling that none of the other kids were taking it seriously. If there were thirty of us in a classroom, ten were doing it in earnest. There wasn't a ton of competition motivating me, and I became disinterested in going to class. After feeling like I'd finally found a learning environment that was going to speak to me, I was back to being the kind of student I was in high school. I started to wonder why I'd wanted to go there in the first place. I wanted badly to be a legitimate cook—I knew enough about commercial kitchens to know how much work I still had to do. But as always, I was too far ahead of myself. I wanted to be done with school even before I started, and I was too cocky to understand the value of learning the basics.

Like the formative years of my adolescent life, I wanted to skip ahead and get right to the good stuff. Fundamentals didn't excite me, and it didn't take long for my grades to start slipping. Like anything, you only get out what you put in, and I wasn't giving school much of myself at all. I realized

that even though I knew my future was in the kitchen, it was not going to include a culinary degree. After my first year, I rolled up my knives and went back to the city.

* * *

I'm often asked today about culinary school: Is it worth the time? The investment? Or is it better to work through the ranks, paying dues and taking *stages* in Michelin-starred kitchens, being mentored by famous chefs and picking it up as you go along? I can't say I have the answers to those questions, but I can say that with the right attitude, there is value to every learning experience. Dedication means not only peeling potatoes twelve hours a day, trying to get faster, to get more accurate, to minimize waste and mistakes. It also means understanding *why* things are done a certain way, being cognizant of history and technique and not just memorizing something because you're a foot soldier, but because being intellectually tied to and curious about the craft will *always* keep you a cut above.

In my case, I think a little knowledge was a dangerous thing. I didn't think I needed the formal training, and later realized so many times that I really could have used it (that aspic did rear its wobbly head, and those French techniques I didn't care to learn crop up in almost every cuisine).

Where you choose to do your learning—whether in an accredited institution or under the mentorship of some industry leader who is generous with their time—won't matter as much as how you choose to put those skills to use. Some paths may be more available than others. Culinary school comes with a price tag, and it's a rising one. It can be prohibitive for some aspiring cooks, depending on where they're coming from, but luckily more scholarships are being established, and schools are making more room for kids who maybe can't afford full tuition. The beauty of this profession has always been its welcoming, egalitarian nature. Now, more than ever, it's an industry open to everyone, and there are lots of avenues to a successful career.

As an older chef, I now romanticize those school days when screwing up a sauce as a student just meant having to start from scratch, when no hungry

diners were counting on you, and no cooks were breathing down your neck, tallying your food cost.

Had I known when I decided to cut my cooking education short that I was about to have a culinary baptism by fire—that the real world I wanted so badly to be working in was so high stakes—I might've thought twice before I walked away from the classroom.

CHAPTER TEN

NUEVO LATINO 101

When I got back to New York in 1995, it seemed like I was finally going to start living the life I'd been waiting to lead since I was sixteen years old. I traded a Providence dorm for an East Side apartment, and my blue JWU necktie for a pair of proper checks. With a pocketful of subway tokens, I was back in my city, a grown man at long last.

But even a grown man isn't foolish enough to deny a little help from his mama when she's willing to offer. She had very few things to say about my abrupt departure from the world of higher learning, but she got one very important message across: "You're grown now," she told me. "Go make your money."

Fortunately, she didn't have to hound me on that front. All I could think about was getting myself into the kitchen and getting paid. My mom always made sure we were taken care of, but there were absolutely no handouts beyond that. Even in high school, I had to work for every dollar. I had some rich-kid friends at my private school, and a lot of them were getting serious allowances to blow on whatever they deemed worthy that week. As an adult and a father now, I'm grateful for the way she raised us. I learned the value of money as a very young man, and it never occurred to me to hit my mom up for cash. I also knew I was going to want to start taking some ladies out on the town, and I would need some padding in my bank account for that. No woman in her right mind was going to waste her time with some lowly cook trying to take her to Gray's Papaya on a first date.

My mom wasn't making any more financial investments in my future after cooking school, but she did offer something a lot more valuable—her pull. She and I sat down one Sunday over dinner and talked about options.

She knew the New York restaurant scene and its major players better than any headhunter, and she had a few folks in mind who might be able to help me out, in particular at a spot called Gramercy Tavern. Danny Meyer was the restaurateur behind it, and he'd already made a name for himself with Union Square Café and other restaurants. It seemed like everything he touched became New York City gold. Gramercy Tavern was gorgeous; it had a wood-fired grill and served simple but unbelievable food that diners and critics were going bananas for (and still are more than twenty years later). It was also turning out some killer talent. The chef and co-owner at the time was a young gun by the name of Tom Colicchio.

Mom made a few phone calls, wrote a name and address down on a piece of paper. "Go see this man," she told me. "He's expecting you."

I wasted no time printing out my résumé and hitting the pavement for my interview. But on my walk down Twentieth Street from the train, fate intervened. Gramercy Tavern was within spitting distance when the sign of another restaurant caught my eye. *Patria*. I knew that name for some reason, but I had to search my memory for where I'd heard it before. It dawned on me that my mom mentioned it to me once after she'd had dinner there. She raved about the pan-Latin flavors and ingenuity of the chef, Douglas Rodriguez, and it stuck in my mind as a place to check out when I had the time.

I looked ahead at Gramercy, and then back to Patria. The door was open, and inside I could see the familiar pre-opening hustle of a restaurant in preparation for the day. There were a bunch of Latino-looking folks, and I just had a feeling about the place. I had a little time to kill, so I saw no harm in taking a quick detour to see what it was about.

I walked in the door and got a full look at the place. It was a stunner— a huge, glamorous space with three tiers. There was a beautiful kitchen in the back with a big raw-bar area where I later learned the ceviche was made fresh. I had never seen a Latin restaurant looking so nice in my life. That kind of food had always been home style to me. But this was a *fine* restaurant.

I was wearing slacks and a white button-down, carrying nothing but my CV. I had never really been on a job interview before, and I wanted to look the part. I was suddenly feeling a lot more nervous, which made me realize how badly I wanted Chef Douglas to like me. I introduced myself and asked

to speak to the chef. In retrospect, it seems like a ridiculously ballsy move for some random kid stepping in off the street to demand an unscheduled meeting with a chef of his caliber. Luckily, I didn't know any better. I was young enough not to understand that I had no business being so brash; if I had, maybe I would have hesitated.

Before I knew it, Chef Douglas was in front of me, pulled away from his kitchen to have an audience with me, to hear what *I* had to say. Which was that I—a nineteen-year-old with no prior professional New York cooking experience and fresh out of culinary school (sans degree), without a meeting or any warning—wanted to work for him.

Douglas is a tall dude with a thick head of black hair. He commanded a presence instantly, and he sized me up through these cool black glasses that were his signature. Looking at me a little sideways with a bar towel in hand, he asked me, "Do you speak Spanish, son?"

"Yes, sir," I told him, and switched languages, in case he needed me to prove it.

He seemed satisfied. I'd later understand that very little English was spoken in his kitchen; he needed to know if I would be able to communicate with his crew. It was the first of many, *many* times in my career that I would be so thankful my mom made sure we kept up with our Spanish.

I was starting to sweat a little when he looked at his watch. "Can you work right now?" he asked.

It was not at all the reaction I was expecting—nor was I exactly prepared to head into the kitchen in my interview clothes. But that didn't stop me, and I instinctively heard myself saying, "Absolutely, Chef."

Forty-five minutes later, I was in the basement peeling a mountain of shrimp instead of sitting in a meeting with Mr. Colicchio. (I remind Tom of this when I see him now. Of course, when I say, "Remember when I almost worked for you?" his response is, "Who says I would have hired your ass?" Touché, Tom.)

I didn't yet realize it, but the team behind Patria was a fucking *powerhouse* group. It felt like the *Ocean's Eleven* lineup of New York City's Latin dining scene. We had Phil Suarez—this really charismatic Puerto Rican guy who grew up in Washington Heights. Total mover and shaker, a truly self-made

man, he was an advertising legend before he became a restaurateur. He met his partner, Bob Giraldi, playing basketball. Bob's main gig was directing music videos and commercials. You may have heard of one in particular: a little joint called *Thriller*, by a dude named Michael Jackson. Bob was brilliant, and those two guys had a production company before they started dabbling in the restaurant world. Phil had his eye on another chef he found dining at a four-star restaurant named Lafayette, a young French immigrant who'd come to New York to cook called Jean-Georges (I don't think I need to include his last name here; he's basically the Madonna of fine dining). They recruited him and opened JoJo, which was quickly named Restaurant of the Year.

Douglas had been working in Miami, where he grew up, and had a restaurant called Yuca on Lincoln Road. He was churning out some mind-blowing food, taking traditional Grandma-style Latin dishes and elevating them with modern technique and impeccable ingredients. It was such a hit that Phil and Bob took notice all the way from New York. They convinced Douglas to come up north, on the promise of partnering on a restaurant that would change the way diners knew Latin food in the city. With that all-star heavyweight lineup, Patria was born.

The place opened to a reception they couldn't possibly have imagined for Latin food. The city, it seemed, was starving for it. Patria was bold and energetic, but still refined and elegant. A few years later, when Ruth Reichl reviewed it in 1996, she wrote, "I walked in tired and jaded, convinced that I had eaten everything. I walked out with an entirely new attitude: Douglas Rodriguez is having such fun in the kitchen that his exuberance is impossible to resist." I can attest to that last part without question—the restaurant crew had that energy every day.

My first few days were such a rush. I couldn't believe my luck. Not only was I finally living the life I'd been daydreaming about since I was sixteen, I was doing it in one of the hottest kitchens in New York City with some of the most creative Latin cuisine I'd ever seen, under a ridiculous assembly of talent.

It wasn't just Douglas and the masterminds behind the creation of Patria. Every single one of the hands on deck behind the swinging doors was impressive to me. Right off the bat, I met Alex García and Michael Cressotti. They had known Douglas in Miami, where they worked for a chef named

Robin Haas. Douglas then tapped them to come to New York to help open Patria. They didn't stay very long—they'd only come on board to get things going, and then moved onto other gigs—but both became fixtures in my life, both professionally and personally (Mikey even went on to be the best man at my wedding).

Alex was this big, gregarious, and lovable teddy bear. He was Cuban born, raised in Puerto Rico. We hit it off, and he was like an older brother for me. Mikey was the only white boy in the crew, but he still got all the respect from the Latinos because he was unbelievably fast.

Then there was Adrian Leon, "The Ceviche Master," a Mexico City–born dude who has opened several restaurants in the decades since; Ray Mohan, a guy from Guyana who had worked with Jean-Georges, which we all knew was a big fucking deal; Pierre Schultz, who came from Vong and worked sauté. The list goes on. Needless to say with that kind of talent around me, I had to do my best to keep up. I was cocky, and I'd managed to earn respect from an older, arguably surlier and less civilized kitchen staff already in my day. I was also extremely green and terrified that it would show, but I wasn't afraid to bust my ass to make up for what I lacked in experience. I was determined to earn my keep, and I had to make sure they saw me try.

Even in that high-level, high-pressure kitchen, we partied as hard as we worked. We got in all kinds of trouble after hours, but we toughened up when we needed to. Douglas liked to have a good time, too, but he was always very present. He led by example just like my mom, and that was something I took to heart.

Douglas showed up every day; he demonstrated how to have respect for and pride in Latin food, and the importance of knowing its roots. He was inspired by a trailblazer named Felipe Lombardi Rojas. Felipe was a Peruvian guy and a chef, and he wrote a beautifully in-depth book in 1986 called *The Art of South American Cooking*. It's a text I still look at often for inspiration; it was so ahead of its time. And a lot of the stuff we did at Patria under Douglas had the essence of the stuff Felipe did, but more elevated, modernized for the mid-'90s palate.

In that sense, it wasn't just my first big-league job; it was also a formal education in all things Latin. I grew up with Mexican food—that was already

in my veins. But in that kitchen, there was so much more. Guatemalan, Argentine, Venezuelan, Chilean—the influences were far ranging, and the food was exploding with color and flavor. I learned about the diversity of Latin cuisines as much as the cultures behind them. It was like the United Nations of Latin countries in there. I was working with people from Ecuador, the Dominican Republic, Puerto Rico, Peru. I learned the nuances of their accents and dialects, I got to know their rich histories through the dishes they made for family meal, and it influenced the way I cooked and looked at the world. I was used to speaking Mexican Spanish, but I spent so much time with that diverse team that even my accent changed. A little while after he left Patria, I met up with Alex. "You've been hanging out with a lot of Caribbeans, man," he said to me. "I can hear it."

We had a lot of Latina women at Patria, too, one in particular who we just called Mama. She must've been about sixty-five years old, and she was in charge of making all the *empanadas*. It was something I learned in that kitchen as well, that in Latin culture, it was often the women who did the really technical, detailed work—tamales and sauces and breads. Our pastry chef was a Dominican woman named Sonja. We were just a big, multicultural family, and I think we all felt pretty welcome and accepted.

And the food—the food was unbelievable. We were known for a dish called "Fire & Ice"—a coconut ceviche with tuna and ginger and tons of chile, served out of a coconut shell over ice, surrounded by a flurry of snow-white coconut shavings. Or *ceviche negra*, octopus and scallops served in an emulsion of black-as-night squid ink. Golden *arepas* were made fresh, one side with yellow and the other with white corn, stuffed with a satiny black bean puree and farmers cheese, served with blistered heirloom tomatoes and finished with a fire-branded star. The stuff coming out of that kitchen was creative and beautiful and completely unique. We had a dessert *burro* made to look like a cigar; we called it the "Smokeless Cuban." It was stuffed with dulce de leche and chocolate mousse, rolled in tons of cocoa powder and served with matches made from spun sugar and a whipped coffee custard—even a cigar band with the restaurant's name. Every night I went to work so proud to be putting my small stamp on each of those dishes.

One of the things that really struck me at Patria was that, in my expe-

rience up till then, Latinos were the dudes washing the dishes, or working the graveyard shift cleaning house. They were *not* the garde manger, the sous chef, or the executive, and certainly not the owners. Their names weren't on the menus or the signs; they were never in the papers. But this restaurant changed all that. It revolutionized what was possible for Latin food; the idea of doing haute cuisine that wasn't French or Italian was unheard of before Douglas. But it also reset the expectation for Latinos in the kitchen. That's not to say that the industry instantly adopted this new paradigm. It's been decades since my days at Patria, and I think we're only now seeing major progress in immigrant representation at the highest levels of the food business. But the team that those guys built at Patria was definitely a starting point. I felt really fortunate to be a part of that—it was something special.

I also saw the significance of my mom's restaurant in helping to make way for a place like Patria. She was the first to start opening up diners' minds, and in the fact that we could prepare the foods of our heritage in a way that wasn't kitschy or cheap or commoditized, I recognized a direct connection to her work. We could create our food with quality ingredients and sound technique, skill, and nuance. And when it was done with love and authenticity and genuine care, people responded, big time.

I watched the phenomenon of our diversity being embraced in the dining room and talked about in the newspapers, and new dreams started taking shape in my mind. At the time, Food Network and food television still weren't on anyone's radar as a way to enhance a cooking career. But at Patria, for the first time I saw bigger opportunities for my future. As a Latino, I knew I could work in a kitchen, but now I saw that I could also open my own restaurant, write my own script—as long as I had something to say.

In the meantime, though, I was still a low man on the totem pole. I woke up in the morning, grabbed my whites, flipped on my Walkman, and made my way to Gramercy Park. Every day was exciting. The way the schedule was set up, we had to work three double shifts to get two days off back-to-back, so essentially we had to open and close one station. I had to prep and stock my own shit, work my own service, take a lull, prep, stock, and work service again, and then close.

I was fine with that, because I lived for the job. I loved all the staying

up late, going out to drink afterward. I loved pushing it hard, and I had no problem getting up to do it all again. There were girls here and there, but mostly my personal life was limited to a few post-shift beers with the crew even though I was still the baby of the group, not even old enough to legally drink. Because of skipping out on culinary school, I was once again years ahead of my brother and peers in terms of some life steps. At nineteen, they were all in their sophomore year, drinking Zima and white zinfandel spritzers, having dorm room hookups and sleeping it off between classes. I was working sixteen-hour double shifts, bandaging salamander burns, paying city prices for rent, and doing my own laundry when I wasn't falling asleep face down the minute I got home. I had to take care of myself, and I definitely didn't have time for goofing off.

I started to develop my confidence as a cook at Patria, but I also made and learned from some serious mistakes. One Mother's Day, Douglas had this bright idea to take beaucoup reservations; we had five hundred covers between brunch and dinner, when typically we were used to doing maybe two hundred or two-fifty. I should say for the record: Now I know that I'd rather work three New Year's Eves in a row than do one single Mother's Day. It's a holiday notorious for tons of substitutions and special requests, and it gets a pretty bad rap from most restaurant workers.

But a restaurant is only as good as its busiest days, and I hadn't formed those opinions just yet. I loved a challenge, so I was raring to go. I was on the grill when we really got rolling around noon. By three o'clock, the place was a shit show. We had dudes downstairs prepping stations because we were running out of everything, and I couldn't see because I was sweating so heavily. I felt like even though everyone was in the weeds, I was the one most clearly drowning.

At the time, my sous chef was a guy named Georgie. He'd been a merchant marine in Peru and was a real tough son of a bitch whom I had a lot of respect for. That made it feel even worse when he came to me during the brief lull between services.

"Hey, man," he said to me, quietly enough that I was could tell he wasn't trying to call me out in front of everyone. "You look like shit. Your uniform looks like shit, your station looks like shit. I want you to go downstairs, change

your uniform, wash your face, get something to eat, and then come back." He was discreet, and it was a reasonable suggestion. He could have easily thrown me out the door, and I'd heard plenty of horror stories from a lot of my peers in traditional French kitchens about the kind of red-faced, short-fused maniac chefs who would embarrass cooks for sport. I'm fortunate to have never experienced that—not then, and not since then. Chef Paul didn't run his ship that way, and neither did my mom or Douglas. But still, I felt humiliated and demoralized. I took it as if I was being thrown off my station.

I finished the night and called my mom when I got through. "You won't believe what happened today." I told her the story. I expected, or maybe I just hoped for, some consoling, some level of collegial understanding. I should have remembered my call to her from that pay phone in New Orleans. There was a familiar silence on the other end of the line for a minute before she spoke.

"You're a fucking disgrace," she said. "You call me, complaining like a baby. You need to get organized, work cleaner, be tougher." I was stunned. "You have my name and my legacy," she said, again giving me déjà vu. "Do a better job." *Click.*

The next day, not long after I went to work for my shift, my mom showed up at Patria, wearing her own chef coat. We weren't open yet, so she had the full attention of the whole crew.

"Apparently my son doesn't know how to properly work the grill," she said, addressing my whole team. "Do I have to come in and do it for him?" she asked them.

There was a chorus of "Ooooh," and of course, I was the laughingstock of the entire kitchen. For weeks afterward, I had to listen to, "Dude let me get this right—your *mom* came in here to school you?" or "You got that, Aarón, or should we call your mom?"

I had a little bit of a chip on my shoulder for a bit after that public whipping. I knew I needed to step it up and prove myself, so I doubled down and ground it out even harder. I wanted respect more than I wanted anything in my life. During another super-intense service on the grill a few weeks later, we did about four hundred covers. I threw it into high gear. All my steaks were perfect, everything I pulled off the fire was totally on point, and by the time

we stabbed the last ticket, I was so proud of myself. I knew I pulled a perfect shift and I was due some recognition, so after we cleaned up, I waited for it.

It never came.

Before I hung it up for the night, I went and found Georgie.

"Chef," I said to him. "I cooked all my steaks, my *churrascos* were right, I got perfect temperatures and nobody complained. Everything I did was all good. How come you guys all jump down my throat when I do one little thing wrong, but no one ever tells me I did a good job?"

He looked at me like I'd just asked why a steak needed salt and said, "*Cabrón*, this is the big leagues." His tone made me instantly regret my question. "My job is not to fucking stroke your ego. When I don't say anything to you, that means you did *your* job."

It was the first lesson for me in what being a professional is all about. I never forgot that moment, and in retrospect, I realize that I *was* being treated like an equal. He was regarding me the same way, and with the same expectations, as everyone else on the line. I never opened my mouth with a question like that again.

Years later, when Georgie and I had both left Patria and crossed paths elsewhere, we were reminiscing about the old days. "Aarón," he told me, "there were so many times we wanted to fire your ass, but I always saw the potential in you. I knew you were going to be great." It meant so much to me even then, because it made me realize how fortunate I was to have such nurturing mentors. It would have been much easier to throw me out on the street, to fire me and replace me with one of the hundreds of other cooks who would have scratched and clawed for a position in that kitchen. Instead, that crew invested in me—their time, energy, and resources. Georgie and Douglas created an environment in which I could grow, and they gave me an example that I still try to implement in my own restaurants today.

I was at Patria for two years, and the experience was fundamental to the food I'd later become known for. It was where I had the chance to start expanding my culinary repertoire. I needed to separate myself from an exclusively Mexican vernacular to define my work independent of mom's legacy, to not be forced to live in her shadow. The relationships carried me well beyond the walls of that kitchen; Chef Douglas ran a beautiful restau-

rant and an organized kitchen, and Patria was a coaching tree that produced accomplished, serious chefs. I am proud and lucky to have been one of them.

But his real legacy is what Douglas was able to accomplish for Latin food. He legitimized it; he defined it and put it on a pedestal. He singlehandedly transformed it into a cuisine that could live on the same level as a Daniel or Le Bernardin. For a restaurant that didn't specialize in the old-guard European fare, earning those three stars was not just unusual—it was unheard of. And for all of us working there, a crew of Latinos who came from over the place, the pride we were able to take in what we did every day was immeasurable. My bonds with the Patria crew were deep, because our accomplishments always felt like they carried more weight than just catering to a trend or palate. We were justifying our existence in what was for a lot of the team an adopted country, one that was not always hospitable. We weren't just cooking, we were improving the value of our very cultures.

That sense of self-worth was something that, as a Mexican in the kitchen, I was going to need to remember many times over the coming years.

MIXED SEAFOOD CEVICHE NEGRO WITH CITRUS AND CHILES

I learned to make this dish during my Patria years, specifically from Adrian Leon. He was the first guy I was paired with when I was cooking, and one of the first stations I worked was ceviche. It was so foreign to me that a ceviche could be this black in color. I admit I was a little skeptical, but when I had my first bite, the flavor blew me away. What an eye opener.

If you're intimidated by poaching shellfish at home, don't hesitate to buy pre-poached shrimp, squid, or crabmeat to get yourself started.

½ pound (225 g) sea scallops

½ pound (225 g) cleaned squid

½ pound (225 g) large shrimp, shelled and deveined

½ pound (225 g) white fish fillets (such as halibut or red snapper), skin removed

1 jalapeño or serrano pepper, seeds and membranes removed, thinly sliced

1¼ cups (300 ml) lime juice

¼ cup (10 g) fresh cilantro, chopped

2 tablespoons orange juice

2 tablespoons olive oil

1 teaspoon squid ink

1 teaspoon kosher salt

½ teaspoon dried Mexican oregano

¼ teaspoon ground cumin

1 small cucumber

1 medium ripe tomato (4 to 6 ounces/110 to 170 g)

1 avocado, diced

1. Cut the seafood into roughly ½-inch (12 mm) pieces (cut the scallops crosswise first, slice the squid into rings, dice the shrimp, and so forth). Place all the seafood and the sliced pepper in a large nonreactive bowl.
2. Pour 1 cup (240 ml) of the lime juice all over the seafood and give it a good stir. Cover and set aside for 2 hours, until the seafood is opaque and the fish flakes easily. Stir a couple of times while it marinates to make sure it's all evenly coated. Drain and discard the juice.
3. In a small bowl, combine the remaining ¼ cup (60 ml) lime juice with the cilantro, orange juice, oil, squid ink, salt, oregano, and cumin. Pour into seafood bowl and gently toss to coat.
4. Halve the cucumber lengthwise and scrape out the seeds; seed the tomato as well. Cut them and the avocado into ¼- to ½-inch (6 mm to 12 mm) dice, fold them into the ceviche, and serve immediately.

CHAPTER ELEVEN

CALIFORNIA DREAMING

After a couple of years at Patria, I was starting to recognize an itch that would become very familiar throughout my career and my life. I think most cooks are born with a restless soul. Douglas was an incredible teacher and mentor, but I wanted to keep learning, and I felt like I'd hit a plateau at Patria. I was ready to move on, to see what else might be out there for me.

It was good timing, because Alex García and his wife were about to open a new spot downtown. Alex and I didn't have a ton of overlap during my time at Patria; he was really there only in my early days, helping get systems in place. But it was long enough that I had developed a strong bond with him. He's about five years older than me, but was always really approachable, and I loved his cooking style. He must've seen something he liked in me, too, because he came looking for me. His new restaurant, Erizo Latino, was an amazing little shoebox of a place in SoHo on West Broadway between Prince and Spring—an amazing location. He needed to build a small team, and when he called, I was ready for him.

Going to Erizo felt like advancement—the perfect next step. I would have more responsibility and get to cook more. I knew enough about the cuisine that I wouldn't be starting from scratch, but I was also going to get an education in getting a restaurant up and running. That meant working with Alex to develop new dishes, getting a sense of the nuts and bolts of startup. As tough as it was to leave the restaurant that had been home to me for two years, I accepted the offer. I thanked Douglas for the opportunity, and for taking a chance on me when I really had no business being a part of that incredible team. I told him I appreciated all of his advice, so much of which

I knew would stick with me for the rest of my career. Then I said good-bye to the team, packed up my knives again, and headed across town.

Erizo was *tiny*; there were maybe forty seats in the whole place, and the kitchen barely had room for three of us. We only had three stations: grill, sauté, and garde manger, because that was truly all we could fit. Alex had mise en place *everywhere*. Every inch of space on the counters was spoken for. When we were cooking, we were on top of each other; there was just enough room for Marcello, our drunk dishwasher, to squeeze in during service. Being a skeleton crew was tough, but it helped me learn so many facets of the food business. I was wearing a lot more hats than just a cook's skullcap.

And man, was it thrilling. We were doing really cool Latin bistro food. It had hints of what we did at Patria, but it was more accessible and had a playfulness to it. We had a mixed grill of churrasco and sausage, which was served directly on the table in these cool little grill pans we found. Diners got the dish still flaming, and it was a really fun spectacle. We had beautiful ceramic bowls we used for our *chupe de camarones*, a Peruvian-style soup, and people were over the moon for our tangerine-glazed tuna and *fufu* (a buttery plantain mash). Every table was always filled, and it was a constant hustle. Even though it was close quarters, people didn't seem to mind, and it always felt like everyone—cooks included—had a great time in that place.

We were always grinding it out, though, doing our best to make the food as creative as possible with the space that we had, and it was always so fucking hot in that kitchen. During one especially jamming service, I had to stop what I was doing and go to Marcello, who was in the middle of his own work, trying to keep pace with an endless line of dishes. "Brother," I said to him in Spanish, "Please, please get me a bucket of cold water." He looked at me like I might have lost it, wondering what the fuck could possibly be so important. When he came back with it, I just stood in the corner, where diners couldn't see me, and I turned the bucket over my head.

But that restaurant was also a party place. After service, it wasn't uncommon for us to pop open pricey bottles of Champagne and invite all kinds of women in, doors wide open to West Broadway where passersby could see what we were up to. With such a small team, it was a hard restaurant to get

going every morning. We always had a long checklist to get through before we could get started. There were days we were seriously hung over from our antics the night before, but if both Alex and I didn't show up, we literally couldn't open the doors. I admit, that did happen a couple of times.

It was also an open kitchen, which meant executing all of our jobs with some level of grace and decorum. That style of design has been all the rage for the last decade or so now, but it was a pretty new phenomenon in those days, and most cooks hated it. Being in full view of diners presented a *lot* of challenges for the unkempt and unruly crews that ran kitchens. It meant cleaning up your act—not to mention your language and your whites.

The flip side, though, was that we got to see *out* of the fishbowl, too. At Erizo, that meant getting a good look at whoever happened to have a seat at the bar. There was no shortage of beautiful women to keep our minds occupied, even while we tried to focus on filleting the latest delivery of flounder or whisking some stock into submission. But there was just one who got under my skin.

Victoria was a regular. She was a friend of our bartender, Max, and she caught my attention immediately. I'd been seeing a lot of girls in those days, taking full advantage of my official card-carrying chef status. What I had anticipated as part of a cook's life was absolutely true. It was a sex, drugs, and rock 'n' roll kind of business. I'd mostly gotten the drugs part out of my system as a teenager, which left more time to emphasize the other two.

But Victoria was something different, and I knew it right away. She always looked so exotic. She was Guatemalan, with gorgeous dark skin and gleaming, sexy eyes. I stepped off the line every chance I got to go talk her up. I'm still not entirely sure I didn't inadvertently sideline poor Max, but all's fair in love and restaurants, and I moved quickly.

One night, Victoria stuck around during our usual post-shift bacchanalia and drank a little too much. When she got sick outside, I helped get her into a taxi and home safe. She called me to say thank you the next day, and I jumped at the opportunity to ask her out.

Pretty soon Victoria was all I could think about. I didn't have a lot of money for wining and dining her the way I wanted to, but one of the perks of growing up in New York is the ability to naturally play tour guide in one of

the most romantic places on earth. During the summer in the city, it seems like there's something fun, charming, and free happening on every corner. We had a lot of al fresco dates at little cafés, we took long walks and hung around in the parks. Mostly, we spent time just talking, and I got to know what an incredible woman I'd found.

True to form for me, Victoria was older. By ten years. She was working on her doctorate in African American studies, and it was the first time I realized you could make a career in academia—that learning and studying for a living was a possibility. I loved that she was so curious, so intelligent, and had so much to teach me. She was raised in upstate New York, the daughter of a maid, and overcame extreme odds to make it through school. I was so in awe of what she'd accomplished; she wasn't just smart, she was fearless, and fiercely determined. In some ways, being around her actually made me a little insecure. I wasn't very well read, I hadn't gone to college. I worried about keeping up with her. That was daunting to me, but she was also so encouraging, and she always let me know that she thought I was smart. It was such a confidence boost, and Victoria was the woman who got me reading again, who helped get me cultured. In that way, she shared a lot of values with my mother, and was another woman along my path who helped me grow up a lot.

Everything about our relationship seemed so perfect, it was almost too good to be true. Except for one major looming problem: She was only visiting New York. At the end of the summer, she was heading back to Berkeley, California, where she was going to finish school. As happy as I was with Alex at Erizo, I was in love big time, so it didn't take much for me to make up my mind. When the summer was up, I told Victoria, "I'm going with you." I had to follow my heart, and it was headed for San Francisco in a beat-up Honda. I thanked Alex and his wife, made sure they were set up with someone to take my place, and hit the road.

* * *

I also saw the move as a good chance for me to try something new and shake things up a bit. It had been a while since I'd really left New York, and

at that point I'd spent most of my life there. I was itching to see another city, to experience another lifestyle, and I'd never been to California outside my time in the mountains with Outward Bound. Victoria reminded me of the exhilaration of learning and collecting knowledge, the power of being curious. This was a chance for me to continue getting educated. I didn't know what that course would be just yet, but my young mind was open to anything.

When we got settled into our own apartment, Victoria went back into her school routine, and it was time for me to find work. I'd heard all kinds of talk about how San Francisco was the new American food mecca. This was the era of Jeremiah Tower's Stars, Chez Panisse's second wave, and Zuni Café. For a young cook, it was worlds away from the old New York City standbys; these places were influenced by the year-round availability of flawless California produce and the bounty of the Bay. It was thrilling to think about the new creative possibilities as a cook.

Fortunately, the food world is a small one, and I had some connections that gave me a place to start. My sister's best friend, Christina, had married a guy named Tony and moved to Berkeley, where she got a gig as Alice Waters's assistant. Christina was like a sister to me, so I called her up and she gave me the lowdown on the restaurants to check out. One in particular that she mentioned was Rose Pistola. Christina said the chef/owner was a guy called Reed Herring, and that his head man in the kitchen, Scott Warner, was a good guy. She offered to arrange for me to meet him. The women in my life had never steered me wrong, so that's exactly what I did.

It turned out my biggest culinary lessons in San Francisco were going to be about different kinds of food. Rose Pistola was an Italian restaurant. When I was a kid, my mom used to take us to eat at very traditional Italian places— old-school red-sauce restaurants, or maybe to Felidia on fancy occasions. I loved it all. I was passionate about the pasta, the flavors, and the culture of Italian cooking, but I'd never done that kind of food before. I grew up with my mom's Mexican style and then spent three years of my professional life cooking Latin cuisine. I wasn't the kid who'd staged in French and Italian restaurants, and I'd resisted that kind of European training at Johnson & Wales. So this was my first chance to get a taste of some cuisines out of my comfort zone.

When I walked into the kitchen my first day, there were guys breaking down huge fish of all kinds on big wooden tables—some of the most beautiful seafood I'd ever seen, stuff I couldn't even identify, all coming straight from the Bay. It was also my initiation into the world of fresh pasta. My experience up until then had been mostly packaged stuff, but here it was being made by hand. I'll never forget that aroma, watching the combination of moist flour and egg yolk come together into a firm, yellow ball, the speed with which the table was dusted before the dough was rolled out again and again, thinner and more delicate each time. When I stepped into the walk-in, I found shelves of pristine California produce and a flawless pork loin soaking in milk and garlic and sage. When we cooked it later, the aromatics were so intense, it made my mouth water. The food was unlike any I'd cooked before, and I was totally in awe of the place.

It was a beautiful open kitchen, and in the dining room, big windows overlooked Columbus Avenue in North Beach, a traditional Italian neighborhood. Nowadays, it's not uncommon for restaurants to specialize in a specific regional cuisine, whether that's Oaxacan or Basque or Sicilian. But back then, diners hadn't yet been introduced to how varied cuisine from different parts of a country could be. Rose was regional Italian—a Ligurian restaurant. Food from that area of Italy is very light and Mediterranean. We had a lot of salads and antipasti, both cured and *crudo*, as well as pizza and that ethereal pasta. Then we had our grilled items. The menu was designed so diners could choose their protein and then select from five different preparations, such as a braised pork with salsa verde, or a grilled fish with fava bean puree. It was a kind of choose-your-own-adventure, and a super-smart way to run things from a business perspective. Cooking at Rose was also very interesting because it was a stockless kitchen; everything was done with pasta water, which was totally new to me. And the seafood was impeccable: sand dabs and spot prawns from Santa Barbara, aqua gem clams, fresh-cut albacore tuna.

Of course, being in California, this very Italian kitchen was staffed almost entirely by Mexican guys. That was very different coming from New York, where Latinos were from all over South America. But as foreign as the food was for me, it was a comfort to be cooking with my people. The chefs, on

the other hand, were all white. Until then, I had very unusual professional experience for a cook, coming from two restaurants that specialized in Latin cuisine and were headed up by Latino chefs. It was in those days that I started to see and figure out that in the majority of the food world, Latinos were cogs—the worker bees—and not the chefs who got the glory. It definitely wasn't specific just to that restaurant; that was the way of the world, and it was something I'd been sheltered from until then. It got me thinking a lot about how I'd run my own restaurant, how I could make a kitchen more welcoming to and encouraging of the kinds of people who were making it possible for American restaurants to work. Those people were immigrants. They were people like my mom. They were people like me. My dream was always to be a chef and put out creative food, but I was getting a little older and my priorities were shifting. I remembered how good it felt at Patria, like we were giving value to and emphasizing the importance of our diversity. I began feeling a desire and even a responsibility to make a difference in the industry that went beyond creating a few new dishes.

* * *

In the meantime, we were a tight team at Rose, and I wanted to take as much away from this new environment as I could. I worked the grill three days a week, which was a really hard station. It was the first charcoal grill I ever worked, and that son of a bitch was a beast. We had these bone-in halibut steaks, and if I looked away for five seconds too long, the thing would be incinerated. It was so fucking hot and sooty that my white coat would be black by the end of the shift, and I remember going home at night and spitting black snot into the sink, hoping to god I wasn't doing permanent damage.

My other two days a week, I worked pasta—another station that was no joke. It was usually run by a Mexican dude named Armando, and almost no one could stand in for him because you had to be so fast. Even though it was totally new to me, cooking pasta sort of came naturally when I started working it. I think it came from having to keep up at Patria and Erizo, and the pace of a New York kitchen, and somehow I earned that spot when Armando had his days off.

Chef Scott was adamant about not sandbagging it—never cutting corners. If I got three orders of pumpkin ravioli with sage brown butter sauce, I couldn't do all three in one pan. I had to do each one individually. That meant at any given time, I could have up to twelve or fifteen pans going at once. But I loved it, and that's where I picked up some real speed and accuracy in my work. Cooking pasta perfectly required precision timing, and we had just three small pots to work with, which meant every order needed to be on point.

These were good times, and I was a happy man with Victoria back at home. In the mornings, she dropped me off at work and went off to school to do her thing. We weren't seeing each other a ton, but we lived for our days off, when we could take little trips, get away together to Marin County or the coast. I did miss New York from time to time, but California living was so cool.

On my days off when Victoria was busy with school, I went to the markets, walked up and down the Mission, and sought out little spots to try. The diversity in San Francisco was a different kind of diversity than in New York, and I was getting really excited about food again, learning about unfamiliar forms of Latin cuisine. One of my favorite places was this little joint with about fifteen seats called Rincón Peruano, where I learned about the significant Japanese influence in Peruvian cuisine. The chef was this Asian Peruvian guy, and seeing this man who looked Japanese speaking Spanish was such a head trip. He did great traditional stuff I'd never tried like *aguadito de pollo*—a really traditional chicken soup dish—and *causa*—which is this sort of potato terrine—and a stir-fry–style dish called *lomo saltado*. I ate all kinds of food, sometimes seeking out a recommended place, other times just stumbling onto something new. I coupled it all with my experiences in New York, carrying around a notebook and writing everything down, and started to make sense of the regionality of South American food. I got really inspired in those days, and a lot of that research wound up in my first cookbook.

* * *

After about a year at Rose, I got word that Mark Miller was coming to town to open up a new restaurant in Ghirardelli Square, called Loongbar. Mark

was a legend, the godfather of Southwestern cuisine and a huge influence for guys like Bobby Flay. But this restaurant was going to be different: He was planning to open an Asian concept. Again, I found myself drawn in by a cuisine I didn't know much about. The idea of expanding into that world was really exciting to me, so I said *grazie* and *arrivederci* to Reed and Rose, and landed the gig at Loongbar in time for a brand-new opening.

It may have seemed unusual for a guy so well known for Southwestern food to be taking on a pan-Asian restaurant, but Mark also happened to be a professor of Asian antiquities. He's got this totally random, secret life as an expert on things like Ming vases and all this kind of stuff no one ever would expect from him. But his life in academia also shaped his approach to forming a restaurant team. Up until that point, when I'd started in a new place, I was usually asked to trail and observe, that sort of thing. The most formal training was maybe sitting through ServSafe certification, which everyone had done at one time or another for legal reasons. But when I got to this restaurant, before we even turned on the stoves, we had to go to *class*.

Mark had us sitting in a room where he stood at the head and conducted lectures and lessons. We were educated on styles of Asian cuisine, history, and technique, without touching a single piece of kitchen hardware.

Mark also loved to do flavor coaching. One afternoon, he handed each of us a raisin. Just one single, run-of-the-mill raisin. He stood at the front of the class and said, "Okay, I want everyone to taste this raisin."

Of course, we—a bunch of knuckleheads—all just looked around at each other. One by one, we started to eat our ration, not convinced our leader hadn't lost his mind.

"What are you tasting?" Mark asked the class.

The answers were as ridiculous as the question seemed. "Um, grapes?"

The description he went into about a shriveled piece of fruit blew me away: "It starts with a funky, fermented backdrop, there's a pop of sweetness, the astringency of the tannic skin." It was a lesson that terroir had to do with more than wine, and that even the simplest ingredient was never a single note. That raisin could be used for flavor, adding sweetness or funk; it could be a textural element for chew; it could add body and depth to a sauce. And my raisin was different than some of my classmates' raisins, emphasizing

how important it is to *taste* a product before cooking with it, and never assuming you know what Mother Nature has packaged up and delivered. That lesson was going to be so important when we started building dishes for the restaurant, and still informs how I structure my cooking and pairing of ingredients today.

We spent practically a day just on pork from Shandong province, and another just on noodles. For a dude who could never sit still in classes before, I was totally enthralled. It was one of the first times I recognized a real link between history, humanity, culture, and the cuisine that I was going to be cooking. That made a huge impact on me that stuck. Even today, if I find myself with a few spare minutes, or if I can't sleep at night, I find myself researching something about ancient Roman banquets or another geeky historical account of food. I credit Mark for teaching me the importance of knowing where cuisine comes from—not just so I can be a more technically effective cook, but so I can feel a connection to the food.

When we finally got into it, the restaurant was a love letter to Asian culture. Real Restaurant Group, a major player in the Bay Area culinary scene, invested a ton of cash into the buildout. We had huge sweeping windows and a spectacular private dining room upstairs. There was a massive, badass dragon embossed in the walls that swooped around the main dining area, and the open kitchen had a wok station where we used local Dungeness crab in fried rice and had Peking ducks, ready for roasting, hanging in full view of the guests. Mark worked with our chef de cuisine, Jeff Inahara, to come up with a truly ambitious menu. We did whole fish with panang red curry and pickled daikon, *unagi* (eel) with *umeboshi* vinaigrette—dishes that were just unlike anything out there, and totally revolutionary for American diners at the time.

Loongbar was my first introduction to Asian flavors and preparations, and it really blew me away. I got to understand technique and ideology so disparate from anything in Latin or European cultures. Textures and ingredients I'd never worked with before, and the concepts of repetition and precision, mastery, and dedication to perfection were foundational to what we did every day if we wanted to remain authentic to Asian cuisine. I loved it, and every day I felt like I was carrying home new culinary secrets in my pockets.

But that old restlessness kicked in after a year or so. Loongbar was high octane and flashy, and I felt like I needed to take a breather after my stints in super-intense San Francisco restaurants and figure out what that restlessness was telling me. Victoria had a friend who was working as a counselor at a camp for kids up in Marin County, and they needed a cook. She asked me if I had any interest, and I wound up agreeing to this gig, where a group of teenagers were learning how to be more environmentally conscious young people. The deal was that I would cook three meals a day and stay on this property in Marin for a few months. It was a chance to get back outdoors, and it sounded like a nice, low-key kind of job after the grind of those high-impact kitchens.

But when I got out there, they dropped another small detail on me: The food had to be entirely vegetarian. Here I was, an accomplished professional cook with blue ribbon experience on both sides of the country, serving tofu scrambled eggs to a bunch of horny teenagers who just wanted to eat hamburgers and hot dogs. I had to buy all the food myself and bring it back, prep it, and cook it. I did love the gig, though, working with kids and breathing fresh air every day, hours that let me catch up on some of the sleep I'd been so sorely missing. And the parameters of cooking strictly vegetarian actually wound up being a really good challenge in how to layer and add depth of flavor without relying on meat.

My retreat didn't last too long, though, and I had been there only a few weeks when, once again, another old Patria friend intervened. Mikey Cressotti had been approached by a guy looking for a chef to run a new restaurant back in New York. Fernando Saralegui, who had Cuban roots, wanted to do a Gulf Coast bistro, and Mikey tracked me down, thinking my background would make me a perfect fit for the food. The concept was to take influences from Texas, where I'm from; Mexico, my background; and the area around New Orleans. He couldn't imagine a more perfect gig for me.

So Mikey put me in touch with Fernando. I had a phone call with him, by which point Fernando already knew my pedigree and my mom. He asked if I'd come back to the city and cook for him; a short trip later, I was offered a job to help launch the new Gulf Coast restaurant L-Ray, as executive chef.

Along with that familiar itch I mentioned, I also had an ache for New

York City. I was torn because of my relationship with Victoria, but given our schedules, sometimes it already felt like we were having a long-distance relationship. She was considering potential teaching gigs at Harvard down the line, so it seemed logical enough that we could stay together and figure out what would come next when she was done with school and we were both in the Northeast. I told her it was an opportunity I couldn't pass up, and she was encouraging and understanding.

We did make it a few more years, but that was the last time Victoria and I would be together as a couple in the same place, with any semblance of a sturdy relationship. We loved each other, and that never changed, but there were a lot of factors, especially time and distance, that slowly caused our candle to burn out. I was still optimistic, though, when I kissed her good-bye and boarded the plane back east. And in 1998, like a boomerang, I was back in the big city.

PUMPKIN RAVIOLI WITH SAGE BROWN BUTTER

SERVES 4 TO 6

This is the recipe I learned at Rose Pistola in San Francisco. I was working as a line cook, and it was my first real exposure to Italian food. I saw how simple and delicious Italian pasta can be.

Be very mindful of the brown butter—allow it to really coat the ravioli. And don't be afraid of that pasta water if the butter looks a little too thick; a little pasta water goes a long way. Also, be sure the water is well salted.

1 small (2 to 3 pounds/900 g to 1.36 kg) pumpkin or butternut
 squash
1 tablespoon olive oil
2 teaspoons kosher salt
½ teaspoon ground black pepper, plus more for serving
½ teaspoon ground cinnamon
½ teaspoon chili powder
2 cups (250 g) all-purpose flour, plus more as needed
3 large eggs
6 tablespoons (14 g) grated hard cheese, like Parmesan or
 Pecorino-Romano, plus more for serving
¼ cup (½ stick/55 g) unsalted butter, cut into pieces
4 sage leaves

1. Preheat the oven to 400°F (205°C) and line a baking sheet with cooking parchment. Trim and peel the pumpkin, halve it lengthwise, and scoop out the seeds and pulp. Cut into 1-inch (2.5 cm) cubes and toss to coat with 1 tablespoon oil and 1 teaspoon of the salt. Roast until tender, 20 to 30 minutes. Let cool for about 10 minutes.

2. In a food processor, pulse the roasted pumpkin with the black pepper, cinnamon, and chili powder until smooth; do not over-process. It

should be pretty thick, so if you notice extra moisture, transfer it to a skillet and cook over medium-low heat until it cooks out. Refrigerate in an airtight container.

3. To make the dough (see Note), pour the flour onto a work surface and spread it into a wide mound. Make a well in the center and fill it with the eggs and remaining 1 teaspoon salt. Use a fork to scramble the eggs, making sure not to break through the sides of the mound; with short, circular strokes, begin to incorporate the flour, little by little, until it's no longer runny. Use your hands to continue working the flour in (you'll have to put some muscle into it). Once it's completely incorporated, knead for 5 to 10 minutes, until the dough is stiff and smooth. Shape it into a ball, tightly wrap it in plastic or place in a zip-top plastic bag, pressing out as much air as possible, and set aside to rest for 30 minutes.

4. Cut the pasta dough into quarters and roll one at a time, leaving the rest tightly wrapped while you work. Lightly dust it with flour and, with a rolling pin, roll it into a rectangle that's ¼ to ½ inch (6 to 12 mm) thick.

5. Pass the dough through a pasta machine on the widest setting. Fold it in thirds like a letter; gently roll to flatten. Repeat twice more, but don't fold it after the last pass.

6. Dial down the pasta machine by one notch and feed the dough through once. Continue to do this, dusting with flour as needed, until the dough is very pliable and just barely translucent, less than ⅛ inch (3 mm) thick; for most pasta machines, this will be the second- or third-to-last setting. Each sheet will be approximately 5 inches (13 cm) wide and 24 to 10 inches (61 to 30 cm) long. When the dough is ready, set it on a lightly floured surface, dust it with a bit more flour, and cover it with plastic wrap to prevent it from drying while you repeat with the rest of the dough.

7. To make the filling, stir the cheese into the pumpkin puree. Working with one sheet of dough at a time, square off the edges and drop small mounds of filling (about 2 teaspoons) along the length of the sheet, in the center, leaving 1½ to 2 inches (4 to 5 cm) of space between each.

Brush water along the border and between each mound, then gently pull one long edge of the dough up and over the filling, pressing snugly to seal and eliminate air bubbles. Trim away any ragged edges and cut the ravioli into individual pieces. Dust with flour and set aside on a plate or sheet, loosely covered with plastic wrap or a dishtowel. Repeat with the rest.

8. Fill a large pot with well-salted water and bring it to a boil over high heat. Meanwhile, combine the butter and sage leaves in a large skillet over medium-low heat. Cook gently, stirring occasionally, until the butter is lightly browned and very fragrant, then decrease the heat to very low.

9. Drop the ravioli into the boiling water and cook until they float and the pasta is tender, 2 to 3 minutes. Splash a tablespoon or two of starchy pasta water into the brown butter, then gently drain the pasta or fish it out of the water with a spider.

10. To finish the brown butter, increase the heat to medium until it's at an active simmer and the water is incorporated. Gently toss the ravioli to coat in the brown butter and serve right away, topped with more cheese and black pepper.

NOTE: *I like to make this dough in the food processor—some call it cheating, but I'll gladly take a shortcut for homemade pasta, and the food processor's already out. If you choose this route, substitute the following method for Step 3: Crack the eggs into a food processor and pulse a couple times to lightly scramble. Add the flour and salt and continue to process until the dough pulls together in a ball. Transfer it to a floured surface, knead it once or twice until smooth, and tightly wrap in plastic; set aside to rest for 30 minutes.*

CHAPTER TWELVE

RETURN TO NEW YORK

At L-Ray, I was working with a guy named Jimmy Bradley, who owned a restaurant in Chelsea called The Red Cat. He also had a restaurant consultancy company, and he's still a legendary hospitality guy. His job was to come and provide the nuts and bolts, do the training, and find the chef. I worked closely with Jimmy to help put the project together, and he was there for me to get this thing open in a really historic space on West Tenth Street, which had been a restaurant called Texarkana in the 1970s.

It all came together quickly, and it was an amazing time. I still couldn't wrap my head around the fact that I was an executive chef. This was the restaurant where I was going to start building my identity, where people would start spelling my name out in black and white when they wrote about our food. I still have my first piece of press ever from our opening night—it's a shot of me at the raw bar making guacamole. Even though I was twenty-two years old, I look about twelve. It was clear people were going to be paying close attention, and that night was jammed with heavy hitters.

One of our first customers was Gael Greene, a legendary New York restaurant critic. I ran upstairs to the office, where we had a phone and I could speak privately. I was terrified to think what she might say. I called my mom and she offered some typically unconventional advice: "You're probably going to have to fuck her for a good review. You're going to do it, right?" My mom. Never one to be shy about anything, even with her own kids.

"Anything for the restaurant, Mom!" I told her.

"That's my boy." Classic Zarela Martinez.

I did not, for the record, sleep with Gael Greene. But we did get some great press anyway. In the winter of '99, Hal Rubenstein wrote us up in *New*

York magazine, saying "chef Aarón Sánchez has got some new mojo working," describing my food as "happily marked by an energetic but disciplined lust for spices, a congenial harmony in his side dishes, and a penchant for smooth finishes." It felt great, and it was such a relief to know that the food was finding an audience.

But then Ruth Reichl—who actually grew up down the street from the restaurant—reviewed us in the *Times*. Though she had some positive things to say about the food, she ultimately awarded us only one star. Everyone was hoping for two. Instead of staying strong and true to the vision, focusing on improving what we'd already built, I scrambled. I decided we had to reexamine the food, and started making changes. I was totally overwhelmed, and I knew I needed help.

After the initial excitement of getting this incredible offer and moving back to the city, I started to recognize the level of responsibility that came along with all of it. I was always a worker bee before that, helping to realize someone else's vision. Now I had to have my own. It was helpful to have Jimmy, and of course the owners had their ideas about what they wanted for the place. But still, the anticipation was high, and there was so much riding on L-Ray's success for me.

Coming up with the menu had been a collaboration with the owners, who were very particular about what they wanted. I had guacamole, ceviche, stuff that people were looking for in that environment. But they wanted to make it a nicer restaurant than it was. There was some confusion coming from ownership, and trying to find the identity of the restaurant was challenging.

I was completely stressed out all the time. I stopped drinking altogether. I stopped seeing my friends and family, convinced that I was always forgetting something, or doing something wrong. I could never get comfortable; I could never enjoy myself or just relax, even on my days off. Most nights, I left work while the rest of the staff stayed for their shift drinks and debriefing of the night's service, and went straight to my apartment. I sat there, unable to sleep, staring at the ceiling and replaying the day in my head over and over again, wondering if I'd done everything right, or what I could have done differently.

It was the deepest funk I had ever been in, and I didn't know how to get out of it. I felt trapped by my situation, and I didn't want to give in to the pressure or feel as if I couldn't hack it as the head of a kitchen.

I went to the owners and let them know I thought we could use another pair of hands, but in truth, I really needed some guidance. I called Georgie up; I told him what was happening and, in not so many words, that I was in over my head. I thought I had great ideas, and I was a good cook, but I also knew I had no idea how to make a restaurant profitable. I asked him to come on board, and when he agreed, it seemed like the best decision I could have made as a leader, that maybe recognizing my shortcomings and admitting I couldn't pull it off alone was a mature move.

Unfortunately, my bright idea kind of backfired. I got a call one day from Fernando that he wanted to have a meeting. There was a place called Joe's Junior around the corner from the restaurant, and I met them there, thinking we were going to have a regular status update, maybe talk about the menu, staff changes—the usual stuff. But when I walked in, Fernando and his partner were there, and Georgie was, too. Georgie wasn't looking at me. He had his head down, and his eyes were anywhere but on me. That's when I knew what was coming.

"Look," Fernando said. "We believe in you, Aarón. We think you have a lot of talent, but we need someone who is more experienced, someone with more poise, ready to take this job on and manage costs and be consistent." He went on. That they needed more structure. They were concerned that there was a lot of turnover. I didn't know how to manage a kitchen, and Georgie did. "We have an investment to protect." That was the final word. They couldn't support two chefs, so they chose experience over youth and ideas.

I understood, but it didn't make it easier to swallow, and I was fighting tears when I thanked them for the opportunity. It was my first and last time that I was shown the door, and it was a huge lesson for me. People are expendable. Talent is replaceable. Ideas, food execution, and energy are only a fraction of the total picture. A restaurant has to have results. Positive reviews. Happy, paying customers sitting in seats.

Before I left Joe's, Fernando stopped me. "Are you okay?" he asked. "I mean, personally." He said he never saw me drinking, but worried that I

always seemed wound up. "You don't do drugs, do you?" I was a little taken aback by the question.

"No, I don't do any of that," I told him, truthfully. I was clean as a whistle, probably more so than any other time in my life. In that moment, I figured it out. I was depressed. That kind of depression for me has always been characterized by a sense of total desperation. It feels like a lack of oxygen, like I'm always gasping and never catching my breath, and the whole world can come crashing down any minute. I thought I was doing a good job keeping it under wraps, that no one could sense it since I was sitting home at night, staring at the walls around me and living it all out inside my own head. But it was visible to the folks around me, and it was affecting my work. That, more than being dismissed from the restaurant, is what sent me reeling. I knew I needed to get it together, and fast. Not just for the sake of my career, but for my own survival.

* * *

As crushing as what happened at L-Ray was, to be honest, I was a little relieved. I had a chance to reevaluate, which was probably the best thing for me at the time. I'd been on a hamster wheel for so long, I never gave myself a chance to really feel what I was going through, and try to evaluate my life or career with any real perspective. What I needed most was some advice, because I didn't know where to go from there. I called up the one person I knew would give me an honest, unbiased opinion, and shortly after I hung up my whites at L-Ray, I was boarding a plane for New Orleans for a meeting with my White Sage: I had arranged an appointment with Chef Paul.

The beauty of the chef world is that sense of care and community. For as eccentric as a lot of cooks can be (okay, almost all cooks), they're also people who like to take care of others—that's at the heart of what we do. Nurturing other chefs is something that gets taken seriously, even when you don't work together anymore. Even if you never have. It's just the code. And I knew Chef Paul was always going to be there for me.

When I got down to my old stomping grounds, I sat with him and asked

him the questions that had been on my mind. What should I do next, Chef? Do I take a sous chef job? Do I try for another head chef job? Chef Paul was cut-and-dry with me, and true to form, he didn't give me any definitive answers, but instead told me stories from his own career. He told me about how many jobs he'd been hired and fired from, and how long it took him to get established. He told me about the doubts he'd had and mistakes he'd made, and he made me laugh for the first time in ages. We had a really poignant conversation, and even though I didn't exactly have a road map when I walked out the door, I finally felt like I was going to be okay.

I stayed in New Orleans for five days, and it helped me clear my head. I visited with old friends, went to K-Paul's, and hung out with some of the guys, who all gave me shit for going city on them. I got a lot of love, and at that time it was so important. I needed to feel that comfort and belonging. I needed Chef Paul's guidance and leadership. I needed reaffirmation from the guys that I was still a part of the family. I needed someone to build me up again. I think I realized then that it may not have been a cure for depression, but that kind of attention and care went a long way in at least soothing what ailed me.

* * *

Back in New York, I was feeling a little better but still in professional limbo, vacillating and fielding some offers, still questioning what I should do next. While my conversation with Chef Paul didn't provide a crystal-clear direction, it did give me a pass—to be a little less hard on myself, to take a beat and think through things, and to not feel like taking a step back would be the end of my career.

At the same time, I still needed to make a living. Enter Alex García once again—the Patria tree just kept on giving fruit. He tipped me off to a gig with a former fashion magazine editor named Diane Ghioto, who was opening a restaurant on Downing Street called Isla. She needed a chef. I needed a job.

Diane wanted to do a Nuevo Cubano–style spot—a love letter to Batista-era Cuba, when there was this cool yacht club culture, and it was referred

to as the Paris of the Caribbean. The food was very posh, and she wanted to capture and celebrate that. I had relevant experience, and it seemed like a good transitional gig for me.

Pretty soon, I found myself in yet another beautiful restaurant. Diane invested a ton into it. She had this exorbitantly expensive blue cement brought in for the floors. There were white banquettes and white tables, and stunning sconces that cast light on chic couples who came to eat and be seen.

We got some good press and reviews early on, but no restaurant is smooth sailing all the time. There was one walk-in, which had a compressor that would kick on and off periodically. The menu featured a beautiful raw bar platter of different kinds of fresh shellfish and ceviche. One Sunday afternoon a few months in—my only day off—I got a frantic call from the kitchen that diners were getting sick. I ran to the restaurant and realized that the compressor went down sometime on Saturday for longer than usual. By the time our sous arrived Sunday morning, it had kicked back on, so he never noticed a problem. But it was too late—the shellfish had already gone bad. Now the crew had been serving foul oysters and shellfish all day, and folks were getting sick left and right. I remember this moment every time I leave my restaurants today, constantly checking (and double- and triple-checking) on equipment, taking temperatures, and always reminding my teams *never* to take for granted that machinery or technology is always going to do its job.

The staff at Isla looked desperate that afternoon, asking me what to do next, stressed out and scared to death of what the health department might do and how many other guests might be afflicted.

"What do we do, Chef?" my sous chef asked.

I would later go on to give a very stern lecture about food safety. In that moment, though, it was about what needed to be done right away: organizing comped meals and obviously killing any dish that might have ingredients from that cooler. I tried to keep everyone calm, letting them know that in the restaurant business, shit happens—literally too fast for us to keep up with, that day. I looked around at the restaurant, which had cleared out considerably, and told him the most important thing that needed to be addressed right away. "First of all," I told him, "go get more toilet paper."

* * *

After a while, I left Isla. Being back in the kitchen full time kept my mind occupied, but it was just another way to avoid addressing the root of my issues. I needed to consider other employment options for a little while and dedicate time to getting my head right, or I was going to wind up right back where I landed at L-Ray.

I finally decided to talk to my mom. "I think I need to see somebody," I told her. The perception of mental health disorders was really distressing to me. I still felt like that was a scarlet letter, and I was really uncomfortable about having that conversation with my tough-as-nails mother. I think for her, though, it was at that moment she realized this was serious. She could tell I felt very vulnerable, and she knew I never would have come to her if I wasn't in real pain. She sat me down and explained how deeply depression ran in our family. That it was not uncommon, and that even she had experienced it. Hearing that history made me realize maybe there were more reasons for the way I was feeling, and that it wasn't just because I was a fuck-up, damaged goods, not man enough to handle my business.

When I went to see a therapist, I was prescribed an antidepressant. At the time, Prozac was in the news a lot, and people were talking about it like it was a miracle drug. It opened the door for a whole new class of medications to be validated and accepted, and I started taking Zoloft, another of the SSRI antidepressants. Taking it felt strange to me, and every morning when I opened that little bottle, I had to talk myself into feeling like it was okay. I was so desperate to feel better, to be without that dull, persistent ache I'd been feeling for so much of my life, I probably would have put a hot poker in my eyes if they said it would help. My therapist was really clear, though, that the medication was not a magic pill, and that it had to be coupled with ongoing therapy. I was going to have to work through it, revisit some of the more painful stuff I had avoided, and dedicate time and energy to getting well.

It's not something I shared with a lot of people. The food business wasn't exactly the most progressive-thinking industry at the time. It's also always been a breeding ground for challenges to mental health—something only recently being recognized. The lifestyle attracts a very specific kind of person;

hospitality workers tend to be sensitive and empathetic, but also often troubled, and susceptible to stress and suffering. The truth is, even when I was with Victoria, even when I was in a busy restaurant, serving tons of guests, surrounded by a team of colleagues, I was lonely. I craved love and intimacy and connection. I think I've been that way my whole life. My mom was never the type to hug and kiss and console her kids; she's more the tough-love type, and I didn't have my dad long enough to know how he'd have reacted when I really needed help. I was always left to imagine what he'd say. Would he have been proud of my career? Disappointed in my dropping out of school? Accepting of my decision to take an antidepressant, or would he think I was weak? Those were questions to which I'd never have answers, and wondering about them sometimes drove me up a wall.

Coming off L-Ray was a low point. The pressure of that job triggered what had been dormant during the years of Patria and San Francisco, when I was numbing myself with work and filling my time with distractions. But somehow, somewhere in my mind, I knew I was going to get through it. I needed to understand my limitations, and that biting off more than I could chew was going to be very dangerous for me in my life. That I may have been more fragile than others in that way. Managing expectations, understanding my vulnerabilities as well as my abilities, and being real with myself that those external factors—the press, family legacy, reviewers—would always affect not only my pride but my health.

Slowly, I started to feel better. It took a lot of time and work, but I knew what I had to do: I had to stay true to my craft and have a clear vision. I had to be self-aware, and be honest with myself when I wasn't doing well. I had to know that it was okay if I wasn't always perfect.

Of course, that didn't mean I wasn't going to try.

CHAPTER THIRTEEN

LIVING THE DREAM

After I left Isla, I decided to dial it back a bit. I had been approached about doing some consulting in the past, but I couldn't fit it into a working restaurant schedule. Now seemed like a good time to revisit those conversations: to take a step back, get some perspective, and see what else was out there for me while I prioritized working through some personal stuff.

One of my main gigs was with a guy named Eddie, who had a chain of Mexican restaurants in New York called Mary Ann's, with about six locations. Eddie found me through Alex García. At the time, it seemed that when any Latin or Latin-adjacent restaurant opened in New York, a couple of names were thrown around—mine included. We were the Ghostbusters of getting a Mexican restaurant open; they all knew who they were gonna call.

Eddie contracted me to help him make specials for his menu. He'd married a Dominican woman named Gloria; all the people in the kitchen were Dominican, a lot of them her relatives, and I felt right at home working with that crew to get them set up. I was really living right; I'd go to one of the locations from eight to five P.M., teach the guys three or four new dishes, and then get paid cash—about $700 a week. That was a ton of money back then for what felt like not a ton of work compared to the grueling back-of-house gigs I was used to. And mercifully, my name wasn't on the menu, so even though I wanted to do a good job for my clients, I didn't feel anywhere near that same level of pressure for press and perfection. It was a great opportunity to stretch my culinary legs again, getting some of my creative mojo back by developing menus on someone else's dime, where the stakes weren't so high.

Eventually, I started running into a guy named Eamon Furlong, a bartender at the Mary Ann's location on Fifth Street and Second Avenue, and

I would see him regularly when I stopped in to meet with the team. Eamon was this very avant-garde, artistic Irish dude, one of the few sober bartenders I knew, and an artist on the side who loved building things with his hands. He and I had a nice little rapport going; he was this typical New York guy, and I could tell he wanted more in life than slinging margaritas at some downtown chain.

One afternoon, after I had wrapped up with Eddie's kitchen crew, he pulled me aside. "I want to open a restaurant," he told me. "But I need a chef." He asked if I might be interested in doing a little consulting, but I had a feeling about Eamon, and I wanted to hear more about the project. We agreed to have a bigger conversation and set up a time to meet at a coffee shop uptown near where I was living at the time. When we did, I was impressed by how far along Eamon was in the process. I'd heard countless folks over the years tell me they wanted to open up a restaurant, and most of the time it was all talk. That was not the case here. Eamon had already hooked up with business partners—a guy named Howie who owned a chain of kitchen supply stores, and the former child actor Mason Reese, who I knew from commercials in which he starred in the '70s. Stuff like Raisin Bran and Dunkin' Donuts, and Underwood Deviled Ham. Google him; you might recognize him, too.

The crew already also had a location. The Lower East Side was an up-and-coming neighborhood, and Howie had a space on Ludlow. He'd been running a burger joint, but it didn't work out, and he still had the lease. He told Eamon he could do essentially whatever he wanted with it, and Eamon already had an idea in mind.

Paladar means "palate" in Spanish, but Eamon knew the word also referred to these Cuban eateries he'd become enamored with during a visit there. All over the country, there are little private restaurants that are, in essence, a person's home, called *paladares*. They were once illegal, underground establishments. Later, they were legalized when self-employment licenses were issued in the '90s, but they stayed a major part of the culture. He recalled loving the vibe of those places, and he wanted to bring that feeling to New York.

The more he talked about his concept, the more excited I became. Eamon was so inspired and enthusiastic about it, but he also had the plans in place

to back it all up. They were only missing one piece: a chef. When he got to the point—the question of whether I'd consider consulting for them—I immediately declined.

"No," I told him, unequivocally. "I want to be an owner," I said.

We worked on the deal for a little while, but Eamon and his partners were very receptive to the idea of cutting me in. I was still gun-shy about getting back into the saddle, wary about what the pressure of opening a new restaurant would do to me after what I'd been through, how I would be able to process it now that I'd had a little distance. But just the negotiations helped give me some confidence to take on the project. I surprised even myself at how clearly I was able to articulate what I wanted, how much, and when. It was the first time I really recognized my value, and I was assertive in making sure that was observed in the final contract. So many chefs struggle with the business side of the job. After all, we're cooks, not MBAs. Little by little, over the course of my career, I've learned that if I wanted any kind of stability and longevity, I was going to have to become a businessman, too. Paladar was the first time I really started to build and strengthen that acumen.

I guess I felt like I had nothing to lose—I didn't really *need* the gig. I easily could have continued consulting for a while. That was the beauty of it, that I did it because I wanted it, because I was passionate about creating Paladar. I knew how difficult it might be, and I'd been strengthening myself mentally for the next step in my career. I thought about my days at Outward Bound, and in New Orleans. All the times I thought I might not be able to make it in a certain situation. I thought about what my mom would do. And my dad. And suddenly, I just felt ready. After all the partying I'd done, after the pain and self-punishment I went through, it was time for the real fiesta to begin.

* * *

Opening Paladar was everything I'd always dreamed about when I started cooking. Howie and Mason were more or less silent partners; the place really belonged to Eamon and me. We spent months developing the style, but our agreement was clear-cut. He was going to handle the business side, and the food was all mine.

Today, the New York restaurant scene is nothing like it was for us. Rents have made it nearly impossible for independent operators to risk investing in a small spot. More often, they need the backing of some major restaurant group, and bootstrapping your own place has mostly become a thing of the past. But we were able to make Paladar into a reality on a shoestring. We financed and built it out for about a hundred grand. We had four thousand square feet and eighty seats for $4,200 a month—a number that would probably make small business owners in that area weep today. My contribution was sweat, blood, and skill in the kitchen.

Before I could cook a single *carne asada*, though, I was helping Eamon with the construction so we could be as economically conservative as possible. No one was consulting on the design side—no ordering fancy fixtures imported from Europe, no concern for whether our tables were strategically placed for optimal Instagram lighting. This was a totally traditional kind of place. Decisions were all designed to make it as easy as possible for us to do the best job we could for the least overhead. We would open for dinner during the week, and brunch Saturday and Sunday. We were cash only. We'd have a small, tight staff. Anything we could accomplish on our own, we did, with me in the kitchen and Eamon on bar.

The aesthetic was super-funky, Lower East Side kitschy-chic, and Eamon was putting his art skills to use for every element. He was handy and resourceful, and he knew how to use simple, inexpensive materials to make big splashes. He found fabric for vintage Latin curtains with a pattern of banana and mango and cut pieces of it to put on the tabletops, which he covered with liquid plastic. With so many small touches, he turned what someone might consider junk into an eye-catching fixture or piece of furniture.

When it came time to turn on the stoves, I was raring to go. Creatively, I was in the zone, and it wasn't hard to find inspiration. New York's dining scene was *en fuego*, and the Lower East Side felt like the epicenter. It was eclectic, full of weird, quirky people and diners who were fully willing to embrace more artistic, but honest, cuisine. When I wasn't cooking, I was out there eating it all up. I spent more evenings than I can count at Prune, where Gabrielle Hamilton was showing the world that simple, rustic cooking in an authentic, no-bullshit kind of space could capture the hearts of guests

just craving a spot that felt like home. Around the corner from Paladar, another little restaurant called wd~50 had opened up. It was named after the address (50 Clinton Street), and its chef's initials, a young dude named Wylie Dufresne. I sat at the bar many nights and watched diners come in and claim reservations they'd waited months for, so they could taste Wylie's revolutionary food. I was witnessing the beginnings of a movement known as molecular gastronomy, a whole new frontier, and I was just as awed by his brilliance whether I was tasting his take on "bagels and lox" or the deconstructed eggs Benedict that set the culinary world on fire.

On Saturday mornings, I would get up first thing and hit the Union Square Greenmarket. It was like a convention of the biggest culinary stars in the city and was the first time I really started to see and feel part of a chef community. We all ran into one another, talked about what was new and exciting, swapped ideas and stories about restaurant life. It was also my first experience connecting with growers and producers, getting up close and personal with the product and having them be able to educate me on the spot about where something came from, the best methods of preparation, and care. Prior to that, I'd always ordered stuff from a big purveyor that delivered stuff to the restaurant in giant boxes and bags, handed over by disinterested delivery dudes. There was nothing romantic or noble about that, but at the market, I finally felt like I was connecting with my food, helping out the little guy, and improving my understanding of ingredients.

I met Colin Alevras, the chef at a restaurant in Nolita called The Tasting Room, and the guy was a total market nut. He was the one who really started to explain how things worked to me. He had this tiny kitchen and made a new menu every day. That kind of thinking is what today's publicists and media refer to as "market-driven." But what Colin was doing wasn't about trends or buzz; it was just how he thought about cooking—that freshness and less fussing and manipulation made the best meal—which was still really unusual and progressive for the time. He was a knowledgeable and generous guy, and any time I had a question about something I leaned on him.

When I went back to Paladar, I tinkered with new dishes based on whatever I picked up that day. It was a small, stripped-down operation that felt honest and true, and that restaurant was a rebirth for me. The menu was a

reflection of so many things I'd picked up over the years, not just in the Latin kitchens of Patria and Erizo, but the European and Asian ones, too. At the heart of it, the cuisine was pan-Latin bistro food, but I ruled nothing out—I wanted to cook without limits. I just wanted to make what was exciting to me, and I paid attention to what my diners and cooks responded to.

I made beef empanadas with a smoked-tomato pico de gallo. I did whole grilled sirloin with *yuca frita* and bitter greens salad with *chimichurri*. I did *sofrito*-stuffed pork chop with grapefruit *mojo*—a sauce made with tons of crispy garlic, grapefruit segments, and chiles—over a Cuban yam puree. I steamed mussels with smoked chipotle broth. Customers went wild for the coconut seafood stew. We had a conch dish: big slivers of sautéed, tenderized conch, served up over salt, which was then flambéed with rum. They were dishes and presentations that, at the time, were pretty fucking avant-garde. And I loved every minute coming up with them.

I went into the Paladar opening with a thicker skin, mentally preparing myself for whatever reviewers might have to say. I couldn't let that bother me now—this was *my* restaurant, and I couldn't fall apart over a bad review. Fortunately, I didn't have to worry. Critical praise came early and often for us. *New York* magazine called Paladar "a colorful, lively circus of a restaurant that's equal parts serious cooking and serious partying." Then I had my redemption in the *New York Times*, when Eric Asimov featured us in his "$25 and Under" column, reporting that our food was "deft and controlled." He went on to write that, regarding the "fad" of Nuevo Latino cuisine, "as long as Paladar and a few other solid restaurants continue to employ the Nuevo Latino vernacular in a sound and appealing way, it's clear that it was deeper than a passing fancy," he wrote. To me, the idea that what we were doing at our restaurant was solidifying this kind of food as a formidable, serious cuisine was a compliment far more rewarding than praise for any one dish.

I was thrilled with the critical reception, but it was the diners who really got me fired up. They came from all over. The Lower East Side wasn't exactly a destination neighborhood in those days, so a lot of our patrons were regulars who lived in the area and returned often, sometimes once a week, some of them even every day.

It was so gratifying and humbling to see that these people were inter-

ested in what I was cooking, enough to bring their friends and family and spend money on our food—something I never took for granted—but also that Latin cuisine was not just some exotic, try-it-and-check-it-off-the-list kind of thing for them. Diners were incorporating it into their daily lives; they craved and came back for these dishes, and it was so cool to know that I could directly credit people I personally knew for making that possible. People like my mom. And Douglas. They blazed a trail that was now wide open for me to build upon, and it was my turn to take those next steps down the path. Thanks to their work, diners' palates were primed and ready for fiery flavors and complex, layered dishes beyond the "margarita mill" staples of tacos and burritos. They were game for just about anything I dared to put on the menu. Our customers supported me, and I was so fulfilled every service, watching as people I'd come to think of as family enjoyed the food we cooked for them.

* * *

This was about where my tattoo habit got a little intense, too (or, my mom might argue, totally out of hand). When I was living in San Francisco, I had my first rendezvous with the needle—some little cross number on my back that didn't make too much of an impression on me and has since been covered up.

Today, it seems like every cook has a collection of tattoos that could rival the sleeve I saw on Chef Bundy at K-Paul's when I was sixteen, but back then it wasn't something you saw much of. Hell, most kitchen workers couldn't afford to foot the bill to cover their arms or legs in ink. Plus, many folks in New York weren't getting tattooed at all; the practice had been banned in the 1960s after a hepatitis outbreak. In 1997, though, the ban was lifted. I liked the idea of getting some more art done, and it was around that time a little tattoo shop called Daredevil opened across from Paladar, owned by these ultra-hip artists, Michelle and Brad. The crew was coming in all the time for meals, and we started kicking it and became friends. I got the bright idea to start bartering my work for theirs, getting new stuff as fast as I could turn out tacos (which was pretty damn fast).

I loved the feeling of getting tattooed and the creative collaboration of working with an artist I knew and trusted to come up with something so enduring. Permanence, for me, was an almost entirely foreign concept until the first time I stepped into a tattoo shop. I'm not a person who keeps a lot of things around, and I don't attach sentimentally to objects. But when everything else in my life changes, I have memories, ideals, and experiences captured in indelible marks that I can carry around.

There was also something to those tattoos that felt like a real commitment to my craft. At some point, you have to look in the mirror and say, okay, fuck it, I'm never going to be an accountant or a doctor. I was locking myself in the kitchen and throwing away the key. As fate would have it, tattooing also provided another avenue of economic opportunity, when Michelle came to me a few years later and asked if I'd consider partnering with them to buy the building where Daredevil was operating (their lease was coming to an end and rent was about to go through the roof). We got together and put up enough cash so they could buy the building and stay, and I got to diversify my business a bit.

That crew was part of our tight little LES clan. When Michelle was featured on a TLC show called *Tattoo Wars*, we had a huge viewing party at the restaurant with a bunch of bikers and tough, tattooed men and women, who were actually some of the sweetest people to come through. I catered Daredevil's anniversary parties the same way I did the old Latino couple's down the street.

At Paladar, it felt so fulfilling to have a family of patrons as a reminder of why I chose the career path I did. For a kid who grew up pretty far from aunts and uncles, cousins and grandparents, I was floored by the feeling of love every day. I was able to make relationships with strangers that I knew I'd rely on for the rest of my life.

They also reminded me what a restaurant is really all about. Early immigrants to New York and the States found connections to one another by communing in churches and places of worship, when services were inevitably followed by a meal regardless of religious association. Irish pubs, Jewish delis—they weren't just centers of commerce and a means of eco-

nomic stability for people from foreign lands. They were places to gather, to have discourse and discussions, to solidify and strengthen their community. Participation in religious institutions has declined over the decades, but restaurants have remained, places for a community to congregate, to set aside what's weighing on us for a little while. It's not about a chef's ego, or flashy food, but it is about feeding people. The word *restaurer*, which is French for *to restore* or *refresh*, says it all, and I think for a long time I'd lost sight of that mission. Paladar brought it back into focus.

Today's food world seems bent on telling neighborhoods what they want, rather than asking and responding to what they *need*. At Paladar, we tried to really tune in to that, and I think it helped our appeal transcend the Latino community. Our tables brought cultures together that might never have sat in the same restaurant, let alone shared a round of mojitos. I loved the food we were making and the team we'd assembled, but *that* was what I was most proud of.

That ideal restored a lot of my passion for cooking and creating restaurants, and also my love for New York City. But no one could ever have been prepared for the way that love was tested one sunny September morning in 2001.

* * *

We'd been open about a year when terrorists hijacked commercial airplanes and turned them into the torpedoes that took down the World Trade Center. Heading in to work that morning, it felt like I was going into a war zone, which, in reality, I guess it was. I was on the Second Avenue bus heading downtown when the first plane hit, and people were freaking out. Cell phones in those days were a far cry from what they are now, and information was disjointed, inaccurate, and confusing. There were passengers pulling the emergency cord to get off, not knowing exactly what was happening, but responding to a growing sense of panic and dread.

I got off at Houston and Second and headed into Paladar. I let Eamon know I was there and walked over to the shop where I got my coffee every

morning. That's when I saw the news, on the little screen behind the counter. We all stood there, glued to the TV for a while, incapacitated and dumbstruck, speechless and silent.

I finally pulled myself away from the repeating images and returned to the restaurant. We didn't prepare the kitchen. We didn't take the chairs off the tables or open the walk-in to start prep. We didn't turn on the stereo. Instead, we set up a little radio outside on the sidewalk and listened, waiting, though I still don't know what exactly we were waiting for. It was eerily quiet, as if the entire city was just trying to collectively, soundlessly process what was happening to it. Eventually, we saw people walking up from Ground Zero in a daze, bringing the horrifying news to life right before our eyes.

The horror of the scenes downtown was so disorienting, so surreal, it felt like I was in a waking nightmare or some parallel universe. My city was literally up in smoke, and we could do nothing but watch it burn from the restaurant's windows. Like so much of the world, we felt helpless, but everyone in the city, in the country, in the world wanted to do *something*. So at Paladar, we did the only thing we knew how—we cooked.

Drew Nieporent, a friend and restaurateur who owned Tribeca Grill, called me up.

"Aarón, we're down here cooking," he told me. He was getting a phone tree going, rallying the chefs in the area to help feed first responders. "Can you come give us a hand?" I told him I'd do him one better. Eamon and I knew we wouldn't be opening Paladar up that day—actually, we had no idea how long we'd be closed. So we emptied out the walk-in, loaded all the food up in Eamon's old Volvo, and drove across town.

For the next few days, we cooked and prepared chafing dishes full of food, and then set up tables outside on Greenwich for emergency crews to come and have a hot meal. We cooked things we thought would be most nourishing, most comforting and fortifying. We made trays of rice and beans, whole roasted chicken with chipotle. Initially, we were serving the food on dishes, but it became clear quickly that these folks didn't have time to sit around. I grabbed one of the volunteers. "Listen," I told him, "we need to get as many to-go containers as we can out here." When he returned, we started

packaging up meals in containers, then bagging each up with silverware and bottled water so we could hand them off to workers on their way through.

Making those meals didn't just feel like a civic duty; it felt like a human responsibility. It was a moment in history when all of us, from all walks— Latino, Iraqi, Saudi Arabian, Italian, Irish, Russian, Chinese, Japanese, Korean, Vietnamese, Christian, Muslim, Jewish—were just New Yorkers. We were Americans. And it felt like we were feeding family. Taking care of those people who were literally risking their lives to take care of us, men and women who were broken down mentally and physically, was a privilege. They were depleted and demoralized, and though they didn't have the time or energy to sit in a restaurant, they needed to be reassured that there was some good in the world. They needed, more than anything, to be restored.

* * *

After 9/11, somehow, life did go on. Restaurants suffered, especially down-town, but we kept things going at Paladar, and we were a tighter team than ever. The guests and staff felt like adopted family, but it was also a truly family-run operation for me. My sister, Marissa, had left Zarela to come be my general manager and help me get the place in order. Sharing a work environment with a sibling is always a special kind of test. One night, not long after *New York* magazine released a little piece of press that named us the best place for parties of eight without reservations, we were cranking hard. Marissa was seating parties like a maniac, which was great for the bottom line, but in the kitchen we couldn't catch our breath in between tables. I went out to the front of the restaurant to tell her to cool it, but she didn't want to relent. Admittedly, she had our best interest at heart, trying to help us turn tables and take as many customers as possible. But still, we went at it the way only siblings could, scaring the rest of the team into thinking we might actually rip each other's heads off, knowing that at the end of the night all would be forgiven over a margarita and a hug.

Most of the time, though, the restaurant was a really pleasant place to work. My staff were serious professionals, and it was the first time I relied

almost entirely on Latin help. I remembered my experience in San Francisco and in so many of the restaurants I'd been in over the years, and the mission I'd decided on then, to support the Latin community as much as I could, and to try to create an environment for a team to learn and grow. Of course, I hired based on skill and talent, drive and reliability, and I wanted to integrate diversity regardless of background, but the team grew sort of organically toward a Latino crew. If I needed a position filled, I went to Juan or Margarito or one of the other cooks and asked whether they knew anyone who would fit the bill. Before I knew it, I would be training someone's brother or sister or cousin. Of the twenty or so people on staff, about three-quarters at any given time were Latino.

I had a very solid group, some of whom worked with me for nearly the whole time we were open. I also hired a lot of women, who often worked even harder than the guys and also somehow managed to keep a lot of the machismo bullshit in check. We had Yorkie, who was a bartender and server, a Dominican girl from the neighborhood named Bailey, and Midgie, who was Puerto Rican and worked with us for a long time. Maurizio was a bartender who had worked with my mom for many years at Zarela before making his way over to Paladar. And then we had another young Dominican kid named Mariel who was also from the neighborhood. That was what was beautiful about our restaurant: A lot of the crew had grown up on the Lower East Side, which at the time was a very Latino neighborhood. We had kids who had grown up on Avenues C and D when it was 'hood and barrio, and were now working at a more upscale Latin restaurant, not just a corner taco shop. But I still didn't want to change that Latin flavor of the LES, and having the team come straight from the blocks around us helped ensure we never strayed too far from its true character. In turn, they'd invite their family members in for a meal, and we had a really nice community vibe because of the staff.

I ran a very calm operation overall. I wanted to encourage creativity, and high-stress kitchens can strangle that really quickly. I also knew that with Latinos, it's all about respect. I think that's something that gets lost in a lot of kitchens where the "help" is Dominican or Mexican or Puerto Rican and the chef is white. There's not a cultural understanding of how to connect with and manage a Latino crew. I've seen it happen, where there's a

little bit of mutiny in the back, and an overbearing chef who thinks yelling and screaming is going to somehow right the ship doesn't know what hit him. It was a very different thing for me to come and say, "Listen, I speak the language, I'm one of you guys, so don't try to pull that shit with me." I wanted them to know right off the bat that I valued them and I respected them, and I expected the same in return.

For the most part, I was a mild-mannered chef anyway. I'm not a confrontational guy, and if something went wrong, I tried to address it quietly and directly with whomever was responsible. I preferred to instruct and correct rather than yell and scream, and I wasn't into the idea of embarrassing someone in front of the whole crew. I also knew it would be no good for that mutual trust I'd worked so hard to build.

But some things still got me pretty wound up. One night, I got word that we were getting an extra-special VIP: Chef Paul Prudhomme. Chef Paul made a regular pilgrimage annually for the Fancy Food Show at the Jacob Javits Center. He'd go and shake hands, sell and sign a ton of his books, and make a little culinary tour of the city in the evenings.

Never had my team seen me so unhinged. I was breathing down their necks, watching every move, making sure the front of house staff had strict orders and were maintaining a spotless restaurant with hospitality on full blast. I let them all know that we were taking care of my Chef, and that everything had to be fucking *flawless*.

When he came, the crew did me proud, helping me put together a beautiful little tasting so Chef Paul could sample a big range, a few bites from across the menu. We made him *sopes*, little corn tarts with black beans and tomatillo sauce, and my signature empanadas with chicken *picadillo* and smoked tomato salsa. We did a whole snapper fried with coconut conch rice, and a sweet plantain with stewed *bacalao*. I tasted each dish obsessively, making sure it would adhere to the principle Chef Paul most valued in cooking: big flavor. I could hear his voice in my head the entire time: "Make sure you season, boy. I don't want none of that soft stuff."

When he finished his meal, I waited for the judgment to come in. He was sitting at a table right near the kitchen, with his team of about eight people, and I left my post to make an appearance tableside. Chef Paul was

an honest man, and never would pay a compliment if he didn't absolutely mean it. His criticisms were always constructive, and he didn't review a dish or cook without carefully considering every element first. So when he told me he loved the food, that it was creative and flavorful, I nearly cried with pride. Being such a close friend of my mom's, he always visited Zarela on his New York circuit, too. He loved my mom's food, but I was always actively trying to distinguish myself from her, to establish my own culinary voice, and Chef Paul validated my effort that night. "I love how different your food is from your mama's," he told me, and it was a compliment that helped solidify the confidence I'd so struggled to find in the years of cooking in the same city as my mother.

The rest of the conversation was, as it always was with Chef Paul, about life. "Are you busy here, boy?" he wanted to know. "Are you making money? Taking care of the business?" I told him I was trying to make him proud across the board. And that was the truth. I had Chef Paul in mind with so many of my decisions, from seasoning a fish to mentoring some young punk who might otherwise be getting in trouble if he weren't in my kitchen peeling shrimp and cutting bell peppers.

Serving Chef Paul at Paladar was the closest thing I would ever get to feeding my father. His opinion and blessing were just as important as my dad's would have been. Having my chef's approval meant the world, and during my Paladar years, I already felt like I was sitting on top of it. That restaurant was my heart and soul.

The laws of physics say that energy cannot be destroyed. Paladar was an extension of that energy that had been latent in me, that pilot light sparked in New Orleans when I was just sixteen thanks to Chef Paul. I had wanted my own restaurant ever since I'd first set foot in a professional kitchen. What we created at Paladar was rare and real, and maybe only possible in that very spot, at that very moment. I'd find out soon that not everything I touched was bound to turn to gold, and I've spent my entire career since chasing that feeling. But for almost a decade at Paladar, I worked hard, and had pure magic.

BACALAO-STUFFED SWEET PLANTAINS WITH CREMA MEXICANA

SERVES 6

Douglas Rodriguez used to do a riff of this dish with yellow corn arepas. It was amazing how that sweet, salty bacalao with an acidic tomato played against the sweet corn arepa. I wanted to take that same sweetness I remembered and put it in a whole fried plantain instead. There were a lot of unique flavors in the dish, but bacalao is something all the Latinos in the neighborhood knew well, as salt cod is customarily eaten during Lent. This was one of the dishes on the menu when we opened Paladar, and the community loved it immediately.

Plan carefully when making this dish at home, as the bacalao needs to be desalted for 24 to 48 hours. And for a DIY crema substitute, you can add 1 tablespoon lime juice to ½ cup (120 ml) crème fraîche.

½ pound (225 g) salt cod
2 cups (480 ml) whole milk
7 large yellow plantains (about 12 ounces/340 g each)
¼ cup (60 ml) olive oil, plus more for baking
3 cloves garlic, peeled
1 teaspoon kosher salt, plus more for cooking
¼ cup (10 g) fresh cilantro, finely chopped, plus more for serving
½ cup (120 ml) crema Mexicana

1. To desalt the cod, rinse the salt off the surface, then submerge the fish in several inches of water in an airtight container. Let stand for 24 to 48 hours (the fish is preserved so you can do this at room temperature), changing the water at least twice and preferably at least four times. Drain.
2. Preheat the oven to 375°F (190°C) and line a baking sheet with cooking parchment.
3. In a small saucepan, cover the cod with the milk. Bring to a very gentle simmer over medium heat, stirring regularly, and cook until the cod

flakes easily, 12 to 18 minutes. With a sieve set over a bowl, drain the fish, reserving the milk. When the fish is cool enough to handle, flake the meat into a blender or the bowl of a food processor, removing the tiny pin bones with tweezers as you go.

4. Peel one plantain, chop it into a few pieces, and place it in a clean saucepan filled with well-salted water to cover. Bring to a boil over high heat, then decrease the heat slightly and cook until the plantain is very tender, about 20 minutes. Drain, then return the cooked plantain to the saucepan along with ⅓ cup (75 ml) of the reserved milk from the cod; mash over low heat until smooth. Scrape it into the blender or bowl of the food processor with the flaked fish.

5. In a small skillet or saucepan, heat the oil over medium heat until very warm. Grate in the garlic with a Microplane, allowing it to toast and become fragrant, then remove it from the heat.

6. In the blender or food processor, puree the mashed plantain and flaked fish until smooth; if the mixture is too thick, add another tablespoon or two of the reserved milk, just enough to loosen it. With the motor still going, slowly stream in the garlicky oil, and continue to process or blend until very smooth and well emulsified.

7. Peel the other 6 plantains by trimming both ends, cutting a shallow slit in the peel (not into the plantain itself), and pulling the peel away; retain all of the peels. Lightly coat the plantains with oil and season with the kosher salt, then rewrap them in their peels and bake on the lined sheet for 20 to 30 minutes, until tender but still holding their integrity; the skins will have blackened.

8. When the plantains are cool enough to handle, remove the peels, lay the plantains flat on the baking sheet, and slit them lengthwise along their tops, leaving about an inch (2.5 cm) intact at either end. Use your knife to gently push out the sides to make space for the filling.

9. Fill the plantains with the puree and bake for 15 to 20 minutes, until lightly browned on top. Meanwhile, stir the cilantro into the crema. Serve the plantains warm, garnished with the cilantro crema and more fresh cilantro.

CHAPTER FOURTEEN

FOOD GETS FAMOUS

As much as I have learned and changed over the years, some traits are so ingrained in your personality that no matter what your evolution, they come along with the package. For me, that's a sense of restlessness. Regardless of where I've been or what I was doing, I've been unable to sit still for very long. A lot of people consider multitasking a defining trait of the millennial generation. Techie kids who need seventeen apps running on their phones, playing Candy Crush with one hand and piloting some hybrid car with the other, all while talking on Bluetooth and running a *Fortune* 500 company. They're masters of doing it all, all at once.

Well, fuck that, I say. Because let me tell you, chefs perfected the art of the split focus long before any millennial was even a sparkle in their parents' eyes. And we've done it with maximum efficiency. Go ahead and try searing a steak, stirring a sauce, stabbing a ticket, and pulling some bubbling skillet from a salamander in the space of thirty seconds, surrounded by screaming servers and a boss bearing down on you threatening not only your job but your life. Man, will you learn to juggle tasks quick. It's total chaos, but that's what we crave.

So tackling multiple endeavors at once never felt like overreaching, overachieving, or a manic effort to stay ahead of the curve. It's just what comes naturally to a cook, and it always felt natural to me. You could say I was classically trained in keeping a lot of irons in the fire, and by the time Paladar was open, I'd already been doing some unusual moonlighting—under the stage lights of a Midtown television studio.

A strange thing had begun happening sometime in the mid-'90s. Cooking on television wasn't new; legends like Julia Child and Graham Kerr, the

Galloping Gourmet, had already had long and impressive careers inspiring folks in home kitchens with their public-television shows, teaching the finer points of how to flip an omelet or make an easy family dinner for a weeknight. But never had there been an appetite for an entire *network* dedicated to food.

So in 1993, when Food Network launched, it seemed like a serious stretch. How could you possibly fill an entire channel with content about *food* and expect more than a few zealous hobbyists to tune in? Cooking was nothing glamorous, and food was functional, there to fill empty stomachs and provide fuel. Restaurants were spots to see and be seen in, and were more about the social aspect than any culinary creation.

Which is why, when I was first asked to make an appearance on the network, I didn't think too much of it. I agreed; it sounded like fun. I always liked a little stage time and rarely got a chance to do much of anything outside the walls of a kitchen. Especially once I had Paladar, it seemed like a great way to get some publicity, help put some butts in seats. But no one was talking about a *future* in television for cooks; I didn't take the gig for money or fame. Chefs were working class—we were the help. We were not the focus of anyone's feature story, we weren't dating supermodels, and we were rarely even the face of a restaurant. That role usually went to the owner.

It happened first during my days at L-Ray. My mom had a good friend who was a critic for the *New York Daily News*—a really well-known New York food guy named Arthur Schwartz who wrote a book called *Naples at the Table* in 1998. There was a party to celebrate the release, and my mom invited me along, suggesting it would be a good chance for me to get to know some more of the city's culinary movers and shakers, now that I was back from the West Coast. I'd worked in New York before, but now that I'd been in the business in earnest for several years and was an executive chef at L-Ray, I think my mom saw that I was taking it seriously, and that I was in it for the long haul.

This was before things had started to go south at L-Ray; I still felt like I had a good thing going there. But the food industry was then—and still

is—rarely static for long. My friends in advertising or banking found their gig and stayed put for a decade or two. But in the food business, there was a constant churning. Chefs are nomads, and restaurants—even the most celebrated ones—never felt like a safe place to stash all your eggs. Everyone knew it, and made it a priority to position themselves as favorably as possible for the moment the health department might want to shut down your main source of income, or some mercurial restaurateur decided on a career change, or the public palate suddenly turned toward another trend.

The party was at a small tapas spot called Solera on Fifty-Third and Third that has since closed. But it was a really inviting, bilevel space, and it was perfect for this event, which was a proper cocktail party. I had to get all gussied up, and it really felt like some sort of culinary industry coming-out party. And man, what a way to do it. I looked around the room at faces I knew well: Gael Greene; Hal Rubenstein; Michael Whiteman, who founded *Restaurant News* in the '60s; Leonard Pickell (pre-scandal) from the James Beard Foundation; and Sara Moulton, who was the chef in charge at *Gourmet* magazine. It was all the old guard, the most influential writers in the business.

The scene at a food industry party was so different at that time, when food journalists and cookbook authors carried enormous weight. They were held with such reverence and regard, from Jillian Duffy, the editor in chief of *New York* magazine, to William Grimes, Ruth Reichl, and Brian Miller from the *New York Times*: established voices with mature careers coming from legacy publications. Also, it was not so much about chefs as it was the restaurateurs—they were the real stars and focus of media attention. It was a generationally deep industry, where seniority still ruled. That's not at all the DNA of such a party now, or the scenario in the industry at large. Today, that crowd would be made up of television stars and young influencers, bloggers, and Instagrammers.

But that night, I didn't even know half of those terms yet. I was just trying not to trip over the words I did know—or use them much at all. My mom's advice was to stand beside her, smile, and look cute. "You're going to shut up, and I'm going to tell you everybody you need to know," she told me.

So the night was a whole lot of, "This is so-and-so, that's so-and-so." I smiled and shook a ton of hands. It was small talk, but honestly, I liked that sort of thing. Some chefs aren't hugely social—it's why they gravitate toward a life behind the swinging doors, where they don't have to interact much with the public. They prefer to be cloistered in a 95-degree closet than entertain customers. But that's never been my style. I love talking to people, I love mixing it up and learning where folks are coming from, what they do, and what they have to say. Maybe that's part of the reason David Rosengarten took an interest in me.

David had been an editor for *Gourmet* during its heyday, and he was in charge of the restaurant reviews there as well. He was a chef and writer, and in '94, he'd picked up a gig hosting a food TV program on this new channel, Food Network. At the time of our meeting, he was cohosting a spot called *In Food Today* with Donna Hanover, a New York TV reporter and actor who was at the time Rudy Giuliani's second wife. But it was not a cooking show. It was a *talk* show. They had popular chefs of the moment come and visit, discuss trends and the hottest tables in town, that sort of thing.

Prior to *In Food Today*, David hosted a show called *Food News & Views* and another called *Taste*. All three were totally foreign concepts in the food world. Today, the "stand and stir" instructional-style shows have really fallen out of favor unless you flip on the Cooking Channel or PBS in an insomniac fit at three in the morning. But back then, deviating from that formula seemed radical. Teaching someone how to cook at least had quantifiable value for viewers. But *talking* about food? Why bother? It wouldn't be long before that question was answered, but David was definitely paving the way before it had been proven that the public did, in fact, care about such things.

"What do you do?" David asked after my mom introduced us.

"I cook at this spot called L-Ray." I described the restaurant for him, talked a little about my role as executive chef.

Someone like David had his finger on the pulse of the food scene—he was already pretty hip to any openings and closings in the city. But he listened, and after a little while he said, "I'd love to have you on my show." It sounded like fun, and I told him so. We exchanged information and went about our nights. I left the party, I went home, and promptly forgot about it.

It was probably about a month that passed before the phone rang: "Aarón, I'd like to have you on my show." It was David on the line. I had to remind myself of our conversation, but once I had total recall, I happily accepted. Food Network was still this unproven commodity, and honestly, it wasn't exactly like I was watching a lot of television. Like most chefs, I was preoccupied with working like an animal. But still, there were a lot of whispers around the industry, folks saying it was worth looking into and keeping an eye on.

"Low budget" doesn't even begin to describe the conditions of production at that time. The first offices were in what was basically an old business building, and if I wanted to do a recipe, I had to bring everything myself, do all my own prep, take care of the entire business. Today, whole teams of people make sure a featured chef has everything they need, from ingredients to food styling to hair and makeup. But none of us knew what we were missing in those days—we were just excited to be a part of this thing, and to be doing something a little different from our day-to-day.

That morning, I woke up excited, though a little bit terrified. I agonized over what to wear. Wardrobe was super stressful for me. I loved to get dressed up for a date or to hit the clubs when I had the occasion to detach from the kitchen. Outside of that, like most cooks, I was most at ease in my checks and a white coat. But part of the idea was to make cooking more approachable, and that included giving chefs the impression of being more relatable. It was nice, and it started changing the norm—it started humanizing chefs in a way that the world hadn't seen before. Until then, TV chefs all wore whites or some kind of standard uniform (blues in the case of Julia Child, of course). But in the meantime, I had to go through half a dozen options.

I swallowed as much coffee as I could stomach and bounced to the train basically a walking ball of nerves and caffeinated energy. I headed to the studio on Fifty-Second and Eleventh, where shows were shot for a few years.

The expectation was for me to do a dish, and I decided on a simple but flavorful seafood stew with coconut, chipotle, and chiles. My stove situation was a small induction burner, a rig that looked awfully questionable to me. When it was time to explain the process to the camera, I got myself all amped up and ready, and when they started rolling I got going on my mentally rehearsed instruction. Immediately I was shocked at what a challenge it was

to cook and talk at the same time. And that would have been the case even if everything had gone flawlessly—which it did not.

"Now, what you want to do is get this pan *screeching* hot, so that when you put all the shellfish to release the juices . . ." and as I was speaking, I dropped a huge handful of seafood into the pan and waited for the sizzle—which never came. The pan was ice cold. The induction burner had never fired up. And very quickly, I was indoctrinated into the world of on-screen improv. I had to pull a redirect and try to keep things moving without letting on that anything had gone wrong.

Despite the debacle, I was asked to come back, and I happily agreed. When I returned, a little more prepared, it was to showcase how to do a whole turkey with Mexican flair. There was no way to ready this thing in the studio, knowing how long the cook would take, and in those days producers didn't quite have the old *switcheroo* perfected, where we put a roast in the oven and have an alternate fully cooked and ready to roll, effectively "time traveling" right on screen.

So instead, I cooked this thing at home in my apartment, and had to transfer it from my front door to the studio. There I was, coming up Sixth Avenue in the back of a cab with a whole roasted turkey in my lap, the back seat stinking to high heaven like a Mexican Thanksgiving gone wrong, and spilling all over my carefully pressed pants. Today, there's a team of sixty people working in those kitchens, solely dedicated to making sure the food is immaculately presented and looks and tastes delicious. My turkey had no such crew waiting for him. By the time I got the damn thing in the door (after tossing the cabbie an extra-big tip), it looked like that bird had been through—well, through a shitty Manhattan commute. A few of the crew members and I got him on a prep table to do some cosmetic surgery, trying our best to gussy this thing up to make it presentable on camera despite the fact that it was dripping with cold, chile-spiked juices and had been cooked three hours prior in my half-sized home oven.

After a few initial shoots with David, I started getting calls from the network now and then to do appearances and guest spots on other shows. At that point, I'd met a lot of really influential folks in the food business. But

when I was asked to be on Sara Moulton's show, I was equal parts thrilled and petrified. Meeting her for the first time one on one, I was totally star-struck. Sara wasn't just a Food Network star; she'd had the food industry on lockdown for decades as the food editor for *Good Morning America*, as well as a chef-in-residence at *Gourmet* for twenty years.

She could have balked at me, asked who the hell this Mexican kid thought he was, but as talented and accomplished as she was, she couldn't have been sweeter or more welcoming. When I arrived on set, she was gentle, guiding, and encouraging. She could easily have been a teacher or a nurse—a caregiver of some kind. In fact, she could have been your mom—if your mom was a food TV star and one of the most important professionals of her generation.

It turned out I probably could have used my own mom a little while later when, during a test run for the spot, I nearly cut my fucking finger off. I was demonstrating how to break down a chicken, using a wicked-sharp, brand-new boning knife—which, while I talked to the camera about the finer points of butchering the bird, I managed to run directly through the tip of my finger. I watched it happen but I didn't want to interrupt the flow. So as subtly as I could, I wrapped it up, put my hand behind my back, and kept right on going, gesturing with one hand. When the director yelled cut, I was way ahead of him. I shocked even the crew when I revealed my hand, which was totally soaked in blood.

Fortunately for the future of my cooking career, not all my gaffes were so life threatening. Working with the IEM (that's the fancy industry abbre-viation for In-Ear Monitor) definitely took some getting used to. Trying to listen, talk, and cook at the same time was like trying to scratch your belly and rub your head while walking on hot coals. Alex García, my old buddy from Patria, had been called to the network to do some shows, too, and he had similar difficulty handling that challenge.

Alex would start out strong, cooking his dish. When a producer wanted to let him know that something he was doing was blocking the camera, they'd try to relay the message in his ear: "Alex, move the bowl."

And of course, Alex would react—"Okay, Bill!"—and dutifully move the bowl.

"DON'T ANSWER BACK TO *ME*, ALEX!" It was hysterical.

But we were all having a great time learning as we went. We had no idea Food Network was going to be what it was. We just thought it was a fun thing to do. Today, chefs are getting paid sick money, but I never did it for the cash—which is a good thing, because I made maybe $500 a pop for those first shows.

I got to work with Sara a few times, then I was a contestant on a program called *Ready, Set, Cook* with Tyler Florence, back when we were practically babies. The show was kind of a precursor to *Iron Chef* in that it was a competition. There was a studio audience, and it was up to them to choose the winner. Each contestant was assigned a piece of produce—for example, a tomato or a pepper. When it came time to vote, the audience showed their favorite by holding up a card with the image of that tomato or pepper that was tallied to determine the winner. It was so silly and old school, but we had a blast.

After a while, I slowly gained the confidence to take some chances. I started to feel myself settling in, loosening up, and letting my personality come through a little more. I danced and joked around—with the crew, and on screen. Sometimes I invented words. "Okay, baby," I'd tell the camera. "Today, I'm going to be making a sofrito; it's a *chilified* sauce."

"Uh, Aarón," the producers would say between takes. "Is *chilified* a word?"

"Hmm, no. I don't believe it is a word," I'd respond. "But I like it!"

I wasn't the only one getting creative. With some success came the realization that the public liked for us to be a little playful. To not be so serious. Prior to that, food shows were staunchly informational. Measurements, steps, instructions. The Food Network crew realized that cooking didn't just have to be about function and started giving people permission to have a little fun in the kitchen.

Eventually, a new concept called *Melting Pot* came up. It was going to be five different groups of chefs doing their own unique cuisines. It was Mediterranean with Rocco DiSpirito and Cat Cora, Eastern European with Michael Symon and Wayne Harley Brachman, and something called "Padma's

Passport" with Padma Lakshmi. And finally, they wanted to include a Nuevo Latino segment—featuring me and my old buddy Alex García.

As much as we all felt we were adjusting to our new TV-host titles, we were still cooks, not actors or broadcasters with any kind of formal education in the field. Knowing how to look at the camera, how to speak in soundbites, that sort of thing—that was all still new to us, and we were learning as we went along. Ultimately, when we started to get some traction and were preparing for *Melting Pot*, the network arranged for us to attend training with a media professional named Lou Ekus.

Lou had a company called AirTyme that had been training culinary talent since before most "culinary talent" saw the light of day outside of a kitchen, let alone soundstage lights. We were all rounded up to have a session with this guy, who was such a character. He told us, when we were all seated and attentive, that what sells television is something he called "PFE." A lot of blank faces looked back at Lou, waiting for him to spell it out for us: passion, fun, and energy.

Maybe some of it seemed a little goofy, but honestly, I learned some great stuff from that dude—a lot of techniques I still use today. He broke it down in a way that we could digest.

He told us to behave as if we weren't talking to forty million people, but to just one. He made sure we knew to look up, and to look at the camera. He reminded us that we weren't in the confines of a restaurant kitchen, but transmitting into the homes of viewers around the country. Opening up to the lens, including the person we were speaking to if someone else was on screen, knowing how to clip your statements so they could be edited later—that was all part of being an appealing and effective host.

He was also really emphatic about us avoiding the tendency to describe food with what he called "useless modifiers." This is something I've come to recognize as a sure tell of someone new to television: "Oh, this macaroni and cheese is wonderful, the flavor is fantastic," they'll say. But those words—wonderful, fantastic—they don't really *say* anything. Remembering that those people watching can't taste or smell what we're talking about was something Lou really impressed on us.

Instead, a much more engaging way to describe it would be: "This macaroni and cheese is really fantastic because we used a super-aromatic three-layer cheese blend of aged Gouda, Monterey jack, and cheddar, which all have a different purpose: one is salty, one has moisture, and one brings texture. And when you take a forkful and break that golden, crispy crust, the blend creates that epic cheese pull, and the toasted breadcrumbs just give a perfect crunch and a little nuttiness when you take a bite." Descriptions like that really sell a dish, make mouths water, and let people in on the flavors and textures and aromas when they can't experience it themselves.

They were invaluable lessons that still serve me today, whether I'm endorsing a product, working with time constraints, or sharing the airtime with a cohost. There are countless nuances and layers to media training that I am so grateful to have had. Dedicated training gave me an advantage early in my TV career that allowed me to continue to book those gigs. There are tons of talented chefs out there who tried their hand at hosting but couldn't keep people engaged on television. It came at the perfect time, because *Melting Pot* was a jumping-off point for a lot of us, and for me it was the first time I was helping to steward a show.

When I walked in the first morning, the studio was big and dark, and the crew was just getting set up. I saw a few familiar cameramen that I'd worked with in the past, which gave me a little comfort. The kitchen was right next door, and there were towering stacks of pots and pans. I approached the staff to talk with them about what I'd be making and to run through the recipes. The way it worked for *Melting Pot* was different from the shows I'd done previously (we'd finally gotten to the point where I didn't have to carry my own poultry into the studio!). Part of our jobs as hosts was to give the team instructions in advance, and they'd spend a few days testing and tweaking to make sure the steps would fall into the timeframe of the segment, while allowing our cohost time to do his or her dish. It was a major step up, and I was excited to have that kind of support and collaboration.

I had just discovered food from the Yucatán, and I was totally bonkers about it. I made this Yucatán-style pork with *achiote*. It felt like a great choice because it was a highly versatile recipe; it had six ingredients, and could be

made not only with pork, but with chicken or fish, which was always a bonus for the home viewer.

By then, I understood that making a TV show is all about dialing it in. In a lot of ways, it's not so different from opening a restaurant—always a series of wrinkles that have to be ironed out. I can confidently say now that that's the case no matter what your level, budget, or network.

Even though I had some insight, and Lou's words in my ears (along with my producer's via IEM), I was still nervous about steering the ship on a brand-new show. But I felt like I wasn't going to be any more prepared than I was right then, so I told the crew I was ready.

"All right," I said standing at the counter. "Let's do this."

We got rolling, and I started going through the steps, but the producers on the show kept stopping me, asking me to begin again. Every time we rolled, I thought, *Okay, you got it—you're doing a great job!* But then I'd get stopped again. It was a harsh realization when a producer came down from the booth to give me the laundry list of things I wasn't doing right: "Look, Aarón, you're doing great, but you didn't tease the next recipes. You didn't mention the story about your mom. You didn't give enough time to Alex."

We did a bunch of takes, which meant making a lot of the same stuff over and over. It was frustrating, and so challenging to keep up my energy when inside I was becoming increasingly discouraged. But I didn't want it to break me down or force me to step away from giving this a real shot, which I had seen happen to some other cooks. Slowly, surely, it changed the way my mind worked, and over time, I began understanding what was important, and that it was about much more than what dish I thought would look cool on TV.

It was all a little trial by fire, and everything about the network felt scrappy at that time. That really appealed to me. I loved being a part of building something, and there was a great vibe between chefs taking those gigs early on. We stuck around sometimes to catch each other's segments, exchanged encouragement, and became a little family of accidental TV stars, figuring it all out together, from the major challenges right down to the smallest rewards. Once, while Alex and I were watching a filming of "Padma's Passport," we went back to say hello to her after they wrapped. We noticed

that behind the cooking station, Padma had a giant bowl of Hershey's Kisses. Alex and I asked her about it, curious what kind of dish she was planning to use all that candy for.

"Oh, they're for me," Padma told us. "I love Hershey's Kisses; they calm me down before I go on camera." We must've looked pretty confused, because then she told us, "You know, you can ask for that kind of stuff, guys." *Boom.* Our minds were fucking blown at that idea. We just thought Padma was such a baller, they were giving her free Hershey's Kisses! It never even occurred to us to ask for something like that.

Because the studios were based in New York, and those early productions had pretty tight budgets, most of the time it meant relying on talent that was local and based in the city. Most of us saw each other outside the studio, too—we ate at one another's restaurants, ran into one another at farmers' markets, and sometimes grabbed a beer or got together socially. The fact that none of us had any clue what we were stepping into built a strong camaraderie. We traded tips and commiserated over what we'd fucked up, sharing lessons we'd learned. Most of the time, we just showed up and tried our best to do our jobs and not burn the studio down. Then we collected our less-than-impressive paychecks and went back to cheffing gigs. After all, no matter how much Lou and the producers tried to polish us up, we were still just misfit cooks at heart, and we had no reason to believe that would ever change.

No precedent had been set for the celebrity chef. There were culinary stars like Wolfgang Puck, people who had made their mark in the industry, whose names traveled beyond their restaurant walls, but they were few and far between. Maybe an early indication that food was becoming fashionable was that the most fashionable people—from Hollywood, from the music business, from political spheres—were suddenly making restaurants more than just places to eat. They were becoming destinations, they were becoming scenes. Spago in Beverly Hills was never anything less than a star-studded affair, and Stars in San Francisco was a notorious hot spot under Jeremiah Tower's splashy, colorful reign.

And as we started gaining our own visibility in show business, emerging from behind the stoves to sidle up beside a home cook at the counter through

the magic of television, there was a palpable sea change. You no longer had to be in the "it" crowd to taste a celebrated chef's food. Not only could you read about where Hollywood was having dinner, you could cook that food right in your own kitchen and get to know the chef who created the dish, too. Our stock shot through the roof, not just as craftspeople, but as entertainers and household names.

CHAPTER FIFTEEN

MEXICAN COOKING ON CAMERA

Maybe the first time we really started to understand how powerful television was going to be for the evolution of our profession was with *Iron Chef: America*, and *The Next Iron Chef*, adaptations of the wildly popular Japanese television programs. That's when chefs started being catapulted into another stratosphere. By setting us up in a competitive atmosphere, creating this scenario where we were "warriors," the chefs gained an almost godlike quality. It was an odd thing to witness, especially knowing the truth about where we were all coming from.

That didn't stop me from participating, though. The first season of *Iron Chef: America* was such a massive hit for the network. Competitors were huge names in the culinary sphere—Ming Tsai, Michael Laiskonis, Rick Bayless. But by season two, when it was clear how much traction these competitors were getting from being on the show regardless of whether they went home with a victory or defeat, the production attracted some seriously big guns: Traci Des Jardins, Todd English, and Wylie Dufresne all took on Batali; barbecue master Adam Perry Lang and Southwestern food superstars Mary Sue Milliken and Susan Feniger (aka Too Hot Tamales) battled Bobby Flay. The list of talent slated to take a spot in Kitchen Stadium was a who's who of what was cooking in the food scene across the country at that moment.

So when Bruce Seidel called me up to tell me one of those episode spots had my name on it, I was more than a little amped. That is, until I found out who I was going up against: Masaharu Morimoto. He was the only one of the Iron Chefs at the time (the others being Cat Cora, Mario Batali, and Bobby Flay) who was from the original Japanese version. I felt like I was a

fucking sacrificial lamb. I'd seen the man cook and compete. He had ten years of experience on me, restaurants all over the world, and he was not *ever* messing around. In fact, I don't think I had even once seen the dude crack a smile. And here I was, this goofy, skinny kid coming in from my little Latin bistro on the Lower East Side, all bravado and big ideas.

But there was no way I was about to turn it down. Paladar was still my baby, and I couldn't think of a better opportunity to get people paying attention to my restaurant. I enlisted Mikey Cressotti, who was working at Sushi Samba, and Colin Alvares from The Tasting Room, to be my two sous chefs, and we got together to powwow on what the secret ingredient might be. Initially, all we could do was speculate, but we were spot-on in guessing that with Morimoto in the mix, it would probably be some kind of seafood.

The way the competition worked, prior to the shoot we were given a list of three possible ingredients that might be the focus of the battle. We wouldn't know exactly which one we'd get stuck with until we showed up on the day of, but since we'd have to create a unique five-course tasting menu, we were able to request up to $500 worth of pantry ingredients in advance that could be used to accompany those options. Our three possibilities were crawfish, black bass, and veal breast.

Right away, we ruled out veal breast. We figured there was no way they'd give us something we couldn't prepare properly in the forty-five-minute cook time. That left crawfish and black bass. Seafood, of course. I thought maybe, given my Louisiana connection, they might throw crawfish our way. We agonized about what preparations might work for both of those ingredients, narrowing down the list of pantry and produce items we wanted to request. It was spring, so I knew I wanted ramps. I had this idea to wrap the fish in the leaves and sauté the stems with some fresh peas for a really light, seasonal preparation that would highlight the fish very purely.

In the meantime, my buddy Bobby Flay, another Iron Chef, offered me a piece of ambiguous advice. He obviously couldn't have steered me toward the secret ingredient, and I don't think he would have known what it was anyway. But he had personally participated in a battle not long before in which the secret ingredient was trout. "All I can tell you," he said to me, "is you've

got to go down to Chinatown and time yourself with a stopwatch whacking a fish, bro." It was a just-in-case kind of thing.

So the next thing my team knew, I had us all down in Chinatown picking up live fish. From there, we transported them back to the kitchen in a plastic bag filled with water, like a giant goldfish at a county fair. We spent the afternoon trying to determine the best way to 86 a fish—did I use a meat hammer? Or go full-on Randy "Macho Man" Savage on this thing? The crew would time me with a stopwatch to see how fast I could figure out how to prepare the thing for cooking. And let me tell you, those were some resilient motherfuckers.

<p style="text-align:center">* * *</p>

While taking Bobby's words under advisement, a few days before the battle I was at the Union Square Greenmarket doing my usual thing for Paladar. Rick Bishop of Mountain Sweet Berry Farms (whose tristar strawberries are still a draw for swooning chefs every season) is to this day probably one of the most well-known farmers in the tri-state area and is a friend of mine. It was pretty common knowledge that I was preparing for battle. I never stopped talking about it, mostly because of my own case of nerves. So Rick was in the know when he pulled me aside to drop a little piece of information.

"Aarón," he said. "Someone just stopped by and asked for a receipt with their purchase. It was a credit card from Food Network."

My heart stopped. "What'd they buy? Rick, what'd they buy?!"

Among other things, this mystery shopper had picked up one of Rick's hottest items of the moment: ramps.

I called Mikey and Colin immediately. "It's fucking bass!" I told them. Ramps were an ingredient on my pantry request list for the bass, so there was no question in my mind—I was not even considering there could be *any* other reason Food Network might want one of the most popular ingredients of the season. We went all in, strategizing and working with what felt like stolen intel. But hey, all's fair in culinary warfare.

The day of the shoot, we got to the studio and Mikey started having a meltdown. "What if it's crawfish, bro? If it's crawfish, we're going to be fucked, bro!" He told me he needed to smoke, so I followed him into the bathroom on the eighth floor, trying to talk him down so we didn't get thrown out of the place faster than the chairman could say *Allez, cuisine.*

Fortunately, we pulled it together by the time the pumped-in theatrical smoke cleared and I was due on stage. When they revealed the secret ingredient, our intuition turned out to be on point. We were about to cook five courses of sea bass.

The experience of cooking in Kitchen Stadium was every bit as intense as it seems on TV; that pressure and the ticking clock are extremely real. We sweated our balls off, trying to stick to the plan we'd so meticulously mapped out, to keep our eyes on our own cutting boards and not be distracted by what was happening on Morimoto's side, or Alton Brown's running commentary. Somehow, we managed to pull off everything we'd hoped to in the time allotted, and I was super proud of my team. We didn't take home the glory, exactly, but we did make history for the show as the first challenger to ever tie an Iron Chef. That alone felt like a win to me; I could walk away with my head held high.

But my run-in with the *Iron Chef* franchise was not yet over. I later competed on the first season of *The Next Iron Chef.* I made it to the final four, and to settle the score, they sent John Besh, Chris Cosentino, Michael Symon, and me to Munich, Germany, to face off, where Symon ultimately wound up winning. Those were some pivotal moments not only for me as a chef, but also for the network and all those people who subsequently appeared on its programs: Food Network was now in the business of manufacturing true celebrities, and changing the way the public looked at our profession.

Iron Chef proved a lot of things—that chefs could carry a show, that programming could be focused on more than just the instructional stuff, and that food could be about entertainment, not only function. With that in mind, along with the general television landscape of reality-dominated programming, a whole cavalcade of new shows debuted.

* * *

The idea behind *Chopped* sounded basic enough when I was first told about it. One host. Four contestants. Three judges. The format of the mystery ingredient that was so captivating in the *Iron Chef* battles showed up here, but amplified. Instead of a single ingredient and five courses, it was three courses—appetizer, entrée, dessert—with three mystery ingredients for each, presented in the iconic, otherwise comforting and innocuous picnic basket.

The network could never have known when they decided to shoot a pilot that *Chopped* would run for more than ten years and hundreds of episodes (with no end in sight), but one thing seemed quickly clear: They'd bottled lightning. It was a great concept for a lot of reasons, though I think a lot of the magic of that program came from the rapport between those of us at the judges' table. It all came about in a very organic way, and again, it was that New York connection. For a show that they were just testing out, the original group of us asked to judge was a city-based crew: Alex Guarnaschelli, Marcus Samuelsson, Scott Conant. When I was first approached, I loved the idea and was honored to be invited to the judging panel for the inaugural episode. (I went on to be a part of the show for twenty-nine subsequent seasons.) We all felt as soon as we wrapped that this was a game-changing game show.

Chopped also provided a loose framework that was replicated dozens of ways, from Food Network's own shows like *Cutthroat Kitchen* and countless one-off specials, to those on other providers attempting to capitalize on its success. It was storytelling, it was cooking, it was teaching. And it was quick! Both for the viewer and for the production team. For *Chopped*, *Iron Chef*'s one-hour run time was cut to a bite-sized twenty-two-minute episode, and on the back end, we were cranking out episodes. Producers got it down to a science fast, and instead of the twenty-hour shoot day common of *Iron Chef*, we were pulling off all the different subplots of *Chopped* within a ten-hour workday. It was cheaper, more efficient, and pretty damn impressive, even to those of us behind the scenes who had watched the process evolve.

I enjoyed doing that show a ton, and it meant getting to keep working with my friends, who had become family. We'd all been working together for a long time and had a lot more tolerance for each other's bullshit. We had camaraderie and community in that core group, the kind of thing that only comes with time together in the trenches (not to mention the avenues

of Manhattan's *real* restaurant scene), and I think that came across on screen. It was also really amazing to add Ted Allen to the mix—he and I got along great. For two dudes who couldn't have appeared more different outwardly, we had a ton in common. We had the same sense of humor, for one thing. And his studious approach to cuisine appealed to my curious side. We liked to read the same style of food books—ones about history, culture, and science. *Chopped* was exciting to make and to watch, it became an instant hit that reached audiences far beyond the food world.

* * *

The show launched careers—of its contestants, and sometimes of its judges. A lot started changing quickly after that. It was the beginning of a new era, and it wasn't long before major brands and companies caught on to the idea that maybe there was something to all this attention that cooks were getting. Chefs, myself included, realized there was a whole new world of business opportunities that could come along with this—but we also realized that few of us were equipped with the acumen (or the free time) to handle the contracts, negotiations, and paperwork that were going to come along with it all. If you had told any of us when we were in cooking school, or when we first picked up a knife to chop carrots or peel potatoes, that someday we were going to need talent agents, managers, and publicists? Well, we probably would have asked you what the hell those people even do.

But just like that, we went from being restaurant workers—workhorses who were once just happy to have their dish called out or typeset on a menu somewhere—to bona fide walking, talking brand names. It was an early lesson in how to rely on other people, too, which was something that required me to relinquish some control. I'd always been extremely hands-on in everything I'd done, but I had to accept that this was uncharted territory for me; I had neither the time or the know-how to manage these new parts of my career.

Once I had a team in place, the trickle of endorsement deals became a river. I started working with brands that I felt aligned with my own values, like the Mexican Avocado Board, and Cacique (which I still work with today); I did a line of cookware with TJ Maxx, HomeGoods and Marshalls.

Those deals were very valuable ones, and my work with brands continues to be both a major part of my income, allowing me to keep doing what I do. Making money from a restaurant isn't just a challenge—in many cases, it's nearly impossible. A lot of chefs doing ultra-high-end fine dining today will tell you that despite the appearance of a packed house or the price tag of their tasting menu, their businesses benefit significantly from the revenue other avenues provide: personal appearances, endorsements, cookbooks, speaking engagements, and television all help supplement their income and allow them to keep the lights on and the paychecks going. It's something a lot of young cooks don't necessarily understand when they go sinking some family member's hard-earned good-faith investment into an ambitious restaurant project with nothing else to rely on or back them up. They think, *if so-and-so can do it, why can't I?*

A lot of chefs began taking shit for accepting gigs on food television and endorsement deals. We started to hear rumblings that we were selling out, like we were some indie band gone major label. But the thing is, it alleviated a lot of pressure from my restaurants, and I think in some ways it allowed them to have a longer life than they would have under different circumstances. I'd worked with cooks who told me horror stories about how their checks were shorted because an owner couldn't make payroll, or a restaurant would close way before its time because it was undercapitalized. Ultimately, chefs had been dependent on the restaurant's revenue for their own income, and if they couldn't support themselves or keep the lights on and ingredients coming in, they certainly couldn't keep a staff of cooks, no matter how badly they might've needed them. Now there was earning potential outside the kitchen, and it changed everything for me as an owner. I could prioritize the restaurant, and not necessarily have to draw a paycheck from my place.

Imagine how that changed the way a chef could create. We were no longer forced to react to tastes and markets. With a little backup strategy, we could take time to hone menus, develop a style and a strong team, build neighborhood ties, and cultivate regular customers. I could write an entire book about the pros and cons of the situation after all these years—up to and including the fact that we may have seriously warped the perception of the value of food and service by funding a restaurant through extracurric-

ulars. But love it or hate it, a chef's ability to make some cash outside their restaurants' doors has forever changed the way we eat out.

* * *

As much value as I was getting from television and brands that chose to align themselves with me, I realized that I had a particular value to the network and the food world, too. I had seen some of the interest in Latin cuisine through my experience with Paladar. It seemed that the powers that be were taking notice, too. From the get-go, I was usually approached to do guest appearances on Mexican-focused episodes of other shows, such as holiday specials with a Latino twist. It seemed like for anything that involved a taco or tamale, there was a phone call to Aarón Sánchez. I was the token Latino, and I didn't know how I felt about that at first. I didn't necessarily want to be pigeonholed, but it did feel good to have that validation—to be regarded as an expert in a certain cuisine.

It also felt like an extension of what my mom had done in the '80s. She used her platform, her restaurant, to illuminate what she was most passionate about, and to share it with her community. She didn't have the benefit of this newly indoctrinated food audience, with their television programs and fancy cooking tools from stores like Williams Sonoma, or their recipe websites. And today, it's changed again. Millennials eat with their eyes on Instagram. Every generation has had to adapt and figure out how to best utilize those avenues new to them.

With food television, this was *my* chance to do something major for my culture. Rather than seeing it as restrictive, I started to view at it as an opportunity to bring some respect to the Latino population that had been the backbone of the food and service industries for so long, unseen, unrecognized, and in thankless roles. It wasn't a post I asked for, and it's not why I got into cooking in the first place. But sometimes responsibility lands in your lap, and had that come to me as a younger man, I might not have been up to the challenge. By the time big brands and TV producers were taking notice, though, I was ready to take the reins.

SEAFOOD STEW WITH COCONUT AND CHIPOTLE

SERVES 4 TO 6

My mom used to have a dish with coconut shrimp that everybody loved. I wanted to riff off that flavor profile, but make it more like a bouillabaisse. The inspiration behind this dish was to have those same Latin flavors with different kinds of seafood. This is when I was really into the whole Nuevo Latino movement, and I wanted to represent that and my love of tropical and Caribbean influences.

This is also a cool opportunity to use a half a coconut as a serving vessel, which makes this an impressive dish for a dinner party.

½ pound (225 g) clams, scrubbed

1 tablespoon cornmeal

1 pound (455 g) Yukon Gold potatoes, cut into ½- to
 1-inch (12 mm to 2.5 cm) pieces

¼ cup (60 ml) canola or grapeseed oil

1 yellow onion, thinly sliced

1 large tomato (10 to 12 ounces/280 to 340 g), diced

4 cloves garlic, finely chopped

¼ cup (60 ml) Chipotle Love (recipe follows)

2 tablespoons minced fresh ginger

¼ cup (60 ml) white wine

½ pound (225 g) mussels, scrubbed

3 cups (720 ml) seafood stock

1½ cups (360 ml) unsweetened coconut milk

¾ pound (340 g) white fish fillets, such as grouper or snapper

¾ pound (340 g) large shrimp, shelled and deveined

2 cups (290 g) corn kernels (from about 2 ears)

¼ cup (10 g) lightly packed cilantro leaves, chopped

2 tablespoons fresh chives, minced

1 lime, cut into 6 wedges

1. Rinse the clams and place them in a bowl with the cornmeal. Cover with about 2 inches (5 cm) of water and set aside; this helps remove any grit.
2. In a large pot filled with well-salted water, bring the potatoes to a boil over high heat, then immediately adjust the heat to medium and simmer until the potatoes are tender but not falling apart, 10 to 15 minutes. Drain and set aside.
3. In the same pot, warm the oil over medium heat. Sauté the onion until soft and translucent, then add the tomato and cook for about 5 minutes, or until the tomato melts and the sauce thickens. Stir in the garlic, chipotle love, and ginger, and cook for another minute or two, until fragrant. Add the wine and scrape any browned bits from the bottom of the pot.
4. Drain the clams and add them along with the mussels to the pot and partly cover. After about 5 minutes, when most of the shells have opened, pour in the stock and coconut milk. Bring to a simmer over medium-high heat. Discard any clams and mussels that have not opened.
5. Meanwhile, cut the fish and shrimp into 1-inch (2.5 cm) pieces.
6. Adjust the heat to medium and add the potatoes, corn, fish, and shrimp. Cook for 4 to 5 minutes, until the fish and shrimp are firm and opaque. Garnish with the cilantro, chives, and a squeeze of lime.

CHIPOTLE LOVE

MAKES 1¾ CUPS (300 ML)

1 cup (200 ml) canola oil
24 cloves garlic, peeled
½ cup (20 g) cilantro
6 tablespoons (100 g) chopped canned chipotle chiles
2 teaspoons kosher salt
Zest of 2 limes (about 4 teaspoons)

1. Preheat the oven to 300°F (150°C).
2. Pour the oil into a small oven-safe saucepan and add the garlic. Cover with foil or a lid and bake until the garlic turns a nutty brown and is soft like cream cheese, 40 to 50 minutes. Remove the pan from the oven and let the garlic and oil cool to room temperature.
3. Using a slotted spoon, transfer the garlic to a food processor and puree it with the cilantro, chipotles, salt, and lime zest. With the machine still running, stream in the garlic-infused oil and continue to process until the mixture is very smooth. Use right away or store refrigerated in an airtight container up to 2 weeks.

CHAPTER SIXTEEN

CENTRICO

Before I knew it, I had become the face of Latino culture on cooking television. It was a new kind of pressure, but I was committed to taking it on. TV and sponsorships had further made my "brand" synonymous with Mexican food, and that was all well and good except for one little detail: I had never really *cooked* Mexican food. Not professionally, and not exclusively, anyway.

My mom was such a massive figure in the world of Mexican food that it was always a struggle for me to dip a toe into that water. It was her territory—she had an ocean of knowledge, while my understanding at the time was only a drop in the bucket of what Mexican cuisine really was. And believe me, she let me know it. She didn't feel as if I'd done the work and the research, or put in the kind of commitment that would be necessary to do the food justice. Considering how much of her own life she dedicated to the study of Mexican cuisine—the traveling and tinkering, the constantly honing and refining her understanding of regionality—I now understand that.

But not exactly having the academic work down wasn't the reason I shied from immersing myself in the Mexican side. I wanted badly to be my own man. It was what drew me to the Nuevo Latino movement in the first place—the idea that I could carve out a unique niche, learn a cuisine that felt like it was my own, and of my generation and my experience, was attractive to me. I was born Mexican, but my life in New York provided me a different perspective than my mom's upbringing. Unlike her, I'd been exposed to all different kinds of Latino culture, and as I began working it felt authentic to me that my cooking should reflect that diversity.

But as I got a bit older, I felt this call to further explore my personal heritage. It started with that experience shooting *Taste of Mexico* with Alex,

and by the time I was approached to do a second restaurant, I had gathered both the interest and the confidence to take that challenge on. I was young and headstrong, and now I had a successful restaurant and a television career on the rise. I felt it was time to make my mark on Mexican food, ready or not.

The opportunity arose when I met with Drew Nieporent, one of the top restaurateurs in the country. He had heavy-hitter spots like Nobu and Tribeca Grill, and we already had a rapport; it was his restaurant from which we'd served those first responders post 9/11. Drew's whole approach was focused on spotting new talent, creating platforms for them, and partnering, which is what a lot of restaurateurs do today. He was definitely before his time in that sense. Paladar was invaluable experience in getting a place up and running in the most economical, stripped-down way—a step I think a lot of young chefs try to bypass these days—but I was also interested in seeing what it was like to be part of a group, and it seemed like the time was right. I knew I could learn from Drew, and we also thought we could do something that would push the envelope a little.

He had a space in Tribeca, which felt like the perfect neighborhood for what I had in mind. After I'd witnessed the embrace of Latin food on the Lower East Side, I started to think there was real potential to reach new audiences. I wanted a place that felt like the next natural step—a more mature menu, something a little more upscale and reflective of my progression as a chef, a refinement of my skills. The goal was to get people excited about Mexican food in a new light. It was meant to demonstrate that the food of my heritage had just as much right to be served with the same elegance as any European cuisine. That it—and its people—deserved the same kind of value.

With that mission in mind, we got to work building the place. I loved the development of that restaurant. I was really proud of what we were able to accomplish with the buildout at Paladar on a shoestring budget, but this was the first time I had a chance to dream big when it came to designing the dining experience. That didn't mean I left behind the people that inspired me; even though Eamon wasn't a partner in this venture, he still came and did some of the construction, so there were through lines between the two restaurants thanks to his thoughtful touches.

When it came time to write the menu for Centrico, I realized I had accumulated a repertoire of dishes that could be considered my signature staples. Figuring that out is a very important moment in a chef's career. In a lot of ways, TV helped me refine my culinary identity. During those first few years on television, I needed to give myself a crash course on cooking specific things, refining and honing my approach so I would know what the fuck I was talking about when I got on camera. It forced me to get good, to get smart, to get serious and articulate about what I was cooking, and why.

I wanted the food to do that speaking now, to highlight those ideals, with an emphasis on clean, elemental cooking. The menu was simple, straightforward stuff that celebrated the beauty of our ingredients: a New York strip over roasted poblanos, cactus, and caramelized onion, served with *epazote* compound butter; a whole chicken marinated in chipotle on a bed of hominy with au jus. It wasn't very traditional in the composition of starch, vegetable, sauce, protein; instead, it was my attempt to polish Mexican food and make it sexier. We did some tastings, built a tight team, trained up an experienced service staff, dialed in our infrastructure, and were off to a fast start.

Centrico opened up to great initial press, and I was super proud of the place, but the real test was my mom's opinion. When she came for the first time, I made a point to cook for her personally. I roasted a lamb loin with a pomegranate ancho chile sauce that she loved. I did a whole roasted suckling pig, *cocina de pibil* style, slow-roasting the pork in a marinade with pickled onions with habanero, served with a big cracklin' on top and fresh tortillas on the side. I made a simple sautéed fish with lime, serrano, cilantro, and olive oil. I think she recognized the effort I was making, what I was trying to do, and that I had a clear vision—and that was really important for her to see. She commented on how stripped down the dishes were; she thought that approach was unique and worthy, and I was more than a little relieved to find her so supportive of my first real steps into her territory.

That was a good thing, because we were both about to get knocked down a few pegs. My experience with food critics up until Centrico had been more or less positive. Patria was a swift initiation to the success that comes tethered to those tiny, black-and-white stars, and most of the restaurants I'd worked

at in between were well received, too. Paladar wasn't eligible to be reviewed for stars (something that has changed in the years since); in those days, spots under a certain price point stayed out of the crosshairs of whoever happened to be staffing the critic's desk. The powers that be still smiled upon us, and public opinion was largely praised.

My mom's entire career was kick-started by supportive critics, by influential folks like Craig Claiborne, who celebrated and championed her before she even set foot in the city. The media, especially given my recently minted status as a television personality, was more of a blessing than a curse for both of us. That said, I'd certainly seen what a critic could do with their venerable authority when they hefted their words onto the other side of the scale. It wasn't uncommon to see a perfectly reasonable chef totally lose his or her shit over a bad review—or worse, watch a solid restaurant wither and die after a less-than-favorable write-up. It was always a risk with every endeavor.

What I never expected, though, was what *New York Times* critic Frank Bruni chose to do shortly after Centrico got rolling. I hadn't ever in my life seen a review take on two restaurants at the same time, let alone two restaurants that, to be honest, didn't even really live in the same stratosphere stylistically—they just happened to be owned by family members. Zarela and Centrico were both inspired by Mexican culture, and that's where the similarities ended. But Bruni decided to make efficient work with my mom and me, when he reviewed Centrico for the first time and re-reviewed Zarela in the same piece.

It was a dismantling of both of us. "Mr. Sánchez is braising on his mother's turf," he wrote. "He also happens to be besting her. At Centrico, you can bet on a meal that will be at least somewhat pleasing. Zarela, in contrast, is a crapshoot." In the end, he gave Centrico one star, and zero to Zarela. Naturally, either of those reviews on their own would have been a blow. Together, though, they did more than damage just our individual egos and businesses. The relationship between my mother and me always had a tenuous element, a hint of competitiveness between two highly driven professionals who shared a genetic, obsessive sense of ambition. What can I say? The tomatillo doesn't fall far from the tree. We both strived to make sure our work represented our own efforts, our own philosophies. For my mom, who was on the fence

about whether I was even worthy or mature enough to be cooking Mexican cuisine, I'm sure it was insulting to be coupled with a young cook like me, twenty years her junior in expertise, regardless of the relationship. And for me, always struggling to separate myself from my mother's legacy and carve my own path, it was yet another reminder of how difficult that would always be.

We both had a very hard time swallowing the bitter pill of Bruni's write-up, but honestly, my restaurant was already suffering. People seemed to like it, reviews aside, but that was only when they actually showed up. I was leaning on Drew to create buzz, to bring some of that Tribeca Grill crowd, but that association was all we could rely on. I realized early on that drawing people to that neighborhood was going to be very difficult, especially in the wintertime. Centrico also had a bit of an identity crisis. It wasn't high end enough to live among those three-star spots—we didn't charge enough and the decor didn't reflect it—but it also wasn't funky enough to be casual. We were in a weird sort of no-man's land.

That doesn't mean we didn't have some great times. I was working a ton, but I didn't mind it, because I was honestly living my dream. Having one restaurant in New York would have been thrilling. Having two different, equally creative and satisfying spots made me feel like I'd arrived. It may not seem all that unusual now, especially for a chef with some buzz, but this was a different time, before the corporatization of restaurants—back when having multiple spots meant really running them yourself. There was a lot to be done every day, and when both restaurants were at their peaks, I worked six days a week. I took Sundays off, and would do either a Friday or Saturday at one of the restaurants; Friday night at Paladar, Saturday at Centrico, or vice versa. During the week, I bounced around and made the trip between them a lot. I could have done that route in my sleep—in fact, sometimes I actually may have been sleepwalking.

There was a lot of synergy between the two places. Whether we were borrowing staff or ingredients, they never totally felt like separate entities, even though the ownership wasn't the same. They were family restaurants in that sense, and I tried to make sure they felt that way to the people working with me, too. I remembered the way the staff at Zarela always felt like a big family, and I tried to bring a little of that to my own restaurants. Every year

on the Fourth of July, I hosted a big friendly soccer game in a city park near Hudson and Bank in the West Village; each restaurant was its own team, and they played against each other.

It was a really special time for me, but the city was changing, and so was my career. Tribeca, which seemed like such a great place to put this concept Mexican restaurant, wasn't the same. Centrico opened in the post-9/11 era. A recession was setting in, and all of us in the restaurant business went through hard times. Even after construction of the Freedom Tower was underway, there was still a very somber feeling in the area. It was difficult to get diners out on the patio, to drink margaritas and let loose in the shadow of what felt like a still-open wound for the city.

Outside the restaurants, things were also getting hectic. I was doing *Chopped*, but I also was doing travel shows: *Chefs vs. City*, with Chris Cosentino, and *Heat Seekers*, with Roger Mooking, a Canadian chef and musician. I didn't want my staff to start wondering when and if I'd ever be in town, and that really concerned me. In fact, I realized some guests were surprised to see me in my own restaurant. As a proprietor, I had always intended to be at my restaurants—most of the time I couldn't sleep at night if I was in town and not on the floor or in the kitchen. But as chefs started dropping pins all over the country, sticking their names on restaurants from Hollywood to Vegas to Miami and every major city and airport in between, it was impossible for them to be everywhere at once. Folks started to assume maybe we didn't actually cook at all. At Centrico, one couple seemed straight up star-struck to see me. They told me they drove all the way from Buffalo just to try my food.

"We love you so much!" the woman told me, holding a photo she'd brought along and giving me a dish she'd made herself and carried all the way from upstate (which I appreciated, but I have to admit, I did not eat—you just never know, dude). They both quoted me, they talked about the dishes they'd tried to re-create at home, and asked me to sign some photos they had with them. When they thanked me for helping them become better cooks, I was floored. It was the first time the whole TV thing started sinking in. I wasn't just a New York chef anymore. I was cooking for and with people as far as Food Network was broadcast. I was in their homes while they made

their family dinners, telling them how to stuff a pepper or prepare a scallop ceviche for a dinner party. It was such a head trip.

So the fact that my public profile had been raised to that level, yet we still weren't getting the kind of traffic we needed at Centrico, was even more disturbing to me. It made me realize that no amount of television appearances were going to be able to guarantee absolute success in this business—that's a lesson that huge TV chefs will still tell you today. I try to impress that fact upon young cooks who come up now thinking that getting their own show is going to mean they're set for life. You still have to be relentless about learning and improving your craft, about paying attention to those timeless considerations for a restaurant: location (location, location); reliable, well-trained staff; cost management; word of mouth. The hurdles that have always been there don't disappear just because your face shows up on the screen. If anything, it may be even *more* important, because more people will be paying attention, and the pressure to live up to that hype is exponentially more intense.

Thanks to all my extracurriculars, I was extremely busy regardless of how many patrons we were or were not serving, and if I learned anything from my days at L-Ray, it was that I needed intense focus to be successful. Taking risks has always been a part of my life—it has helped me stumble upon success on more than one occasion. The difference is that with experience, I started to be able to recognize a risk that was worth it versus one that might've been a death sentence. I knew that when I started to feel as if I was straying from a secure zone, I had to reevaluate rather than just push relentlessly, further into the mire.

I also knew at this point that there was a lot more on the line than my ego or personal success. I had staff in both restaurants, many of whom had families. It wouldn't be easy for them if I closed the restaurants, but at least if I planned ahead, went out on my own terms, I could give them plenty of warning and maybe even help them find placement. I was proud of the teams that I had built. I knew what my own jobs and kitchen environments had meant to me when I was coming up, not just professionally, but personally. I wanted my crew to feel that kind of love and fulfillment. If I dropped a last-minute bomb on them, what kind of trust would they have going forward in this business?

As much as I would have loved to have kept it all going, I had to make that judgment call. Between Paladar, Centrico, and an increasingly hectic TV schedule, my attention was fractured; my ambitious concept needed more love than I was able to give it. There's a Mexican saying: "You have to be around to watch the horse get fat." Centrico was my first experience with what so many chefs, especially those with dual careers in food media, are experiencing today. We're pulled in so many directions at once—shooting shows, traveling for endorsements, tending to multiple locations, training staff, making appearances on talk shows. That was the first time I'd been working on a restaurant and feeling that I wasn't giving it 100 percent. And it didn't feel good. It was time to cash in, and so within the space of a year and a half, giving myself enough time to get our affairs in order and prepare my staff, I shuttered both spaces.

By New York standards, both restaurants were successful. Centrico was eight years old when we closed, and Paladar was more than ten—both practically geriatric among the city's dining establishments. Especially today, in an age when "concepts" are actually intended to have a shelf life, not to become institutions or legacy restaurants handed down through generations.

Running them concurrently was a really important part of my career. It helped me to understand how to ensure each had their own unique culinary identity. With Centrico, I also got an education in working with a restaurant group. That was invaluable given the direction restaurants have taken since then; it's rare nowadays to find any restaurants run by sole proprietors or partnerships anywhere, let alone in New York City. Fortunately, Drew was a great partner and mentor, but it was up to me to make sure I could figure out how to keep pace with the rest of his portfolio, to stand out, to live up to expectations and earn the resources that were being dedicated to my operation. A lot of consideration has to go into selecting a group that will be the best fit. I cannot stress enough to young cooks the importance of being business savvy and doing your homework when choosing partners. It is extremely easy, especially when you're young and hungry, to be seduced by the first offer that comes your way, but values, vision, and philosophy—those things have to be settled before you can consider the bottom line. Work hard and focus on your craft, and the cash will come.

When I was coming up with Paladar, it was a golden age. You could do a charming restaurant with some exposed brick and cheap paintings, but have great food and service, and still do well. That was no longer the case. The change in dynamic left a lot of people longing for something more special. I think my mom was included in that group; this was not the world she walked into in the '80s. This was not even the one I'd walked into at Patria in the '90s. I was watching careers being built up and destroyed in new ways, and I felt like I needed to take a step back and reevaluate. My goal for my career had to be longevity, and I needed to be smart about the next steps. I knew enough to know I didn't know what was coming down the pike, and I wanted to have a better understanding.

Another major thing happened during the latter days of Paladar and Centrico that changed everything about my world, and contributed to my decision to take a step back from businesses operations. For the second time in my life, I fell in love. With all the plates I was balancing, I also added two more titles to my résumé: husband and father.

SAUTÉED HOMINY WITH PICO DE GALLO AND OREGANO

SERVES 4 TO 6

This is a hearty, rich side dish, and it is a great way to use leftover pico de gallo. I originally developed this at Centrico, where I served it with a roasted half chicken. But with its oregano flavor, and its simplicity and versatility, it can go with just about anything.

For this recipe, look for canned hominy, which is very easy to find. You want the whole, big kernels; "dry hominy" is split into smaller pieces and doesn't cook the same way. Just be sure to wash it well after draining the solution in the can.

4 heaping cups drained hominy (from about three 15-ounce/440 g cans)

1 small white onion, finely chopped

2 medium ripe tomatoes, cored and finely chopped

2 green onions, thinly sliced, plus more for serving

1 jalapeño or serrano pepper, grated or minced

½ cup (20 g) fresh cilantro, chopped

2 tablespoons lime juice

2 teaspoons dried Mexican oregano

1 teaspoon kosher salt

2 tablespoons grapeseed or vegetable oil

2 tablespoons unsalted butter

4 strips bacon, diced

2 tablespoons fresh oregano, chopped

2 cloves garlic, finely chopped

1. Rinse the hominy well, spread it in a single layer, and blot dry.
2. Make the pico de gallo: In a mixing bowl, combine half of the onion with the tomatoes, green onions, pepper, cilantro, lime juice, 1 teaspoon of the dried oregano, and the salt.

3. Make the hominy: In a large skillet (preferably cast-iron), heat the oil and butter over medium heat. Meanwhile, line a plate with paper towels. When the butter stops bubbling, add the bacon and let it render its fat, stirring only occasionally, for 5 to 10 minutes. When it gets crispy, use a slotted spoon to transfer it to the lined plate, leaving the fat behind.

4. Add the remaining half of the onion and remaining 1 teaspoon dried oregano to the pan. Sauté for about 5 minutes, until the onion is golden and soft. Stir in the fresh oregano and garlic and cook for about a minute before folding in the hominy. Cook for another minute or two, until the hominy browns lightly along the edges, then add the bacon.

5. With a slotted spoon, scoop all but ½ cup (120 g) of the pico de gallo into the pan, allowing excess juice to drain into the bowl. Adjust the heat to medium-high for a minute or two, until the juice reduces. Serve warm, garnished with the remaining pico de gallo and sliced green onions.

CHAPTER SEVENTEEN

IFE & YUMA

I have always thought autumn is the most romantic time of year. When I was a kid, I loved the vibrancy of the season and how the city came alive: pumpkins taking over the sidewalk displays outside corner bodegas, carved-up jack-o'-lanterns sitting on stoops watching people pass by, and the way the crisp air smells so clean you could practically bathe in it—like a deep breath could cleanse anything still stuck to you after the sweltering days of summer. It felt like a time for a new beginning, a fresh start. So it makes sense that it was three days after Thanksgiving, as the foliage was at its peak in dusty reds and radiant oranges, when I fell completely and utterly in love.

In her time off from managing Paladar (which was limited, thanks to our shared genetic predisposition to work an unreasonable amount of hours), my sister Marissa had taken up yoga. Food industry workers have a notoriously hard time chilling out, and it was the one hour a few times a week that Marissa was forced to slow down. It was also a great social outlet for her. Working a restaurant, your coworkers definitely become family, which can be a nice, supportive feeling. But let's face it, sometimes you just want to get the fuck away from the people you work with.

I had my chef friends from other restaurants, plus my amigos at the tattoo shop. I was doing a little dating when I could find the time. Marissa found a community in her yoga classes, where she made some new friends. During those days, it was rare for both Marissa and me to have the same evening free. But the Sunday of that holiday weekend, after a few busy days of dinner services—not to mention my cooking at my mom's for the holiday—we happened to have the right cocktail of coverage so we could both

take the night off. Marissa was planning to head to a party hosted by the dudes in her yoga class.

"You should come with me," she said. I was exhausted; what I really felt like doing was lying on the floor and staring into space or watching some TV for a few hours. Solitude, peace, and quiet—those were scarce commodities of extreme value to me, and I wasn't interested in socializing after such an ass-kicking couple of days. I also knew what happens when you say no to everything. It's a slippery slope to becoming a full-blown recluse, and I knew too many chefs (I *still* know too many chefs) who never took the time for a personal life. Off duty, they wind up practically hermetically sealed in their apartments, with aluminum foil covering their windows.

So, I rallied. Partly to save myself from such a fate, but also partly because it was just a good chance to show off some spankin' new Adidas Stan Smiths I'd just gotten my hands on. They were these super-flashy gold sneakers that I'd been eyeing forever. I fucking loved them, and taking them for a spin was good enough motivation for getting my butt out the door at least for a little while. It's amazing when you have the benefit of time and distance to see what tiny things define your path. Sometimes I wonder, if I hadn't had those sneakers, what kind of turn my life might have taken. Because a few hours later, I heard the first words my future wife would ever speak to me: "Nice shoes."

By then, I'd already been keeping tabs on Ife from across the room. The party was cool, Marissa's fellow yogis weren't as crunchy as I expected them to be, and I was having a pretty good time. From the minute she walked in the door with her sister, I was totally distracted by this woman. She had long, thick black hair and arched eyebrows, and a pristine complexion with high, round cheekbones that crowded her dark eyes when she smiled, which she was doing a lot of that night. Big, Native American–looking feather earrings framed her face, and she looked totally rock 'n' roll, wearing all black leather. I later learned that she was half Mexican, half African American, and she had these beautiful elements of both cultures. She just had *it*. That indescribable thing that made it utterly impossible for me to take my eyes off her. She was working the room, talking people up, doing her thing. But we kept making

eye contact. When she finally came up to me and complimented my kicks, I had already made my decision.

"I'm going to kiss you good night," I told her after a few minutes of small talk, feeling pretty bold for a dude wearing a Hawaiian-style button-down shirt and jeans.

"No, you're not," she said, but she was smiling, too, those cheekbones doing their thing and driving me wild. I took it for a pretty good sign. She was coy and confident, and I loved flirting with her.

We talked for a while, and by the time the night was winding down, she let me make good on my promise. People talk about fireworks when they describe a first kiss. But this was no explosion. This was a smolder, the start of something way more consequential than a bang and burnout. It was the kind of connection that ignites a pilot light, a flame that felt like it'd already been there all our lives, just waiting for someone to flip the starter switch and turn up the heat.

So much of our love felt predestined. I found out that Ife lived only six doors down from me, on Ridge. Not that it really mattered, because she spent the next two weeks holed up in my apartment. On my couch, at my kitchen table, in my bed, in my arms. We made out and made love, and in between I made dinner, and a lot of excuses to not leave the house. We listened to music and stayed up until the sun would gently start to warm the late-autumn air inside my apartment, just rapping and getting to know each other. We were totally swallowed up. I left for work when I had to, but Ife was a musician and didn't have anywhere specific to be most of that time.

It happened so quickly, so subtly, that I almost didn't notice the transition from bachelorhood to committed boyfriend. Another small, otherwise inconsequential fact that probably changed the course of both our lives was that the life's lease was up at the end of the year, and she needed to decide where to go next. Her grandmother had a place across town that she was considering moving into. But she was already spending every waking minute with me, and the idea of her being anywhere that would put even a single extra block between us felt insufferable. It seemed like the natural solution was for her to move in with me.

So, within the span of a month, I went from being a lone wolf, lapping up the spoils of being a single, working chef and restaurateur, to having a girlfriend *and* a roommate. And once again, I was forced into a growth spurt, fast. Not only was I in a suddenly serious relationship, but I had also become a de facto stepdad. Ife had been married before, and she had a daughter, Sofia, who was about eight years old at the time. Sofia lived with her father most of the time, but spent holidays and summers with Ife. She was a great kid and I loved spending time with the two of them, but the change of lifestyle was abrupt. I felt like I had sat down in a nice, comfy chair only to realize that I was strapped into the car of a roller coaster, just as it was about to crest a giant hill before a drop-off.

We didn't have a plan, but we figured we'd figure it out. There were so many things about Ife that made me feel certain it was the right move. She was gorgeous and creative and smart. She was so bohemian, a total free spirit, and she followed steadily in that pattern of strong women that had been so instrumental in my life. She taught me things. She showed me worlds beyond my own. When she talked about music, she made me fall in love with whatever we were listening to, and then by extension more in love with her. She was so passionate; I had always felt that way about cooking and food, and being able to share that level of dedication to a craft made me feel like we understood each other on a different plane.

Ife was also a Buddhist. She was what you call a "Fortune Child," meaning both her parents were Buddhists, and she was born into the practice. I was really curious about it, and early on I spent a lot of time asking her questions, trying to understand it all. Almost immediately, I was drawn to the philosophy. I wasn't raised like a lot of Mexican kids, who came from devoutly Catholic families. My mom was kind of a hippie (she and Ife actually had that bohemian free-spiritedness in common), growing up in Mexico but then going to a Dominican college in Santa Rosa in the late '60s. In fact, when we were born, my mom leaned toward Judaism. She loved the idea of family and community; she gave us Jewish names for that reason: Aarón and Rodrigo Abraham. I was never pushed in one direction or another when it came to religion, and she probably would have supported any path we chose to take, as long as it didn't interfere with our ability to be contrib-

uting members of society. My mom's only faith was in the higher powers of ambition and hard work.

But what she did instill in us were values: how to treat people the way we'd want to be treated, to be diligent and honest, and to take care of the world around us. The ideas of karma, of cause and effect—all elements of Buddhism—made sense to me because of the way she raised us. I hadn't exactly been searching for some kind of affiliation, but the way Ife explained it, and the more I learned about Buddhism, the more I found myself appreciating the simplicity, the logic, the common-sense values. It was very inclusive, not guilt-based like Western religions, and Buddhism at its core is not a religion at all, but a practice. A way of living life. I started studying it then, and it has been a foundation for me ever since.

I think being in love, being with Ife, gave me a sense of purpose that for the first time extended beyond career, and it was a reminder of how much I really loved to take care of people. I gave 110 percent of myself to our relationship. I did things for her whenever I could; I surprised her with a new guitar she'd had her eye on; I schlepped her Marshall amps, which were half my fucking body weight, up and down the stairs of whatever joint she was gigging at. I took a lot of pleasure in taking care of my woman.

And of course, I cooked for her. One of the first days we spent together, I tried to show off a little. She was very interested in Mexican customs, so I figured making a traditional mole would help seal the deal. I seared beautiful pieces of fresh salmon, and as I was getting ready to plate our dinner, I wanted to reheat the sauce I'd prepared earlier. I had the mole in this earthenware dish, and I figured it'd be no problem to set it over a burner for just a few minutes to warm it up. I was very wrong. As soon as I took my eyes off it, the thing shattered. Now, I would have probably been *Chopped* had any of my fellow judges saw the next move, but I managed to salvage enough of the sauce to still serve over our fish—*very* careful not to endanger my new lover with shards of clay. Fortunately, we both survived, and the dish secured a spot as one of her most requested meals during our relationship.

Those early days were beautiful. We were both working on our crafts and sharing our goals; I had my restaurants, and she had her music. We

also worked on our relationship; we were attentive to each other. I wrote her poems, she wrote songs for me. It was a very traditional kind of love.

It was also a really adult love. This was the first time I had to provide for someone else. Victoria had had her own money, and even though we'd lived together, we never really shared finances—just the keys to that shitty Honda. Ife and I combined every aspect of our lives early on. Neither of us were exactly raking it in at the beginning, but we were in it together and talked a lot about the future—about *our* future. It was something so unusual for me; until then, my life was very selfish in a lot of ways. I made decisions based on what *I* wanted, what might be best for *me* and *my* career. I was never concerned with how the choices I made might affect someone else. Honestly, it always felt like the only way to excel in the cheffing world. As a group, we're born nomads and loners. We take whatever jobs might come our way, always prepared to jump ship if we sensed a leak in the hold, a life raft (or a few) at the ready. It's not conducive to sharing a life.

With Ife, it was different. I wanted to include her in the choices I made. I wanted to consider how the things I did would affect her. I was really ready to be a part of a team, to be part of a family. It had been so long since I'd felt that comfort, that love and security, and after so many years of being alone and unmoored, I felt like I'd found home.

* * *

In September of 2009, I was in San Francisco filming *Chefs vs. City* with my buddy Chris Cosentino, and Ife came along for the trip. Something about the Bay Area, the briny air, being away together, I got swept up in the romance of it all.

"Let's do this," I said, and I asked her to marry me, right then and there. It was impulsive and born from some whimsical feeling I could hardly identify. Impulsivity defined a lot of our relationship. We were two devastatingly passionate people who were spontaneous and just going on love. Maybe it wasn't always the wisest way to live, in retrospect, but at least we always knew we were going with our hearts.

So we got married at the courthouse one afternoon, and then had lunch

at this cool, French-style brasserie in Hayes Valley called Absinthe. I'll never forget how full my heart was that day, sitting at that table, holding her hand. My wife's hand. By that point, marrying Ife was not something I was conflicted about; it was a fait accompli. I'd laid the groundwork by letting her know it was what I intended to do, and even asked her father for his blessing, which was deeply important to me. Her dad married a Cuban woman after he and Ife's mom split up, and he really liked the idea of Paladar being a love letter to Latin America. Before we'd left for California, I invited him to the restaurant one Sunday after brunch. I wanted to make an impression, and I thought it might help for him to see a busy service and know that I was a competent business operator with a steady restaurant who could provide for his daughter. I was sweating a little, going over this speech I'd had in my mind. I sat him down at one of the tables Eamon built, suddenly aware of how homemade everything in that restaurant was.

"Sir," I said, with as much respectful authority as I could muster. "I'd like your permission to marry your daughter."

I probably didn't have to worry; the man had five girls, and Ife was the first to be married. His reaction was something along the lines of, "Oh, thank *god*."

My mom, on the other hand, was less receptive. She and Ife never exactly warmed to each other, though to be honest, I'm not sure my mom would have been satisfied with anyone I brought home. She was, and is, very exacting, very demanding of people, family or otherwise. Her standards for herself, her business, and her kids were all equally intense, and that extended to anyone we were involved with. It was disappointing for me, but she brought us up to be very independent, so it wasn't a deal breaker for me to not exactly have her blessing. I'd known a long time ago it was probably never going to happen.

After we were legally married in the Bay Area, Ife and I started planning a party for our friends and family back in New York to celebrate properly. In between, though, something slightly less expected happened: Ife became pregnant. I had always wanted to be a dad, and watching Ife with Sofia gave me a sneak peek at what a wonderful, caring mother she was, as well as a little bit of a crash course in parenting through her experience. She wanted

another child, too, and maybe she would have chosen to wait until after we could at least until put away a Champagne toast with our friends, but we were both thrilled to make that discovery.

Even though we'd talked about it, even though I knew it was what I wanted, the reality was much more powerful than the idea, and I was very emotional when she first told me the news. Sometimes I think the notion of being a dad myself felt like a chance to get back some of what I felt like I'd missed out on with my own father. This instinctual reaction kicked in, and after that point, every action I took, every decision I made, it all carried new weight. I wasn't just making choices for myself, or even for myself and Ife, but for my kid. My legacy. There's a belief in Buddhism that your child is an extension of you. Your purpose in life as a parent is to make sure you set your child up to have a better life than the one you had, and that your child should exceed your own accomplishments. I can't imagine my own mother jumping on board with that philosophy, but for me, every step I took became about what was best for that child.

And like his mother before him, he was going to be a Fortune Child, born to two loving, practicing Buddhist parents. Ife and I wanted to have a Buddhist ceremony, so we booked the cultural center on Fifteenth Street by Union Square. There are a lot of Japanese-style elements to a Buddhist wedding—a really beautiful sake ceremony, a period of chanting prior to the exchange of vows—and it's a very spiritual, thought-provoking custom. I looked around at the room: On one side was Ife's family and friends, her fellow musicians. On my side, people like Jonathan Waxman and Bobby Flay, Alex García, and my best man, Mikey Cressotti, in addition to my mom and Rodrigo, my dad's kids, and my *tias* and *tios*. I felt so blessed to be surrounded by love, sharing that moment with the people who were most special to me.

Less special to all of us was the lead-up to the ceremony. It was the height of a humid New York summer, and the bride was late. Ife's hair appointment ran long, and we had a room packed with people fanning themselves frantically to supplement the circulation of a very sluggish A/C system. They were getting antsy and frustrated, and all I could think was, it's time to get these folks liquored up.

Fortunately, that part we were more than prepared for. Centrico was

operating at its peak, and the restaurant was a perfect place for the occasion. Ife eventually arrived, stunning the whole room with how gorgeous she looked in a knee-length, cap-sleeved white dress, a white flower in her black hair. I wore a black suit and tie, swapped those Stan Smiths for a proper pair of grown-up shoes, and as soon as we sealed the deal, we all hightailed it downtown.

The bride and groom each had specific priorities for the party. For Ife, that meant music, so we actually built a stage right inside the dining room where her friends played our favorite songs and took requests from our guests. I asked them to learn a song by Tyrone Wells called "I'm Thinking of You," which, of course, made us both cry.

And for me, obviously, it was all about the food. Once you're in the hospitality business, you can rely on always being well cared for. That spirit, the desire to look after others, to feed them—that's not contrived. Cooks are exceedingly generous. With their time. With a lesson (whether you want it or not). With a favor whenever you need it. But when it comes to food, it can actually be a threat to your life to be friends with a chef. There's a kind of joke we play on each other when we know another cook is eating at our restaurants: We try to kill each other with food. It's a constant one-upping game; we send out dish after dish after dish until someone finally cries uncle.

So just imagine what it was like to have those same people cater my wedding. The food was not just delicious; it also seemed endless. Most catered events come with mediocre, heat-lamped roast beef and some soggy cavatelli and broccoli. We had the best cooks in the country curating the spread. Alex put together a raw bar with monster crab legs and ceviches. Waxman made his famous chicken. John Besh brought a spread of Louisiana-style specialties. We had a carving station, too, but our dry-aged beauties bore little resemblance to those commodity catered cuts. And we made sure no one went thirsty; we had gallons of margaritas and wine flowing at all times. The music was cranking, everyone was on the dance floor, and it was one of the most epic parties I've ever been to. Given that she was carrying our child, poor Ife couldn't indulge as much as she'd wanted to, so I considered it my first duty as a husband to make sure I drank and danced her share (though I'm not sure she appreciated that as much as I'd hoped).

As a chef, I can't express how it felt for me that day, to have all the people I loved in one place, in my own restaurant, knowing that I was on the cusp of creating a family for myself. My heart was so full, I could have exploded with happiness. Forget that my mom cried during the whole thing—and those were *not* tears of joy. Shit, I was just happy she showed up.

I thought about my dad a lot that afternoon. I could imagine him giving me some advice and fixing my tie before I walked down the aisle, sitting at one of the tables with Marissa and Spanky and Rodrigo afterward. He would be seeing my restaurant for the first time, having made the trip all the way up from El Paso. I'd ask him what he thought of the place. I'd hope he'd say he was proud of me and the man I had become. I pictured giving him the news that Ife was pregnant, just between the two of us, so he could go back to Texas and brag about becoming a grandfather. And of course, I'd have made sure there was plenty of Chivas on hand to toast the future, carrying on his legacy, and three generations of Sánchez men.

* * *

With the wedding behind us, we really focused on planning for our kid's arrival. We wanted to do a natural birth, so we spent a lot of time reading up on the specifics, and attending Lamaze classes together. But Ife was asthmatic, and a few months before her due date, she came down with pneumonia. I was terrified for both my wife and my unborn son. We had to start a round of steroids and make sure she was monitored constantly, and it ruled out the plan for a natural birth. Her labor was complicated, too, because my son was a monster. We joked afterward that it must've had to do with the steroids Ife had to take when she was sick, because he was an enormous baby. The doctor knew immediately there was no way she'd be able to have a traditional birth. They started setting Ife up for a C-section, and though it wasn't her first child, I could see and sense her fear. I wanted to protect her, but I knew the only thing I could really do was hold her hand and silently pray, to be as strong as I possibly could even though I was a big old baby on the verge of tears myself.

But Ife was amazing, powering through it all, and pretty soon we were

blessed with a child. Before I saw Yuma's face, I heard him cry, and the doctor shouting, "This child is *huge!*" I was asked to cut the cord, and that's when I saw him. This slimy, hairy thing. I wondered if that was how all babies were supposed to look. Either way, I was totally in love. The nurses laid him into one of those newborn scales, and let us know that our newborn son was nearly eleven pounds.

"You're the first thing this child is going to see," the doctor said when he turned him over to us. I was melting. Yuma Sánchez. For almost twenty years, I lived without my father. When my son was born, I sat with him in my arms and I felt my dad's presence. As if I was at once taking another step toward making peace with his passing and also having an opportunity to reclaim time with him. My father's blood pumping through this tiny little person's young veins, his whole untarnished life ahead of him.

Having Yuma also bonded Ife and me forever, we knew that. But the unfortunate truth was, we had already started to argue and fracture before we tied the knot. When our son came along, I couldn't have imagined anything more motivating—for my career, for my relationship, for making me a better man and a better husband. I resolved again that day to be that man, that husband, and that father. We'd created life together, and more than ever, I wanted so badly for my new family to have the kind of stability I missed growing up. Our roller coaster was fast and thrilling. Yuma's birth was without a doubt our peak. And while it would have been unreasonable to think we wouldn't have highs and lows, neither of us was prepared for how steep the drop ahead would prove to be.

SEARED SALMON WITH PUMPKIN SEED MOLE

SERVES 4 TO 6

This was the dish I cooked to show off for Ife. It had a wow factor I thought was going to make a real impression, which it did, after I cleaned up the broken dish.

It's uncommon to see seafood or fish with mole. The real beauty of this dish is that salmon, because of its richness and fat content, can stand up well to that strong, nutty sauce.

¾ cup (105 g) pumpkin seeds, toasted, plus more for serving
½ teaspoon cumin seed
4 to 6 (6 ounces/170 g) salmon fillets, with skin
Kosher salt and freshly ground black pepper
4 tomatillos
1 to 2 jalapeño or serrano peppers
½ white onion, chopped
2 cloves garlic, finely chopped
1½ cups (360 ml) chicken stock
1 tablespoon unsalted butter
1½ cups (30 g) baby spinach
1 cup (40 g) fresh cilantro, plus more for serving
1 cup (50 g) flat-leaf parsley
¼ cup (7 g) oregano
1½ tablespoons lime juice
Grapeseed or vegetable oil for frying
Cracked black pepper for serving

1. In a spice grinder or mortar and pestle, finely grind the pumpkin seeds and cumin; set aside. Meanwhile, season the salmon all over with salt and pepper and let it sit at room temperature while you prepare the sauce.

2. Preheat your broiler with a rack 6 inches (15 cm) below the heat source, or place a metal grate directly atop a gas burner on medium-high heat. Char the tomatillos and peppers, turning occasionally, until they're partially blackened all over. When they're cool enough to handle, stem the peppers and cut out the seeds and membranes (or leave them in for a spicier sauce). In a blender or food processor, puree the tomatillos and peppers with the onion, garlic, 1 teaspoon salt, ¼ teaspoon pepper, and 1 cup (240 ml) of the chicken stock. Stir in the ground pumpkin seeds and cumin.

3. In a deep skillet or large saucepan, melt the butter over medium heat. Add the sauce and cook gently, stirring occasionally, until it's slightly thicker and the onion doesn't taste raw, 5 minutes or so.

4. Meanwhile, bring a pot of gently salted water to a boil; have a sieve at the ready and set up an ice bath beside it. Cook the spinach, cilantro, parsley, and oregano for 20 to 30 seconds, just until they turn a more vibrant green, then drain and quickly plunge into the ice bath to halt cooking. Wring dry in a clean dish towel and finely chop. In a blender, puree with the remaining ½ cup (120 ml) stock and the lime juice; season with salt. Swirl it into the pan with the pumpkin seed mole and keep warm on low heat.

5. Coat the bottom of a large skillet with a thin layer of oil and get it sizzling hot over medium-high heat. Cook the salmon, skin side up, until you start to see golden edges along the bottom edge of the fillets, 3 to 4 minutes; the fish should release easily from the pan. Flip and cook another 2 to 3 minutes, or until the skin has begun to crisp up.

6. To serve, line bowls or a serving platter with the sauce and nestle the fillets on top. Top with cilantro, toasted pumpkin seeds, and cracked black pepper.

CHAPTER EIGHTEEN

A PAINFUL SPLIT

Chefs have a notoriously difficult time keeping relationships. I'd be hard pressed to name more than a few of us who have been able to balance a successful cooking career with a happy family life. So many of us wind up divorced, depressed, detached from the outside world. Because I was a restaurateur, it would have been challenging enough for Ife and me. Add in the variables of television, endorsements, and an increasing amount of travel, and things got really complicated.

Shortly after we got together, Food Network started to take off in a way none of us ever could have imagined. It was a little mind-blowing to see how the public reacted to what we were doing. And the more shows I did, the more shows I was asked to do. Real, substantial money started to come along with the work, which felt great. Being able to support my family and give my wife and son a beautiful home, a sense of security—that was my greatest accomplishment to date. The network was definitely developing a sort of core cast of characters, and I felt fortunate that I seemed to be among that group. Getting a lot of additional work on screen also helped drive my restaurant business as well. During the first few years we were together was also when *Chopped* got its footing. Professionally, it was a really exciting time.

It was less exciting for my wife. Not only was I less available—to her, to our son, to our life together—but I was married to a woman who was striving for a sort of commercial creative success of her own. My increasing fame started to create friction. I'm not sure I can say categorically that Ife wasn't happy for me, or that she wasn't proud of me. But her music career was something she worked at with equal passion and diligence, and it was taking more time for her to make small advancements in that extremely

competitive world. It probably didn't help that she was now spending a lot of her time and energy taking care of our kid while I was out working or on the road.

I understood her frustrations, but the way in which our troubles were manifesting was taking a toll on both of us. We had arguments about the usual stuff: bills, childcare, the daily duties of two working parents. Ife felt like I was putting work before family, and I felt like I was between a rock and a fucking hard place. By that point, we'd moved into an apartment in Greenpoint and had a house out on Long Island.

"Do you like the home we're living in now?" I would ask her when it inevitably came to a head. "The vacations we get to take?" I tried to impress on her that I had to work to keep supporting those things. That my absence came with perks. In retrospect, maybe those weren't the things I should have been so focused on providing. Maybe my family would have been better off if I had made a few less dollars and spent a little more time with them at the end of every day. But that kind of insight doesn't always come when you need it most. I was working my ass off, and I felt like that was my job as the primary breadwinner. I thought about my dad and my mom. I thought about how hard they both had to hustle, to make sure my siblings and I were taken care of, that we never wanted for anything. That was my example to follow—that there was nothing more important than that. It meant taking every opportunity, because I also had no idea how long it was all going to last. There was no track record for food TV, and any restaurateur knows success comes with a ticking clock. I was motivated as much by fear and insecurity as I was by accolades and achievement.

But as it does for so many couples, all of those little challenges added up to a lot of heartache. We were sizzling when we started out, and now there was nothing but ice between us. During her pregnancy, Ife expressed feeling abandoned by me. By the time we had Yuma, our relationship became really only about him. Don't get me wrong, my child is the most important thing in my life. But I was grieving at the same time. All that love I had been so fulfilled by when I found Ife was gone, and it felt like the death of a dream.

The intimacy between us dwindled almost to a point of nonexistence, and Ife started to suspect that I was having my needs met elsewhere. In the

early days, she would come on the road with me, but at some point, even before we had Yuma, she decided it wasn't for her. "I'm not getting anything out of this," she told me after a while. I think it was also exacerbating the situation for her to see some of the attention I was getting. It's not that I was some Brad Pitt level of paparazzi bait, but there were women who wanted my autograph or a picture with me from time to time. I can't say it wasn't fun to be stopped on the street and have some couple from Iowa want to take their photo with me. It was still such a trip for me to be recognized at all. I mean, I was just a cook, for fuck's sake—that's all I'd set out to be, and I never asked for the fame part of things, even though it was a welcome development. But for Ife, it was salt in a fresh wound. She stopped kissing me, stopped talking to me for days at a time. I never knew how to react. I'm not a fighter; it's never been in my nature—not in the kitchen, and not at home. Instead I wound up shutting down and retreating, never communicating the way I felt, and that only made things worse.

I started to feel slighted, like I wasn't being appreciated. It was hard to express how much I was sacrificing to do what I was doing. Yes, the recognition felt good. Yes, I was seeing the world and my face was on television, and for once I was getting a few extra dollars in my pocket for the work I was doing. But in some ways, I craved that attention because I felt like I wasn't being recognized at home. And every minute I was on the road, in a television studio, or behind a restaurant stove was another that I wasn't spending with my son, watching his first steps, or being there to take care of my wife when she needed me.

I couldn't make her see it that way. I guess it'd be hard for anyone to make sense of that logic. Our arguments started to get nastier. Instead of spending our free time appreciating one another, it became about catching the other one out in a lie or a cheat, doing something we shouldn't be doing. She was accusing me of flirting with a publicist. I read her emails at night to see who she might be talking to. We were two people in pain, possessed by self-preservation and subconsciously determined to destroy this beautiful thing we had. The trust, the tenderness and understanding, the respect that we'd built the relationship on became something of the past. We started to bring out the worst in each other.

199

When it gets like that, at some point, someone has to say to hell with it, our love is more important than anything else—than any stupid gripe or personal vendetta, or proverbial chip on the shoulder. That didn't happen for us. We needed to take a serious break, to see if there was a way to get some perspective and still salvage our marriage. So we separated.

I was fucking crushed. I was losing my wife, and I was also losing my son. They say history repeats itself, and here I was, splitting up from his mother at about the same age when my parents divorced. I couldn't stand the ache I felt every morning when I woke up without him in the same house. It was like a phantom limb.

I refused to believe it was over, still. In East Williamsburg, I got my own place on Ainsley Street, thinking it was temporary, still convinced we were going to reconcile. It was a beautiful loft and, New York being New York, the move—broker's fees, security, and everything in between—cost me more than ten grand. But I still wanted to have Ife and Yuma visit me and feel like I was providing a proper space for my family. We were apart for about five months when I finally heard the two words I'd been desperate to hear: *Come home*. I didn't hesitate to give it all up. I turned over the keys to the apartment, forfeited the cash I'd put up, packed my bags, and went home.

But the fact was that we'd done way too much damage. We lasted barely six months after that. By the time we'd come to the foregone conclusion, Ife and I were both exhausted. And to be very honest, I found myself kind of wishing for freedom. I wanted to be loved, but I didn't want to battle so hard for it anymore. I realized then that I wanted love to be easy. Maybe that sounds shallow or even weak willed. Ife would say that we had to work for our love—that we were going to have to really fight for it. In theory, I understood what she meant. I'd seen that story in movies, too. But I also felt as if I'd been working desperately hard for love my whole life. My professional life was so challenging, so rigorous, that all I wanted at the end of the day was to come home to a few quiet, happy moments with my family. To lower my defenses and have something soft and sacred. That just wasn't happening for us.

For the second time within a year, I was devastated. And now I was angry, too. It wasn't that we had some sort of dramatic ending where blame could really be cast on one party or the other, but I was pissed that it happened.

I was phenomenally fucked up by the whole thing, and for a little while there I did start to feel like I needed to put it on her. I wanted someone to be responsible for how messed up I felt. I loved women; my whole life I'd been influenced by the women around me—ones who raised me, taught me lessons, showed me how to be a good man. And suddenly I felt like I'd been betrayed. I had met a woman who made me feel there was this dark side I didn't know about, that I was going to have to watch out for now. My trust was rocked, and not because of infidelity or anything—that might have been easier to overcome. It was my trust in love. The idea that something so pure existed and was real was now a hard notion to believe. I felt hopeless, like the kind of family life and connection I had assumed would someday be a part of my life didn't actually exist in the world.

On top of it, after we finalized the divorce, Ife took my son and moved to Los Angeles. I was definitely the one with the stronger income, and maybe I could have fought harder for custody, but my work lifestyle was just not conducive to being a single dad. Earning that cash meant putting in the kind of hours that forced the wedge between us in the first place. There was no way I could give Yuma the kind of one-on-one time I knew he needed, and I could never argue that Ife wasn't a wonderful mother. But that didn't mean I was okay with being three thousand miles away from him, and it didn't mean I felt like less of a failure as a father right out of the gate.

I felt totally alone. I'd never had a close relationship with Rodrigo, and my mom was not the type to dote on me. Friendships were hard to come by, and it was harder still for me to open up to people when I was in pain. I was once again angry that I was without my father, that I couldn't call him up, have a beer with him, and ask his advice. I was desperate for some affection, some connection, and I hated the world for all of it. I had had what I wanted so badly with Ife, and afterward, it felt like someone had cut the heat in my building in the dead of a New York winter.

If the stress and heartbreak of the L-Ray days forced me into some kind of monastic, secluded lifestyle, my split with Ife did the exact opposite. For about a year afterward, I just went at it. I was alone now, no one to answer to, and I figured I might as well get my kicks. I was partying constantly, drinking way too much. I continued to practice Buddhism, but I was definitely not

living true to code. I felt like I was flipping off the world, but the person I was actually treating the worst was myself.

One constant in my life is that when the going gets tough, I get hard on myself. I wish I could explain to these younger versions of me that these things weren't my fault. That it's all part of life, and that everyone goes through some take on their own personal hell. I probably should have called my shrink again and started working through it like an adult. But I wasn't ready. Instead, I internalized, taking my pain and anger out on my own body, doing a disservice to all the hard work I'd put in by getting fucked up all the time.

I wasn't even thinking about my career, which for more than fifteen years was the carrot that kept me walking in a straight line. I'd seen what could happen to people who misbehaved when they had the spotlight—or were even *perceived* as misbehaving. Just because the cameras were off didn't mean I wasn't still being watched, and on the contrary, probably more eyes were on me than ever. Every time I hit the town, acting like a fool, drinking and philandering and staying out till the nine-to-fivers were starting their morning commute, I was jeopardizing everything. The progress I'd made on TV, the relationships I had with the brands I endorsed, not to mention compromising the message I was trying to send Latino kids, or really any of those young people who thought of me as a kind of role model. The thought of all that in the sober light of day only made me more depressed, more hateful toward myself. It was a vicious, miserable cycle.

Maybe the real sign of maturity for me was recognizing it. I woke up one day, looked around, and realized I was on a very familiar path—the wrong one. I'd done the about-face before, when I was younger. I had to remember what it was in those days that pulled me out of it. What were the strategies, the steps I had taken? What were the inspirations that gave me a reason to take them?

I remembered Chef Paul's kitchen. The feeling of being a part of the team—being accepted by those guys who took me in, who taught me lessons and didn't give a shit about my pretty-boy ego. I thought about how good it felt when Chef tasted my gumbo and nodded his quiet approval. How I later learned that Georgie's silence was actually a pat on the back. How my mom's face looked the first time she stepped into Paladar, or when I served

her at Centrico. The way guests at my tables looked when they had their first taste of something new.

I thought about the way I felt when I came up with a new dish—a combination of hand-picked ingredients that I'd invented and written down, researched, and painstakingly put together with meticulous care, or even something I'd come up with on the fly—and it worked perfectly in the plate and on the palate. Every single one of those memories was a moment of magic. Of fulfillment. Of pride. Of *purpose*. I needed to remember those moments, to recall what brought the most light to my life, so I could dig myself out of my darkest hole yet. I had to remember that cooking didn't just put food on the table. Cooking had saved my life.

CALDO GALLEGOS OF WHITE BEAN, CHORIZO, AND SWISS CHARD

SERVES 6

For me, this dish is a statement about the Spanish influence on Cuban cooking. It's a classic recipe I first learned about from researching a trailblazing woman in the food world, Nitza Villapol. She is referred to as "the Julia Child of Cuban cuisine," and this is my personal riff in homage. It has that cassoulet feel to it, and I love the versatility and possibilities. The sausage and pork combinations are endless with this potage.

1 bunch Swiss chard

2 tablespoons olive oil, plus more for serving

4 ounces (115 g) Mexican chorizo

1 yellow onion, chopped

1 teaspoon kosher salt

8 cloves garlic, finely chopped

2 tablespoons oregano, chopped

1 teaspoon smoked paprika

⅔ cup (130 g) dry white beans, soaked overnight and drained

4 ounces (115 g) fully cooked Spanish chorizo, diced

2 bay leaves

1 large Yukon gold potato (about 12 ounces/340 g), diced

1 large turnip (about 12 ounces/340 g), peeled and diced

¼ cup (13 g) flat-leaf parsley, chopped

1. Trim the thick stems from the Swiss chard and cut them into ½-inch (12 mm) dice. Reserve the delicate greens.
2. In a large heavy-bottomed pot, warm the oil over medium heat. Add the Mexican chorizo in a single layer, breaking it up with a spoon, and fry undisturbed until most of its fat has rendered and the sausage is starting to crisp up. Stir in the onion and salt and sauté until the onion

begins to soften, 5 to 8 minutes. Stir in the garlic, oregano, and paprika and toast for another minute.

3. To the pot, add the beans, 2 quarts (2 L) of water, the Spanish chorizo, and the bay leaves. Adjust the heat to medium-high, bring to a simmer, then adjust the heat to medium and cook, stirring occasionally, until the beans just start to soften, 40 to 50 minutes.

4. To the pot, add the potato, turnip, and chard stems and continue to cook until the vegetables are tender and the beans are creamy, another 30 minutes or so. After 20 minutes, tear the reserved Swiss chard leaves into the pot to wilt. Serve warm, topped with fresh parsley and a swirl of oil.

CHAPTER NINETEEN

A WIDER WORLD

The only thing that suffered more than I did during my post-divorce period of debauchery and recklessness was my cooking. "Write drunk, edit sober," Hemingway said. Good thing that dude wasn't a cook, because I don't recommend that strategy if your creative medium requires you to operate a stove and carry a blade the size of a souvenir baseball bat.

Given my family's history with depression and addiction, and my father's alcohol abuse, I figure I'm just lucky that I didn't wind up with bigger problems than a few half-baked recipe ideas. Somehow in my life, I always managed to throttle back just before I hit the point of no return—another strategy I don't recommend testing out. It creates a feeling of constant risk. Always balancing right on the edge requires an awful lot of energy, and the anxiety that comes along with it just isn't worth it.

At different times during my years of therapy, the topic of suicide came up. If I showed up at my lowest, the doctors would check in, to make sure that I wasn't on an especially dark path. There were times when things were so hard, when I felt so worthless, that I wondered if the world wouldn't be better off without me. If I had anything left to be hopeful for or look forward to. But I think I always knew deep down that every life has value, even in the moments when I wasn't clear exactly what mine was. Even as a kid, and later as a practicing Buddhist, I understood that nothing was random. That we all had a role. And when I finally started to get right and emerge from the fog of self-loathing and self-destruction, I remembered the one I was born to play: chef.

I also realized I'd been sorely neglecting rehearsal for that role. Thankfully, somehow, I didn't fuck up my spot on Food Network, which was nothing

short of a miracle. I even kept my restaurants pretty well attended to when they were still open. But the food world had changed. Like all industries in the information age, evolution was accelerated. The progress of tastes and trends that at one point might have taken a decade was happening in the span of a few months. Television was definitely a part of that. I mostly considered that positive, but it also presented some new challenges.

People were no longer coming into Paladar or Centrico unfamiliar with Latin food, having their minds blown by their first bite of an enchilada or carne asada. Many diners now not only had the lexicon of Mexican food down pat, a lot of them were making it at home in their own kitchens.

I loved my restaurants, but I opened each of them with something to say. Now, I felt like I'd plead my case on both counts, and I wasn't contributing anything new to the conversation. I was also no longer the only Latino game in town. I got by on guts and good looks in the beginning, bolstered by hard work and maybe even a little dumb luck. I'd gotten as far as I could on that particular cocktail, but there was no way that shit was going to fly now that the competition was amping up.

Whether or not I had a hand in helping pave that path like my mom did for me and my generation, new Mexican restaurants were popping up all over the place, with diners primed and informed. Even that regional Mexican cooking, the breadth that Zarela pioneered and studied so intensely back in the '80s, was becoming super popular. But just because the interest was there didn't always mean the product was good. I blame the pitcher-sized happy hour margaritas and bottomless baskets of over-fried tortilla chips at corporate chains. The proliferation of Mexican food was becoming a caricature—there was a lot of Mexican food, but in a lot of cases it was *bad* Mexican food. Enchiladas smothered in some unidentifiable red sauce. Rice and beans heaped onto combo platters after hours of sitting heat-lamped in a kitchen where cooking amounted to opening up a plastic bag and dumping it into a hotel pan. Of course, there were some more elevated options out there, and even white chefs were capitalizing on my heritage, staking their claim on what had easily become one of the most popular cuisines in the country.

People started asking me the same questions everywhere I went: What did I think about it all? Was it authentic? Was it *fair*?

I've always been of the mind that a rising tide raises all ships. There was an opportunity in it all, to continue telling the story of Mexican food and culture to a captive audience, hungry for more. Maybe it was even the chance to show people the story of *who* was actually doing the cooking, and why those people deserved credit, better jobs, and, above all, respect. But the bottom line was that it didn't fucking matter what I thought. The train wasn't going to slow down whether or not I liked where it was headed. I could only hope to help steer it in the right direction.

What mattered now was one thing: that I step up my game. If I wanted to continue being a leader for Latino cuisine and a voice for Mexican culture, I knew exactly what I needed to do to prove that I deserved that post, that I knew what I was talking about. I needed to *know* more.

<p style="text-align:center">* * *</p>

By 2012, I was divorced and had turned in the keys to both my restaurants. My son was on the other side of the country, and suddenly my range of responsibilities had narrowed significantly. I was still making television, but they were rigorous production periods punctuated by hiatuses that could last weeks or even months. I looked again to my mom's example. She never had the benefit of culinary school or cooking television to tune into for tips. When she needed to get educated, she had to figure it out herself, and she knew the best way to get schooled was to go straight to the source.

I thought back to the times in my life that were the most thought provoking, the most enriching, both personally and professionally. So much of what I knew came from the mouths of my mentors, but travel was what put it all in perspective. It was on the road, out in the world, that I saw those lessons in practice. I could see where technique was born and, more importantly, *why*. Travel connected the dots. Memorizing instructions will never give you the muscle memory that comes with the repeated practice of grinding chiles, or the insight to determine whether produce is ripe from one good

WHERE I COME FROM

whiff. And reading a recipe a thousand times will never provide the context or the connection that makes it special. The power to give food vibrancy and life. That requires total immersion; it requires connection to the land, the ingredients, and the people.

That was something I learned early in my journeys with Alex during *Taste of Mexico*. I also recalled some other experiences over the years when I'd been able to break away. During the early Paladar years, I traveled to Spain with Jonathan Waxman. The trip was put on by a Spanish tourism organization, and originally six chefs were slated to go, but at the last minute most of them dropped out for one reason or another. So the only ones who wound up on the plane were Waxman and me.

We toured six different regions of Spain. We went to a saffron farm during harvest to watch the picking of those precious, delicate threads. We were introduced to the farmers who lovingly cared for the beautiful, sturdy *cerdos blancos*—white pigs—that would become the mountain region's prized *jamón serrano*. In Valencia, we ate traditional paella from massive pans cooked over an open fire fueled by pine wood, creating the most intoxicating, aromatic smoke. We toured wineries handed down through generations and tasted food that had familiar elements, dishes I'd seen a hundred times in the United States, but with soul that was hard to describe. Eating food where it's grown or where a dish was created, still consumed for the same reasons and by the same people, where tradition runs centuries deep—there's just nothing like it. It's spiritual and emotional. It is humbling beyond words.

I was also exposed to flavors and cooking techniques that explained much about the pre-conquistador connection to Mexico, the ingredients that were exchanged, the history and timeline of events that altered the course of both countries and hugely influenced modern Mexican cuisine. When the conquistadors landed at the port of Veracruz in 1519, they brought ingredients that influenced and enlarged the canon of modern-day Mexican flavors: olive oil, wheat, pigs, and *Vitis vinifera*, the grape vine. And beyond following the trajectory of different foods, when we visited an archival library, I was also able to trace our family back to Spain in the 1500s. I learned my ancestors on

my mom's side are from the Basque country and were once musket makers. It was an influential, insightful trip both professionally and personally, and it intensified my appreciation for understanding where things come from and why—myself included.

Then, several years later in early November 2008, I had a chance to take a trip with the Chilean tourism board. We traveled to San Pedro de Atacama in the northern part of the country, which is the most arid place in the world, even more so than the Sahara and Mojave deserts. I learned about the *machuca* people, natives of a small Andean village where only twenty or so buildings, constructed from clay and cactus wood, comprise the entire town. They lived on and traded llama meat and empanadas, their simple lives heavily reliant on the tourism industry and visitors to their little piece of the globe, and were generous and welcoming to travelers passing through. I was fascinated by these new places, not to mention astonished and humbled. I went to sleep every night exhausted from travel but emotionally invigorated. I was always in awe of something—a landscape or a dish—but also of the human spirit and rich histories come to life.

That trip was historic in so many ways; a few nights into the excursion was the American election in which Barack Obama became the first-ever black president-elect. By then, we'd made our way to a small island off the coast called Chiloé, part of the Chiloé Archipelago. It was a gorgeous destination I easily could have lost myself in. But our group—made up of Americans and Latinos—was also very aware of what was going on back home, and we wanted to make sure we could tune in to keep up with the results. We were in a remote, rural Chilean town and Internet was less than reliable, but we managed to find a small Internet café where we could gather around a small screen when the results came in. When the newscaster made the final call, there was a hush over our group. Hands covered mouths and tears collected in the corners of eyes most of us never imagined would see such a day. Our Chilean hosts could grasp the gravity of the moment; it seemed as if they were sharing our pride and reverence, if not at least showing respect for what we were feeling. It was a profound moment for me as an American, as a person of color. Sharing it with the citizens of

another country, another culture, who could also fundamentally appreciate the significance, as part of a global community of human beings—that's a feeling I'll never forget.

While historic progress was in motion at home, in Chiloé we were later treated to a very special, millennia-old tradition. *Curantos* is a custom of pit cooking with a massive amount of seafood, meant to feed a crowd (or historically, a whole community). Huge leaves, usually from a type of local rhubarb called *nalca*, are used to wrap mussels and clams and all kinds of shellfish, as well as little cakes made from potato and flour called *chapaleles*. All of that goodness gets placed into a pit layered with red-hot stones and covered with earth. It's a celebratory, communal cooking act that shares DNA with a massive Southern barbecue or a New England crab boil.

I could hardly stand the wait sitting by the pit, the aromas of both earth and sea intensifying as the minutes ticked by. But we passed the time getting to know the locals and listening to and telling stories, and after an hour or so, together we unearthed this unbelievable bounty of shellfish. The quantity of food required a group of diners to make sure nothing was wasted, but I don't think that was a risk in our case. Our hosts and benefactors sat with our group, and we passed around charred clams and smoky mussels, and of course the country's staple—those *chapaleles* delivered in their chewy, starchy cake form.

It was amazing to me how something so primitive could be so technically on point. The textures and flavors were the type chefs in professional kitchens work tirelessly every day to capture and compose. Our hosts were just doing what's been done for centuries; no one was putting a garnish on our dish or explaining the locally sourced ingredients, because that wasn't something worth talking about—it was just life. It was a powerful lesson in how simple food can be so flawless, and how eating together, even with strangers, can create an unforgettable experience. To this day, when I close my eyes around a bonfire, I can recapture some of that moment in my mind. The food was delicious, but the company, the international camaraderie, the humanity—they're what made the evening magical.

* * *

Experiences like that had made a massive impact on my cooking, not to mention the way I viewed culture and the world. But when the restaurants were rolling at full steam, getting away was always a challenge. Even when I left to shoot a TV special or some work-related promotion, I always felt like I was neglecting my real job: my restaurants, my diners, and my staff. Now, I was ready to put myself back out there and continue my education.

With any spare time that couldn't be spent in LA with Yuma, I started booking trips. And it wasn't just to Mexico. I took trips to South and Central America as often as I could, for my first real venture into places like Peru and El Salvador, Nicaragua and Costa Rica. I'd been exposed to some of the food and culture while working at Patria, but I'd never seen it up close, never had the chance to shake hands and see and taste and smell at the source.

I was on a mission. I was never without a notebook; I never met someone with whom I didn't have a conversation, of whom I didn't ask questions or extend my curiosity. I wanted to understand their reality, the texture of their day to day. I needed to know the fundamentals of their lives, what motivated them, because those human factors in any culture are what shape the nature of its food.

Fortunately, I'd also proven myself to be a competent host for travel and on-location TV shows, and that afforded me even more opportunities. While Ife and I were still together, I'd gotten an offer to do some work in Argentina. Fox Utilisima, a Spanish-language arm of the network, was interested in having me come down to do some guest spots on cooking programs, which I happily accepted knowing it'd take me south on the company dime. Eventually, they offered me a gig doing my own show called *Tres Minutos con Aarón*, or "Three Minutes with Aarón." The idea was to do some quick and easy recipes that I could demonstrate in those three minutes—kind of a precursor to a lot of today's Internet-based instructionals and webisodes. In total, I was going to shoot about thirty of these spots, so for the next twenty-four months, for three weeks at a time, I was basically living in South America.

The show was a trip, and I got to bring Tio along for the ride. One of the best decisions I made with my new bachelorhood was to take him on as a new roommate. Tio Mario and Tia Gringa had split up not long after I stopped

visiting El Paso regularly, and he'd moved to Denver, remarried, and had twin boys: Javier and Mario. Before I knew it, those boys were young men, and were graduating from high school around the time Ife and I divorced. Mario was fixing to be alone, too, and I was getting to a point in my life and career where I could use someone around who had my back. It seemed like the perfect time to return the favor for all he did for me growing up, so I called him and asked him to come live with me. I flew out to Denver, packed him up, and we road-tripped like the good old days back to Brooklyn, where I was living in a little brownstone in Boerum Hill.

It felt great to be around family again, someone who really knew me and could be an anchoring presence. Just like that, Mario was a fixture in my life again, and whenever I could bring him along for work, I did. In Argentina, they put us up in a hotel, and he loved every minute of it. We had a blast. I was super happy to include him, and the producers actually did me one better. Not only did he accompany me on the journey; Mario got to try his hand at being a television star with a little guest spot on the show as a series regular.

The set was designed to look like a loft where I would do my cooking. I would go through the process of explaining the steps and getting things going, and then we'd have a moment where I'd stop: "Oh, I think I hear the doorbell ringing. Could that be . . . *Tio Mario*?" The idea was for Tio to come in at the end, with either a bottle of wine or a cocktail, and we'd go over what we made, share the meal, and have a toast. That was meant to be the send-off for the show. Somehow, though, Tio would always get himself caught in our fake elevator trying to open the door, and the whole thing was like a damn comedy. We had such a good time improvising our way through, and it felt like a real representation of our relationship.

In our off hours, we explored the Argentinian food scene, and high on my list was authentic *asado*—Argentina's national barbecue. The country has an intense tradition of cattle herding, and as such, they're adamant about respecting this animal that is so central to their culture. It blew my mind after having had some stateside interpretations of *asado* that in Argentina, it's never about putting prime cuts on the grill (or the *parrilla*). They use every

element of an animal in this massive feast. We tasted a dish called *chinchulini*, in which the intestines of the cow are braided—the result looking almost like a pre-baked challah bread—seasoned, and then grilled. Argentines, like people from many cultures, are incredibly resourceful; *asado* also often includes sweetbreads and kidneys and blood sausage called *morcilli*, and it's all served in what is essentially one big party.

As massive a meal as they might have throughout the day, Argentines seem never to be far from something to eat—primarily protein. At night, after dancing and partying (national pastimes that spoke to me as much as the constant snacking), we lined up with locals at street vendors serving *choripán*, a grilled sausage served in a baguette with a red or green chimichurri sauce that was almost like a broth on the side. On the weekends, Tio and I went to these unbelievable fairs where locals set up stands to serve and sell food to families taking a stroll.

I loved the flavors of everything we tasted. Argentine cuisine had such diversity of influences and, more importantly, it was never an afterthought. Food always anchored the day, in large part to create a chance for social gathering. Spending so much time in Argentina was my first immersion into a Latin culture outside Mexico. When we were in town, I learned to adapt quickly to their way of life, not just their food. I learned that above all, respect was key—treating each other well. People were very sweet and very affectionate. Even when men say hello, they kiss each other on the cheek, which was such a far cry from the American bro-hug or macho handshake. Even on set, we all paused to take family meal together. Shooting in the States, schedules were rigorous and stringent, but in Argentina, no one was on their cell phones during dinner, or talking shop when sharing a meal. It didn't mean they weren't serious about getting the job done, just that spending time getting to know one another, and appreciating life outside the studio, was equally imperative.

I loved that folks were so generous sharing their culture. There was nothing better than being able to hook up with other cooks and food people who offered to show me around their hometowns. In Argentina there was a chef named Fernando Trocca, who had a run in New York with a restaurant

called Vandam. He later went back to Argentina to open his restaurants there and had a couple of shows on Fox Utilisima, too. I did a few guest appearances on his shows, and afterward he was more than happy to be my guide for a few days in Argentina. When I visited Colombia, that role went to one of my dear friends and one of the best chefs in Bogotá, Harry Sasson, who showed me the diversity of Colombian food. His namesake restaurant was the first place where I was exposed to really unbelievable empanadas, different stews, and the use of herbs and chiles so common in Colombian cooking.

Through their eyes, and with the time gifted to me by so many friends and generous guiding souls during trips all over the Southern Hemisphere and the world, I started to compile an extensive understanding of not only food, but history, people, and cultures.

<p style="text-align:center">* * *</p>

In 2014, I was offered a very special project. Fox Utilisima had evolved into Fox Life and had developed a show called *MotoChefs*, planned as a Spanish-language limited series. The idea was to discover Mexico through its food—in an unconventional way. Two chefs, one Mexican, one Mexican American (me), would travel by motorcycle from Houston to Mexico City, on a six-week open-road journey, visiting twenty-six different cities, all while cataloging adventures and sharing our findings on camera.

My costar would be Aquiles Chávez, a prominent chef from Mexico. I was super excited about the opportunity, but my shoot schedule back home was tight, and I had one tiny little hurdle to take care of before I could get on a plane to meet the crew in Texas: I needed a motorcycle license, pronto.

I'd ridden motorbikes before, mostly with my cousins in Mexico. But they were more like dirt bikes, and I didn't need any special documentation. Preparing for *MotoChefs* meant the real deal. If I was going to spend a month and a half covering thousands of miles, I was going to have to get good, and fast. I got my learner's permit and had to complete a certain number of hours on the road with a companion rider to supervise me. The whole thing was

216

tremendously stressful because the departure date was looming large, and I was scrambling to complete the requirements. If I didn't pass the test, I couldn't make the show—simple as that.

Fortunately, I somehow pulled it off at the eleventh hour, dashing to the airport with my paperwork fresh off the presses, waving for them to hold the plane, and trying to catch one mode of transportation while proving I was fit to operate another.

When we got out there, I took to riding really naturally. I loved the feeling of the open road, and I couldn't wait to get out into the Mexican countryside on that bike. Aquiles and I got along great immediately. He was known as sort of a renegade, and we had a lot in common that way, but we also presented some cool contrasts. We had very different perspectives about food thanks to our varied upbringings. Even though we shared a heritage, he was Mexican born and raised and I was his Mexican American foil. That was really eye-opening for me. After being considered the authority on Latino culture by Food Network and other media, or even among my circle of friends in high school or college or Chef Paul's kitchen, I was now the inexperienced one. I had moments where I felt self-conscious—about my accent, about my relationship to and understanding of Mexican culture. I had to hang back, follow Aquiles's lead, let him teach me what I needed to know. Being bicultural always presents that challenge; you're never quite American enough north of the border, and never exactly Mexican enough on the other side.

I took home a ton of lessons about the food of each of those regions, of course, but *MotoChefs* was about so much more than food. Instead of us just venturing out to a restaurant or market—the typical stuff for a food/travel program—we incorporated charitable elements as we traveled through the country. In Monterey, we visited a school for blind children, where the plan was to teach them to cook and create a meal together. Aquiles and I were both parents, and though the kids may have been the ones with the visual impairment, I was having a difficult time trying to cook through the tears. To watch how happy they were, how enthusiastic about cooking and eating the food we made, their senses of smell and tastes heightened,

having us as their visitors, and the way they enjoyed and appreciated what we made together was humbling in a way television cameras could never have fully captured.

Even when we set out to be the actual teachers and anthropologists, we were almost always the ones walking away with the most important lessons, making the biggest personal strides. When we visited Teotihuacán, we ate at a restaurant where the plan was to feature its female chef. We talked to her about her food, but we also often had conversations with subjects about their lives and stories. Their hopes and dreams. She told us the thing she most wanted before she died was to someday go up in a hot-air balloon.

Teotihuacán was known for these hot-air balloon tours, and so we strategized. We asked if she would visit a local market with us the next day. That morning, we picked her up, and instead took a detour to a hot-air balloon field, where we'd arranged to take flight. It took her a few minutes to fully process what we were telling her, and before long she'd burst into tears. It was so moving. To know we'd be able to use this medium, this TV show, to truly make someone's dream come true was a powerful thing.

Unfortunately, I wasn't feeling especially powerful myself: I have always *hated* heights. So I was fucking petrified. Watching those balloons take off around us, I was freaking out, pacing back and forth.

"Aarón, are you going to do this?" Our producer was starting to worry that I was going to take off running before we had a chance to lift off.

"I don't know, man. I don't know," I said, and I really didn't. I had never shied away from any adventure before, not for the sake of the show or for my own personal growth. But this one had me worried. I hemmed and hawed, watching our crew prepare this woman for the chance of a lifetime, and I decided this was no time to chicken out, not when she was waiting on me to live out her dream.

I climbed into the basket—wondering how on earth anyone decided this was a good idea in the first place—and my fears about the ability of the thing to actually "fly" were only compounded by the amount of weight we were packing into it. Aquiles, me, our chef, a producer, the shooter with his super heavy camera gear, and of course, the captain. Who, instead of

staying *inside* the basket, decided it was better to actually hang off the side of the thing.

I was shaking my head and trying to bite my tongue. Under my breath, letting our fearless producer know, "This shit ain't fucking cool, bro," every now and then.

After a little while, I got a hold of myself, and at some point during the ascent, the captain stopped us.

"Watch this," he said in Spanish.

I had hardly opened my eyes the entire time, so watching anything didn't seem like it was going to happen for me. But I did as we were told, and I am so grateful I did. I looked up just as we broke the cloud line. Never have I seen something so pure, so peaceful. We all stood, silently absorbing that moment. I forgot my fear about being so high in the air or the size and sturdiness of the basket we were in. I forgot everything, for that matter. Some experiences make you realize your place in the world, that you're just a visitor on the earth, and that some beauty is enduring, eternal, untarnished by civilization. I understood in that moment why this woman had dreamed of this so fiercely, and I couldn't have been more gratified that in some way, I played a role in helping her realize that lifelong desire.

There were powerful moments back on earth, too. The food we tasted was always incredible, but it was the people that blew me away. We went to small ancestral ranches where we were invited in for traditional meals. We met families who'd been doing the same work for generations, farming and growing and harvesting—women making tortillas and tamales by hand, who seemed almost baffled that we were so interested in their craft.

I learned about so much of the region's culinary bounty and diversity on that trip. A taco carne asada in one state is not a taco carne asada in another. The regionality comes from variation in ingredients, but also the variation in the same ingredient depending on where it came from, the soil in which it was grown, how it had been tended and harvested. Technique and preparation added to individuality, each spot making it their own.

I also came to realize how *big* Mexico is. Some days, in the saddle of that bike, it felt like we'd been riding forever. Especially when it was hot or raining,

or when the bags under my eyes started to resemble the ones on the side of the motorcycle. But nothing can take that experience from me. Six weeks exploring the countryside in some of the most unimaginable circumstances, making friends at every new stop and city, would have been priceless no matter what. The fact that it was on someone else's dime—that I was actually getting *paid* to do this—that was something I could never have dreamed of when I first stepped into Chef Paul's kitchen, or into a JWU classroom, or even my early cheffing stints.

I was lucky to have those experiences through my television gigs, but nowadays chefs get opportunities to travel for all kinds of reasons. Press trips or endorsements, research invitations sponsored by wineries or tourism boards. For a lot of chefs, the world of cooking now means exploring the whole world. Once again, I'm aware of how ahead of the curve my mom was in her day; no book ever could have given me the same breadth of knowledge or inspiration that those days in Mexico did.

* * *

Later that same year, I got to host my own show—a special we were calling *Taco Trip*. After recognizing the massive diversity of a single dish from one place in Mexico to another, I loved the idea of celebrating this iconic food and how people all over the United States were doing their own riffs. I wanted it to be a journey highlighting and exposing all the layers of tacos and what the taco could be. From the mom-and-pop shops to the super high end, we wanted to find it all to show viewers the creativity that was out there.

I was just coming off *MotoChefs*, and of course, the idea of traveling to all these different cities greatly appealed to me. It was also the first program where I was the sole talent carrying the show—a huge responsibility, and a very new challenge. But I felt like there was no better vehicle for doing that than getting back out on the road and meeting people.

My favorite thing about *Taco Trip*, aside from eating a *lot* of tacos, was being able to showcase other people's stories, to learn from them—and in the process, teach viewers about a new place or city or culture. I loved that

we were going not just to major metropolitan areas, but also checking out smaller cities like Nashville or Portland, Maine. And we were also showing restaurants and cooks offering their own takes on tacos regardless of whether they were in a Mexican place; some were American regional restaurants that had a taco on the menu.

I knew we'd find some cool stuff out there, but two seasons of the show proved to me that I could never have guessed what people were coming up with. Sometimes that meant taking tacos to the streets in food trucks, in more common tourist destinations like Los Angeles, where Chef Wes Avila of Guerrilla Tacos was making pork belly tacos topped with quail eggs (a nod to his fine dining experience). Or speeding over to Denver's Native American eatery Tocabe, where the owners, Matt Chandra and Ben Jacobs, were representing the Osage Nation and doing Native American food, applying their own breadth of flavors to my beloved tacos. I watched as Ben prepped a whole shoulder of bison—this massive hunk of meat, so arduous to deal with—marinating and grilling the whole thing. It was hard to imagine all that work would be worth it, but when he served it over his house-made fry bread rather than a tortilla, it was totally unusual and completely delicious.

The question of authenticity comes up so much these days, but doing the research for *Taco Trip*, I wasn't worried about whether or not a Korean chef was strictly adhering to traditional carnitas. What was more inspiring was to see how creative cooks were drawing ideas and inspiration from Mexican culture and making it their own. They were innovating and doing things that didn't ever occur to me. Don't get me wrong, I love to find a spot that's really doing it right, by the traditional Mexican playbook. But I think what I've learned in my time in Mexico is that in some ways, the "authentic" Mexican way of doing things means doing it your *own* way. With the ingredients and techniques that come from your own heritage and your own surroundings. We wouldn't expect a homogenous product from Puebla to Veracruz; adaptation based on geography and personal experience *is* making food in the true Mexican spirit.

Mostly, it was humbling to have people open their doors to us. Sometimes they'd write to me afterward to say they saw a spike in business because of

being on the show, or that they had gotten some subsequent press that made a difference for them. That's when making TV felt really rewarding.

* * *

Being back out in the world reawakened something in me. Living in Argentina. Doing Spanish-language shows. Traveling the continents to get to know people from all walks of life, doing inventive and interesting things with the food I knew and loved, and that was at once familiar and totally foreign to me. I got to reconnect with my culture, and for the first time in years, when I got back home, cooking was so much fun again. It was like someone handed me a whole new box of crayons for an old coloring book. Everything was vibrant. I found myself waking up in the morning with a notepad next to my head, full of ideas that I'd scratched out in between dreams. Ingredients I'd never used before. New dishes. New flavors. Ancient inspiration. I started daydreaming again, with a clear mind, and I could see so many possibilities for the future: restaurant concepts, cookbooks, TV shows. It was a period of incredible creativity for me.

It was also when I started to realize that I enjoyed teaching as much as I did learning. When I was with Victoria and I realized that academia could be a way of making a living, I considered that in another life, I might have spent my days studying and learning (a realization that might have been useful when I was actually *in* school). But I needed to be a student of something that meant something to me. And then I began to recognize that in my kitchens, and on television, I loved to pass on what I'd learned from my own mentors and studies. To me, that's the definition of a chef. To be creative and original, to cook great food—all that should be a given. But to earn that title in earnest, you have to pass on the knowledge, *share* what you've learned. You need to leave the industry a little stronger than you found it.

The legacy that chefs leave is often measured by the strength and success of those who come out of their kitchens. I never understood cooks who clung to recipes, guarded them like they're gold, and refused to share. I think what often gets taken for granted with TV is the ability to use it for just such an education. *Chopped* was entertaining, but it was also real. Those people,

their stories, their efforts, their struggles. It was genuine, and I started to find myself wanting to spend more time with the contestants. Hell, I even went on to hire some of them.

After a while, with my feet on the ground, I knew I wanted to figure out how to do more of that. And as I contemplated my next move, as I thought about what would be most satisfying for my career, two major opportunities presented themselves.

CHAPTER TWENTY

NEW ORLEANS CALLING

From the moment Ife and I split, I knew my days in New York were numbered. I loved the city. It had been my place of residence for most of my life, and it had been extremely good to me in a lot of ways. But after traveling, getting a sense of the world, it made me realize that (and I fear I might be burned at the stake for saying this), New York was actually *not* the center of the universe. At least, it wasn't the center of mine.

I know a lot of people who feel there's only one place for them. The small town they grew up in, or some city on the other side of the world they visited once and can't stop dreaming about. For me, I had been without a home enough times throughout my life that I knew I could create that sense of home almost anywhere. That used to make life feel hard. That I never had a place where I felt like I belonged. But over time, I realized that it was actually kind of liberating. I didn't have to *be* anywhere; I could make myself at home wherever I needed to, wherever I was drawn.

But there was one place that did keep calling me back, where the volume of my lifelong restlessness seemed to quiet down, and that was New Orleans.

When I imagined some of the best moments of my life, that's where my mind took me. It's where I realized my calling and my purpose. Where I learned to be a man—one of his word, with an appreciation of good manners, being polite and respectful of other people. Where a community of people—on the line in the restaurant, and out on the street—cared deeply for one another. Where people walked with their chests wide open, tipping hats and saying hello to strangers.

New York will always have a lot of wonderful memories for me, but after Ife, and after closing the doors to my restaurants, it held some painful

reminders, too. Travel helped clear my head, but I couldn't stay on the road forever. I was able to get out there and gain some perspective, but when I came back, the city I'd called home for so long just felt changed.

The food scene was a totally different beast, too. There was a time when almost anyone with a decent understanding of a profit-and-loss statement, a little startup cash, and some solid cooking chops could carve out a little place for themselves in New York and make a decent living. But that wasn't the case anymore. Rents were out of control, and as a result, restaurants were being increasingly corporatized. Chefs and owners couldn't afford to keep the stoves on. They were getting pushed to the outer boroughs, then out of the city altogether. I watched a lot of great friends and a lot of phenomenal cooks lose their leases, their livelihoods, their life savings. I saw decades-old institutions default and disappear, replaced by banks and doctors' offices. The idea of opening a new concept in New York City felt like a bad bet.

And if it was hard for chefs and owners, it was worse for cooks. Young men and women hoofing it on the line or washing dishes couldn't afford to live anywhere near their place of employment on what they were getting paid. Some dude cooking steaks at a trendy Midtown restaurant was now looking at an hour-long commute (or longer) to some part of the city where they could actually afford rent. The lifestyle for hospitality professionals, always a challenge, was now almost completely untenable. I spent countless nights sitting around with other chefs and owners, commiserating over meals about the disturbing shortage of reliable kitchen staff. The struggle, as they say, is fucking real.

The flip side of everything going down in New York, San Francisco, LA, and Chicago was that smaller cities started popping. The Austins and Nashvilles, the Charlestons and Denvers and Louisvilles, they were suddenly turning out James Beard Award–winning cooks and restaurants. The talent in less-established markets was something to be reckoned with. It meant young men and women who wanted to make a living in food didn't need to run off to some big city to be recognized anymore. They could work for world-class chefs, get invaluable mentoring, even open up their own places and invest in their own dreams. And they didn't have to go sleep on a couch

in some shithole studio they shared with five other cooks. They could have a dog and a yard and some actual square footage. They could have a life, for fuck's sake. Maybe even a boyfriend or a girlfriend.

New Orleans has always had a strong food heritage. But this kind of shift away from expensive metro areas only made the city more appealing to me, and it made the diners there savvier and excited to see something new. I'd been killing myself in New York's hyper-competitive dining scene for a long time already—almost twenty years since I first put on an apron, and even longer if you counted the years I just lent a hand for my mom. I was tired. I was still healing from a broken heart. I had watched people in Mexico look at cooking as a way to connect with the earth and with other people—not as a commodity or some kind of angle into a show-business career. Ingredients weren't just an inventory; they were a direct line to ancestors and the earth.

I wanted to cook with that same kind of soul and philosophy, and it didn't feel possible in New York. I certainly wasn't ready to retire my whites, but I wanted a life that was a little slower, a little sweeter. One that gave me a chance to have more satisfaction, not just professional success. What better place to relax a little than the Big Easy?

Buddhism explains that by opening yourself up, the universe will provide what you need most at the time you most need it. And as soon as I started to consider what else might be out there for me, opportunity came knocking.

* * *

John Besh and I knew each other from the epic days of shooting *The Next Iron Chef,* so when we all got together for an annual fishing trip in 2014 with some other chefs in between my travel and shooting, we already had a rapport.

Once a year, a bunch of us had a little tradition of spending a week on the river in Alabama, casting lines, drinking beers, messing with each other, and rustling up whatever we could get our hands on for supper. Whenever you get a bunch of restaurant cooks in one place, you've got the recipe for an endless amount of look-what-I-can-do impromptu cooking competitions.

That summer, one of the guys showed up with a massive haul of Maine lobster, just in case we couldn't catch anything for ourselves (not that anyone would have admitted to doubting their abilities).

Of course—*of course* there had to be little friendly challenge regarding the best way to use the lobster. Some of us older chefs decided to leave it in the hands of the young guns. *Let's see what they can do*, we figured. We loaded up our gear in the morning and gave them a task. We were going to head out to do some fishing and leave them with the lobster. "We want some *Iron Chef*-level shit when we get back," we told them.

We were in a pretty remote area; no one was going to be calling Postmates or Uber Eats if this little experiment went south. But we had beautiful, fresh ingredients and a bunch of professional culinarians, so we figured it was going to be a no-brainer.

When we came back to camp, we couldn't believe our eyes. These numb-nuts stood there with big, proud smiles on their faces, and when I saw what they were trying to feed us, we had one question: "What the *fuck* have you guys been doing all morning?"

They gave us some line about trying to showcase the ingredient, and how they didn't want to mess with the perfection of those Maine lobsters. That might work in a fine-dining restaurant, but not in our little makeshift food competition show. All they had done was whip up some roasted-garlic drawn butter and boil a few potatoes.

We wanted pizzazz. We wanted to be wowed. So we told them, "Step aside, boys. We'll show you how it's done."

We took one look at all those perfect crustaceans, and I knew immediately what to do. "John, help me roll," I told Besh. "I'll make the sauce."

We took swaths of pillowy, tart crème fraîche, salty shredded cheese, and fresh flour tortillas, and together we crafted these beautiful lobster enchiladas drizzled with spicy chipotle cream. Since we both had Louisiana ties, where it's traditional to garnish fish dishes with crab meat, we decided on a finishing touch—we gilded each one with a hefty dose of lump crab. It was everything I never knew that dish was missing.

The guys went wild when they tasted them—buttery lobster with a smoky kick from the sauce, cool crema against the warm, toasted tortilla, all elevated

by mouthfuls of sweet, flaky crab. The dish was something special, and before I could even finish eating, I made a joke: We should open a restaurant, and call it *Johnny Sánchez*. I was kidding, but pretty soon, it began to evolve into a fully formed idea—and we knew it was a good one.

* * *

We didn't wait long to get started. By the time I got home, I'd already scribbled down ideas in my notebook and called my team to let them know to prepare themselves. I've never been the type to agonize too much over any one decision. For better or worse, I almost always go with a gut feeling—whether that's following a sign for Patria instead of taking the extra steps to Gramercy Tavern's front door or lacing up my Stan Smiths instead of lounging at home in my sweatpants. So much of my life has been defined by those small moments, those simple choices. Something in me told me this was my next move. And when something feels right to me, I go for it full throttle.

I'd been doing a little restaurant consulting between shooting TV shows, but I needed a restaurant. Personally, I needed that creative outlet, a platform, a place to teach and mentor, and where I could feed people. Professionally, my team and I felt that doing TV was only a sustainable side gig as long as I continued to maintain a handle on my craft. Too many cooking show stars had had their credibility questioned when they closed restaurants, or when they didn't have them to begin with. I have always—*always*—been a cook first, and a TV personality second (or third, or fourth). I didn't want to lose touch with what my work was really all about, what made my soul feel most satisfied, and I missed working with my hands and a culinary team. I'm also the type of guy who needs a mission: I'm goal oriented, and I work best when I'm busy. It was just time. Everyone was on board pretty quickly, and we immediately jumped into action.

* * *

I went down to New Orleans less than a month later to meet with John and our third business partner, Octavio Mantilla. We decided we were going to

do things the good, old-fashioned way. No investors or lawyers or douchebag suits who pretend they know the business but really just think it's fun to have a place to drink free martinis and take dates. Just the three of us.

We'd identified a spot we thought could be perfect. It used to be a place called Saint Marie's. To make the most of my time in town, we arranged to tour the space with the realtor first, and then take a meeting with the bank to explore our options. We walked in and did some quick assessments, and immediately started to see it taking shape. We could open up these big windows here. We could put an open kitchen there. A patio out front. The location was right near the Superdome, and we were imagining the traffic we could move through on game nights.

We said we wanted it, and to my utter shock, we were handed the keys right then on good faith. We hadn't even been to the bank! We stopped to have a quick coffee and breakfast, and then, feeling like it was a little too good to be true, pulled up our chairs at the loan officer's desk a little while later. I waited for the other shoe to drop and wasn't about to get too comfortable with those keys in my pocket. But before I knew it, each of us had a pen in our hands—$1 million each, signed, sealed, and soon to be delivered.

Coming from New York City, my expectations for quickly closing a deal weren't high. Leases and loans took a lifetime in Manhattan. But in New Orleans, in less than a few hours, I was a new business owner with cash and a location. *Now* this *is how you live*, I kept thinking, and I flew back to New York on cloud nine.

Of course, there was the little detail that I lived fifteen hundred miles away. Maybe that's not uncommon for chefs nowadays, when they have restaurants in cities nationwide and around the world. The Internet, globalization, technology—obviously it all helps make management from afar possible. And it wasn't as if I was going to be an absentee owner, either. John and Octavio were New Orleans based, and we had identified a crack chef de cuisine in Miles Landrem. Miles had been working at August, John's first restaurant, and had proven to be talented, organized, and energetic. We knew we needed someone strong to lead this place, and the time was right for him to take the reins (we'd even forgiven that he was part of that drawn-butter lobster battalion).

I started flying back and forth regularly, leaving Tio to man the Brooklyn homefront. The notion of moving to New Orleans had been forming in my mind since prior to the launch of Johnny Sánchez, even before that fateful fishing trip. Now the pieces were all in place, and all I needed was a plan. As if the move wasn't already written in the stars, a message from above managed to light a fire under me.

During the time I was living in New York and making that commute to New Orleans, my beloved mentor Paul Prudhomme passed away. Though he lived to be older than my father, I still felt as if another patriarch had been taken from me too soon. I thought of him often in those days, and the lessons I'd learned in his kitchen, now that I was running my own again.

So maybe it's no surprise that one night, back in Brooklyn, Chef Paul visited me in a dream. When I woke up, I was in a cold sweat. It was so vivid, so real, I could remember every detail as if I'd just sat down with him down in Louisiana. And as abstract as Chef Paul was with his advice in life, he was direct in my dream: "I need you in New Orleans, boy," he'd said.

I was packing my bags before the sun came up.

* * *

By the time Tio and I got settled in our new digs, I had been contacted with a game-changing offer for the other side of my career. After more than a decade and a half working with Food Network, I was being asked to audition for Fox's *MasterChef*. The show was a powerhouse, with a firebrand at the helm. Gordon Ramsay is one of the most formidable chefs of our generation— throughout his career, the dude has racked up more than a dozen Michelin stars. He's also one of the most polarizing figures the food world has probably ever known. But there was no debating that he was a television superstar whose reach went far beyond the average celebrity chef's.

At the time, the show was bringing in chefs to try out for a rotating series of guest-judge spots. I was still shooting *Chopped*, and there was definitely the question of a conflict of interest. But being involved with *MasterChef* could have so many benefits for me, and it was only a guest spot, anyway. When I got the blessing from Food Network, I made it my sole mission.

I admit, there was a part of me that felt, after having been on television for twenty years, almost frustrated with the idea of auditioning. It was such an introductory step, and I felt like a seasoned professional. But as soon as those feelings started to creep in, I realized there was no better reason to do it. It is always important to accept challenges that take you down a few pegs, that bring you back to earth. The minute you start feeling too big for your britches is exactly when you need to start thinking about how you can grow. I needed to prove myself for the first time in a long time, which was exhilarating and motivating. I decided I was going to lose fifteen pounds, go in there in peak shape, clear headed, with no drama to distract me. I was going to show these cats that I meant business.

I was super nervous when I finally flew to LA for an audition at the Hollywood Hotel. When I showed up, I saw Jose Garces from afar, and it scared the shit out of me. They were bringing in the heavy artillery; these were serious chefs.

The whole thing was so Hollywood. I remember thinking that this is what actors must feel like when they go in for a cattle call. I was brought in, where I met Gordon for the first time. It was an intense moment; the man has an aura and a presence unlike anyone I'd met in the food industry before. We got going and I did my thing, and when we wrapped I felt pretty good about it. I thought I might have a bit of an edge on some of the other chefs I'd seen milling around the lobby, given my media training (thanks again, Lou) and experience both in the studio and on location.

But it was all pretty anticlimactic. They were keeping it close to the vest, and if they thought I did a good job, no one let on. It took probably about a month to get word, but then when they called to ask about my schedule, I knew I'd gotten it. The guest spot was great experience, and I was thankful to have done it, but what I didn't realize is that the entire season, with its rotation of guest judges, was sort of an informal audition for a permanent spot.

When I heard they were looking to fill that role, I instantly felt conflicted. I wanted the job badly, but I was concerned about my relationship with Food Network. I knew I couldn't do both, and I didn't want to lose one gig to take a shot at another.

It wasn't just about the leap of faith in moving to a show and network I had little experience with. It was about loyalty. To me, Food Network was more than an employer, it was a family. I'd been brought in at the beginning and really grown with the team there. They invested in me, and I felt like I had given a lot of myself to them. Over nearly seventeen years I built meaningful relationships with an array of caring, talented, and generous culinary and media pros. I felt a sincere sense of gratitude and love for Food Network, but I also knew I wanted to grow.

Based on initial interactions with Gordon and what I knew about him and his career, I believed working closely with him would be invaluable. Plus, there was another huge benefit to *MasterChef*—it shot in LA. That meant that if I were cast on the show, I would spend at least four months a year in the same city as my son. That was a massive check in the "pro" column when I was considering this move. I had to make a call, and in my head, somehow I knew what I had to do. Fortune favors the bold. Sometimes you've got to put your balls on the line and take a leap of faith. I wanted to grow again, and from what I'd briefly glimpsed, I felt that Gordon's mentorship would be worth the risk.

It was also going to satisfy my own itch to teach. What I find so exciting about *MasterChef* is the nurturing we're able to provide to cooks. I loved *Chopped*, but we had such a short time with the contestants, and no say in what ingredients were chosen for the baskets or whether they made culinary sense. The show was definitely entertaining, and it was a great chance for chefs to get into the spotlight and gain some fame. But we couldn't help them really grow, aside from a few comments and critiques during the judging. But on *MasterChef*, we can invest time into each of those people. Depending on the contestant's experience, there can be an opportunity to have significantly more time to develop relationships, to provide insight and support, guidance and mentorship, so whether they win, lose, or draw, they go home with applicable skills and knowledge that will help them, regardless of their career path. It's a rewarding way to do television, and as much as I miss my Food Network family, taking that step was important to my professional evolution.

* * *

At the same time, Johnny Sánchez was going through a bit of an evolution of its own. When we opened, we had envisioned a sort of high-concept Mexican food. The dishes Miles and I were coming up with pushed the envelope a bit, the way I'd done back in New York. They were small plates, more stylized dishes that picked from different regions of Mexico.

But in our inaugural year we saw major fluctuation in business; the more unfamiliar dishes were sometimes received tepidly. We struggled with the idea of doing something more accessible to the masses while staying true to the identity of the restaurant we'd set out to build. But I realized quickly that the diners in New Orleans, like the city itself, wanted something a little more laid back, a little easier. What they wanted was guacamole, margaritas, and tacos.

It was a hard thing for me to accept as a chef. I had big ideas, a mission to prove that Mexican cuisine was so much more than just those few items. I did a lot of soul searching, but in the end, a realization came back to me from my days at Paladar. A restaurant is a place for the people. It's not my personal stage. Yes, there are opportunities for me to experiment and push forward, but at its core, I had to listen to what the neighborhood wanted, and not try to dictate that for them. I think every chef, if he or she is to have longevity in this business, has a moment like that in their career. It's a gut check, and it can be a little frustrating, a little stifling to one's creativity. But a restaurant is not about a chef's ego.

I remembered the clientele at K-Paul's—that 80 percent or so who were tourists. We had to remember that New Orleans gets more than ten million visitors a year. We weren't catering to the Manhattan diner; we were serving someone who comes from Mississippi for a weekend getaway or family vacation, a business trip or a sporting event. We had spring breakers who wanted mojitos and carne asada. We had musicians touring through looking for a little bit of comfort while on the road.

I started asking people, when they came in, what did they want to see? What were they hungry for? Most of them were just shocked to see me in my restaurant—a reaction that only grew more common as celebrity chef culture intensified. But they weren't necessarily interested in my modernist spin on mole. They wanted to see what I'd been cooking on TV for twenty years.

Miles and I put six tacos on the menu, and immediately business shot up.

I told my team, all right, this is what our audience is demanding. We're here for *them*. I remember Chef Paul's words when I tried to fudge the jalapeño vinegar: *We're not always going to have customers.* That people came to the restaurant in the first place is a humbling thing. There are countless places for them to have a meal in a city like New Orleans. Hospitality is about taking care of those people, and I told the crew we had to remember that.

At its core, that's also what Mexican cooking is all about, so in that sense, we stayed true to the spirit of the culture no matter what we put on the plate. Making concessions when it came to the menu was a business decision: Do we want to have a great restaurant that's not packed, or do the best job doing tacos, but doing them our way, in a fun and approachable style, while using the best ingredients and technique? Could we make a menu and an experience that's friendly and fun and still put our stamp on it?

Even after all the restaurant work I'd done in the past, this was a new learning curve. I'd always worked in cities and environments where I was fortunate to find diners who were game for just about anything. "However the chef recommends," was the answer so many times for questions like "How would you like that cooked?" I was a little spoiled in that way.

But every time you bump up against a wall, you can turn around and go home, you can beat your head against it, trying to force your way through—or you can find another way around. I think young chefs really need to take notice of the fact that cooking food is not always going to be what you want. You can either fall on that sword or adjust and make business decisions. That's the plight of a chef.

So we found that middle ground at Johnny Sánchez. The familiar carnitas are there, but they're made with duck and served with a crispy duck skin cracklin'. You can have your queso *fundido*, but the tortillas are handmade with freshly milled, aromatic corn that hasn't had the soul processed out of it. And we get to nod to our NoLa roots, with crispy Louisiana shrimp served with crunchy jicama slaw. My grandmother's *albóndigas* even make an appearance. We use market-fresh ingredients, we have impeccable technique, and most importantly, we still cook every single thing with a ton of heart. The love for the craft, for the diners, and for each other as a team is—as cheesy as it may sound—still the most important part of the recipe. But that doesn't

mean you have to entirely sacrifice your culinary voice; we stayed creatively satisfied in other ways.

Today, Johnny Sánchez is three years in and we're almost paid off. We're going to start to make serious money soon, and we can start thinking about expansion, maybe other concepts. It happened by being realistic, and under-standing what needed to be done.

<p style="text-align:center">* * *</p>

We listened to the guests at Johnny Sánchez, but I also really like to listen to what new cooks wanted to do. After such a long time in the business, it's great to have fresh blood with enthusiasm for cooking, and I'm so blessed to have a powerhouse team of chefs with great ideas. They have come from all over the country to work with us, and these kids are hungry. That's my struggle as a chef now, to not lose great people. The hardest thing about working with twenty-eight- or thirty-year-olds is keeping them engaged. To invest this time with them, mentoring them and teaching them. The last thing I want is for them to wake up one morning and think, *Shit, I'm doing the same thing here every day.* We decided we could take those risks with our menu and be a little more adventurous with specials or family-style meals a few times a week. We give cooks a platform to experiment and push the boundaries when they have a great idea, or when they've traveled themselves and come home with inspiration, and that keeps me (and them) invigorated.

This is also the first time in my career that I'm working with a team that is not primarily Latino, and very few cooks of Mexican descent. The Latino community in New Orleans is largely Honduran—the city is home to the largest population of Honduran immigrants in the United States. Our restaurant has a very multicultural mix. Our staff is about twenty-five people, and almost half are women. We have a lot of African American kids, and a lot of inner-city kids. We have a lot of young disenfranchised white kids who come in from the country to learn and grow.

In New York or other big US cities, cooks usually come into a restaurant with experience and chops. For us, it's a bit more of a struggle. Thankfully, maybe because of the celebrity reach and TV exposure, we're fortunate to

be approached by a lot of great talent. Still, we teach, teach, teach, trying to turn hungry young workers into chefs. We know that investing in them will be rewarding in the end, for the crew and the guests.

From the get-go, Johnny Sánchez was really in Miles's and my hands. John and Octavio helped us get off the ground, but their roles were always elsewhere in the restaurant group. One of the most important strategies a restaurateur has for keeping his or her chefs happy and retaining great talent is to cut them in on the action. Since opening, we've made Miles a partner, so he would have some skin in the game, remain incentivized, and know how much he's valued. He'd been a strong leader and an exemplary chef, and he deserved to have that ownership. I'm grateful to have had the chance to work with and mentor him, and together, we're always trying to identify people in our organization who will be the future for us, and for the food industry.

* * *

I'm not sure where we'll go next. Being on *MasterChef* comes with a certain amount of cachet, and it's made me want to use this platform to do another restaurant, to challenge myself and prove I deserve that role. After more than two decades of cooking, I know I still have a few more good restaurants in me. I want to collaborate. I want to keep pushing, and I want to provide a restaurant that New Orleans needs—even if they don't quite know they need it yet. We do still want to bring something new to the community, start to slowly develop that palate and interest the way my mom and Douglas did in New York, and maybe not always with just Latin or Mexican food, either.

The beauty of the food world today is that "authenticity" doesn't have to come with handcuffs. My personal authentic experience is as a Mexican American, one who has lived and cooked all over the country, in different kinds of cuisines, and has grown up exposed to and loving them all. It doesn't mean I'm going to open an Italian restaurant tomorrow, but my Mexican background nonetheless shouldn't make me a one-trick pony. Plenty of gringo chefs are doing dozens of styles of food, and no one bats an eye. My hope for the Latino community is that we can do both: experiment with the types of cuisines we've been cooking behind the scenes all over the country for

years (try to find me someone who can work a pasta station faster and more efficiently than a Latino), while also representing our culture in a way that enlightens the masses about who we are and where we came from. There's a beauty in having a breadth of knowledge to draw from when creating a menu, and I never want to be forced to live—or cook—within borders.

* * *

Fortunately, I didn't have to tailor the Johnny Sánchez menu to my son's palate. Early on, when I took Yuma to the restaurant when he first visited New Orleans, I had an incredibly disturbing realization: The kid didn't like tortillas. What Mexican kid doesn't like tortillas? What *gringo* kid doesn't like tortillas, for that matter? I was beside myself. My own flesh and blood. All I could think was, *Here we go . . . just my luck.*

But still, it was so fun to see him there in my new space. He was too small to appreciate Paladar and Centrico when they were in their heyday. At Johnny Sánchez, though, he loved cutting it up. He ran around, terrorizing the restaurant, being a knucklehead. All the staff thought he was so cute, while I was over there about to wring his neck. Being a restaurant kid myself, and probably having given my mom the same kinds of headaches in her early days, I saw this as a perfect example of karma.

(For the record, I should say that he's come around on tortillas now, and so all's right with the world.)

The beauty of *MasterChef* for me is that it shoots in Los Angeles. So about five months a year, I get to be in the same city as my kid. I find an Airbnb spot not too far from him so we can spend time together. I can help him with his homework, and he can help me stay in shape, making me chase him around the yard playing soccer or tossing around a baseball (the kid has a rocket for an arm—sports scouts, you heard it here first).

As he grows older, Yuma inspires me in so many ways. I am astounded by how much I learn from him, through him, and with him. TV has been an interesting tool for our relationship, too. Yuma and I have a similar relationship to the one I had with my own dad, visiting for a few months each year. But when we're not together, he gets to catch my shows and we can

talk about them afterward, which is tremendously cool. It's really important to me that he watches my shows and sees what I do professionally, so he understands what Daddy does and why he's away so much. It's kind of like bring-your-son-to-work day every day. I want him to have an affinity for food, and to understand how I support us.

But I also want to be around for him—and I mean in the long run, not just the day-to-day. I know I need to keep myself healthy so he doesn't have to suffer the way I did, living life without a father. I continue to take antidepressants and I still talk with a therapist every week, to keep those old feelings in check and always run interference. I have tried to cut back on the rosé, but I can't say that I don't enjoy myself when I'm off the clock. Those moments of relaxation and downtime are just as critical for my sanity, and I've learned the importance of maintaining that balance.

Having a child, having a team and a family, having a community of diners willing to come and taste my food, and viewers who care enough to tune in every week for a TV show about cooking—those things have forced me to be a better man. They've helped me get myself together, to understand that life is not all about me, and it never can be again. Not in my restaurants, and not at home. I'm relied upon, for better or worse, to provide. To succeed. And to do the right thing. And I welcome that challenge.

JOHNNY SÁNCHEZ BRUSSELS SPROUTS SALAD WITH BUTTERNUT SQUASH, COTIJA, AND JALAPEÑO VINAIGRETTE

SERVES 4 TO 6

I always say to my chefs, if you can make vegetarian food taste delicious, and create something super-craveable, I think that shows more skill than just throwing pork fat on everything. This salad gets right down to it, utilizing beautiful produce and layering flavors that could satisfy even the most carnivorous guest.

This is a dish that also nods to my original New Orleans roots, with that jalapeño vinaigrette, which is similar to a dressing I learned during my days at K-Paul's.

1 large butternut squash

1 tablespoon extra-virgin olive oil

2 teaspoons kosher salt, plus more for seasoning

1 teaspoon chili powder

½ teaspoon dried Mexican oregano

¼ teaspoon ground cumin

¼ teaspoon ground coriander

¼ teaspoon ground fennel

¼ teaspoon ground yellow mustard

¼ teaspoon sweet paprika

⅛ teaspoon onion powder

⅛ teaspoon garlic powder

8 cups (about 790 g) Brussels sprouts

2 quarts (2 L) canola or vegetable oil for frying

1 cup (120 ml) Roasted Jalapeño Vinaigrette (recipe follows)

½ cup (15 g) cilantro, chopped, plus more for serving

1 serrano pepper, thinly sliced

½ cup (60 g) crumbled cotija cheese

¼ cup (45 g) pomegranate seeds

1. Preheat the oven to 375°F (190°C) and line a baking sheet with cooking parchment. Peel and seed the squash, then cut it into 1-inch (2.5 cm) pieces. Toss with the olive oil, salt, and all the spices, then spread on the sheet in a single layer. Roast until tender with lightly browned edges, 20 to 30 minutes.

2. Meanwhile, halve the Brussels sprouts and trim their tough outer leaves. (If you prefer to roast the Brussels sprouts instead of deep-frying them, see Note.) Pour the canola oil into a large heavy-bottomed pot and clip a thermometer to the side. Line a plate or wire rack with paper towels.

3. Bring the canola oil to 375°F (190°C) over medium-high heat and fry the sprouts in batches until golden brown, about 2 minutes per batch. Use a spider or slotted spoon to transfer them to the lined plate, season with salt, and continue with the rest.

4. Pour the vinaigrette into a large mixing bowl, then gently fold in the squash, Brussels sprouts, cilantro, and serrano pepper to coat. Scatter the cheese and a handful of pomegranate seeds over the top for serving.

NOTE: *To roast the Brussels sprouts, line another baking sheet with cooking parchment and adjust the oven to 400°F (205°C). Prep the sprouts as described in Step 2, then toss them in 2 tablespoons of olive oil, season with salt, and roast until deeply golden, 20 to 25 minutes.*

ROASTED JALAPEÑO VINAIGRETTE

MAKES ABOUT 1½ CUPS (360 ML)

1 to 2 jalapeños
2 green onions
2 cloves garlic, peeled
1 cup (200 ml) grapeseed or vegetable oil
¼ cup (60 ml) rice vinegar
1 tablespoon orange juice
1 tablespoon lime juice
1 tablespoon agave nectar
1 cup (40 g) fresh cilantro
Salt and freshly ground black pepper

1. Preheat your grill to medium-high or place a metal grate directly atop a gas burner on medium-high heat. Set the jalapeños and green onions over the flame and roast, turning occasionally, until they're soft and charred all over. When they're cool enough to handle, peel any papery char from the jalapeño, then remove its stem, seeds, and membranes.

2. Confit the garlic by covering the cloves with the oil in a small saucepan or skillet and gently warming over medium-low heat for 20 to 30 minutes, until it's soft but hasn't built too much color. Remove the garlic when cooked and reserve the oil.

3. Chop the roasted jalapeños and green onions and puree in a blender with the confit garlic, rice vinegar, orange juice, lime juice, agave nectar, and cilantro. With the blender still going, stream in the reserved garlic oil and blend until smooth. Season with salt and pepper. Use right away or store in refrigerator up to 1 week.

TEQUILA-BATTERED CAULIFLOWER TACOS WITH CHIMICHURRI AND CHIPOTLE MAYONNAISE

MAKES 12 SMALL TACOS; SERVES 4 TO 6

A vegetarian dish that stands out on our menu at Johnny Sánchez is this crave-worthy, complex, and crushable tequila-spiked taco. And you don't have to take my word for it—there's a local taco competition in New Orleans, in which many of the city's best taquerias and Mexican restaurants participate, and this won Top Taco two years in a row.

½ cup (120 ml) lime juice

1 tablespoon sugar

Kosher salt

2 jalapeños

1 bunch fresh cilantro, coarsely chopped

2 green onions, coarsely chopped

1 cup (50 g) flat-leaf parsley

2 cloves garlic, peeled

2 tablespoons red wine vinegar

1 tablespoon capers, drained; reserve 1 tablespoon caper brine

¼ cup (60 ml) olive oil

¼ cup (60 ml) grapeseed oil

3 canned chipotle chiles in adobo, finely chopped

½ cup (120 g) mayonnaise

2 quarts (2 L) canola or vegetable oil for frying

2 cups (320 g) rice flour

1 cup (130 g) cornstarch

2 cups (480 ml) club soda

3 tablespoons silver tequila

1 whole head cauliflower, cut into florets (halve or quarter any very
 large pieces)

12 small corn tortillas
1 cup (95 g) queso fresco, shredded
1 lime, cut into 6 wedges

1. Make the pickled jalapeños: In a nonreactive cup, combine the lime juice and sugar with 1 teaspoon salt. Reserve half a jalapeño for the chimichurri and thinly slice the rest. Stir into the lime juice (weight down with a small bowl if they won't stay submerged) and set aside for 1 hour.
2. Make the chimichurri: In a food processor, combine the cilantro, green onions, parsley, reserved jalapeño, garlic, vinegar, capers and brine, and 1 teaspoon salt. Process until the herbs are finely, evenly chopped; while the processor is running, stream in the olive oil and grapeseed oil. Transfer to a large bowl.
3. Make the chipotle mayo: Stir the chipotles into the mayonnaise.
4. Pour the canola oil into a large heavy-bottomed pot (it should be at least 3 inches/7.5 cm deep) and clip a thermometer to the side. Line a baking sheet with paper towels or a wire rack. Bring the oil to 375°F (190°C) over medium-high heat.
5. Meanwhile, in a mixing bowl, with a wire whisk, mix the rice flour, cornstarch, and 1 teaspoon salt. Stir in half the club soda along with the tequila, then gradually add more club soda until the batter is pourable but not runny; you might not need the full amount.
6. Dredge the cauliflower florets in the batter. Working in batches so you don't crowd the pot, fry the florets until crispy and golden, 2 to 3 minutes. With a slotted spoon or spider, transfer them to the lined plate and season immediately with a bit of salt.
7. Toss the fried cauliflower in the chimichurri. To toast the tortillas, set them directly over a gas burner on medium heat, watching closely to make sure they blister in places but don't burn. Smear with the spicy mayonnaise, fill with cauliflower, and garnish with the pickled jalapeños, queso fresco, and a squeeze of lime.

CHAPTER TWENTY-ONE
FEEDING CHANGE

With Johnny Sánchez up and running smoothly, having *MasterChef* on the regular, and moving to New Orleans, I started feeling like I was on steady ground. The food industry had once again helped me find my place, a sense of stability, and a home, as it had so many times over the course of two decades. It wasn't always a cake walk, of course. I had a lot of my own challenges along the way, but the food world was always there for me.

I wish I could sit here and say that it's been so warm and welcoming for all of my colleagues, but unfortunately, not everyone's experience has been as positive as my own. From the early days of my mom's career, when cooks could barely count on scraping out a living, to the soundstages of TV shows, when they first don their chef's whites for cameras, crews, and audiences, I've watched an evolution take place. The very nature of the food world—a lot of traditional macho mentalities coupled with grueling, low-paying gigs, hours that bordered on inhuman, crushing pressure during the work day, and off-duty excess to the extreme—created the perfect environment for bad behavior. And it often came at someone's expense. Add in all these new variables of fame and money and power, and it was a volatile recipe simmering away, with few leaders prepared to keep an eye on the stove.

There are a lot of benefits to fame. Television, events, travel—these were all opportunities to reach people around the globe. It's mind-blowing how far we can transmit a message as cooks these days. And the promise of having that power encourages new, ambitious, determined young professionals to get into the game, which deepens the talent pool and in turn forces the rest of us to step up and stay sharp. The flip side is that, with any level of notoriety or fame, there's a responsibility, whether you want it or not. You become

the subject of a lot of praise and positive attention, but you're also availing yourself to public scrutiny. The visibility chefs have now as "personalities" and "celebrities" puts our lives under a microscope in ways our predecessors never experienced.

We started realizing that a while back, after a few years of Food Network gaining serious traction. Those were such good fucking times. It was the kind of magic that can only come organically, from genuinely surprising success. We weren't trying to force fame, and we had no expectations, because there was no precedent. We were just a bunch of cooks who happened to luck into this wild thing. We figured we'd enjoy it while we could and live it up, because who knew how long that would last. We did our shows, shot our specials, and then we went back to our restaurants and carried on our daily lives.

I think Rocco DiSpirito was one of the first to really see a different side of that fame. Rocco was the food industry's golden boy, which wasn't a shock. The dude had these poster-boy good looks and a charm that the public just devoured. He also had the chops to back it all up.

Rocco starred on *Melting Pot* with us, and he'd developed a following that made him ultra-attractive when NBC decided they wanted a piece of the food-TV pie. In 2003, the network debuted a new show called *The Restaurant*. This came at a time when shows like *The Real World*, *America's Next Top Model*, and *The Bachelor* were getting huge ratings. Food Network was thriving, which proved that TV viewers were hungry for food-related content, and they were finally taking big steps away from the "stand and stir" shows, trying out the documentary- and competition-style stuff that makes up most of their programming now. It was a matter of time before a major network would step into the food reality space.

The Restaurant probably seemed like a sure thing, and it was a simple enough idea: to film the opening of Rocco's new restaurant. Between Rocco's shining star and the naturally high-stakes scenario of getting a new restaurant off the ground in ultra-competitive New York City, it felt like a perfect formula. They probably anticipated the stuff that happened in the first season: doubts about timelines, complications with buildout, staff training, and management, and all the little dramas that spontaneously erupt when you put all these new people together under pressure.

But producers found themselves with a storyline they maybe didn't see coming. Rocco and his business partner bickered a little in early episodes, disagreeing on the usual stuff like menu items, and the extra drama made for good TV. But by season two, it had become an all-out war—one that ultimately resulted in a lawsuit and closure of the restaurant. The public took sides, and to some, Rocco came out the villain. And the world got to watch the whole painful experience. As fellow restaurateurs, we could empathize with so many of the issues, watching our colleague's very personal strife play out on screen. The show was cancelled after two seasons, and Rocco, once the food world's most celebrated rising star, stepped away from cooking in restaurants for more than fifteen years.

For chefs grappling with publicity, problems of personality were the tip of the iceberg. Sometimes attention was sought out, contracts signed, and deals brokered. But other times, the press was a lot less welcome. By 2003, Alex García and I had been crisscrossing paths for nearly ten years, first at Patria and then at Food Network, doing shows like *Melting Pot* and *Taste of Mexico*. I'd seen him in all different capacities: from sous chef to restaurant co-owner to television cohost. But when I saw his name in the food section of the *New York Times* that year, it was a role in which I'd never known him to play: criminal.

The official charges brought against Alex were conspiracy and money laundering. It was alleged that he was involved in a drug ring with his brother and some others, importing hundreds of pounds of cocaine. Restaurants where he was cheffing were implicated as the sites for some of the deals, and the whole thing was a total mess. Alex was found guilty of money laundering. He didn't do any time, but the damage was done—to his own career, and also to the industry as a whole. It was a public-relations nightmare for Food Network, which was known for being home to these squeaky-clean hosts turning out totally innocuous, wholesome television. Personally, it crushed him. He's still out there cooking today, but he has never quite recaptured the momentum he had in those days.

What was really astounding to all of his peers, and the real wake-up call, was that this wasn't just news that circulated in our little food circle. Alex was by no means the first cook to get into a skirmish with the law (or Uncle

Sam, come tax time). But it was definitely one of the first instances where we read about it in the *Times* rather than hearing it through the restaurant gossip chain. Usually this was the kind of thing that traveled between tired cooks and servers over post-shift drinks. Maybe it made it to the Metro Section, but Florence Fabricant's typical beat didn't exactly include exposing crooked characters and criminal activity.

We all started to realize that this whole fame thing was about a lot more than signing a few menus at the end of dinner service. We were going to need to get our shit together. Staying out all night, stepping out on spouses, screaming at staff—that stuff was media gold. It all scared the shit out of me. The first few times I was stopped in my restaurant or recognized on the street and asked to pose for a photo, I got the message loud and clear. How I carried myself, every little thing that I did, whether I was lighting a cigarette or swearing in public or picking my fucking nose, could all wind up on *Page Six*.

Those were early lessons, and there were other scandals over the years that made their way through the food industry. I managed to keep my nose clean, which I like to believe is because I was truly doing the right things. As a Buddhist, I believe in karma, and that the things you choose to do, whether behind closed doors or in full view of the whole world, will come back to bite you if you're not acting right. I'm also kind of a homebody. I still love me a few glasses of wine, and I like to have a good time, but I want to do it in the comfort of my own home. I'm on the road 250 days a year sometimes, so my time alone or with my family is precious to me. And after all those years of partying, first as a teenager, and then again after my divorce, I think I managed to thoroughly get that shit out of my system. I can tell you I get a hell of a lot more satisfaction and joy out of taking Yuma to a petting zoo than I ever did crushing Presidentes after pulling a double shift. It took a long time, but I finally started to balance what's most important to me.

Then, in the fall of 2017, my business partner, John Besh, was accused of sexual harassment and fostering a culture of sexual harassment in some of his restaurants. The newspapers were thorough in their coverage, and the reporting ran deep. I never did witness any of the behavior he was accused of, but from my years of working in restaurant kitchens, seeing the dynamics between powerful (usually white) men in charge and the women and (often)

minorities who work for them, I knew these accusations had to be taken very seriously, and that a long-overdue reckoning was coming. It was clear that John would have to step down from the business. That's what he did, and I turned my focus immediately to the staff. My number-one priority was taking care of my team, making sure my people felt secure and had a way to come forward with any concerns.

So I called an emergency staff meeting at Johnny Sánchez. I needed to reestablish confidence and directly ask if anyone had *ever* had any issues. What was most important to me was having an open dialogue and making sure everyone in my restaurant felt safe. I needed to let them know that management, myself included, was there for them 24/7—the door was always open. We had a human resources professional lead the conversation, some-one who knew what was up and how to handle the gravity of the situation.

An avalanche of similar stories very, *very* quickly broke in the food world, many of which involved people I'd worked with over the years in kitchens and on screens. More reports from around the country and the world poured from media pages and websites. Major players were stepping down and stepping away from restaurants left and right, issuing statements of apology (some that felt genuine and were effective, others not so much), and then going totally off the grid.

At first, it was hard to watch. Not because I didn't believe that it was deserved. This was all a long time coming, as far as I'm concerned. But it was tough because this business—the people in it—had given me support my entire life. The hospitality industry had been my closest family since I was old enough to carry a sheet tray of cookies for Zarela's Catering. To know it was being poisoned from the inside out nauseated me. I thought of how safe and looked-after I'd felt in so many kitchens in my life. It pained me to accept that the same environments that were so nurturing for me were a waking nightmare for so many others.

Our industry has a black eye, and we need to do everything possible to regain the trust of the people who make it work. As devastating as it was—and continues to be, as more chilling stories surface and the industry scrambles to make sense of it all—I believe #MeToo is absolutely necessary. I have always believed women are essential in restaurant kitchens. And as

a minority in the kitchen, I knew how extra hard they had to work to gain respect. With my mom being a chef and having women in her kitchen, and coming up with so many female chefs who were kicking ass, I always saw it as non-negotiable. I've learned from them, felt they were a grounding force among the clichéd machismo that could take over the kitchen otherwise. So many times, I've been blown away by the skill, tenacity, and talent of my female colleagues—they could cook circles around a lot of the dudes I know.

But I'm definitely ignorant of the struggle. It's no secret that kitchens are male dominated—especially at higher echelons. Studies have been done on the pay inequality and the ratio of women to men in head chef positions. The numbers can't be argued with, and in plain English, they fucking suck. We need to put down our knives for a second and take a serious look at how to create a more equitable world for food industry workers. It's all been going on way too long, and we need to prove to history that our generation is finally doing the right thing in setting a positive course for the future.

My hope is that we start embracing a new philosophy of diversity across the board. I count myself extremely lucky that I've gotten to work in establishments where Latinos weren't just grunt workers. They were chefs and leaders. But my experience is far from the norm. Chefs of color, of different races, backgrounds, genders, and sexual orientations, should all have an equal shot at the top if they've got the talent and the drive. It only makes for a more exciting food scene to have those different voices and points of view in the mix.

I think we're finally seeing evidence of change. It saddens me that it took such unspeakable things to get us here, but it feels like we're on the cusp of a new age. The fame that came so unexpectedly to an industry that was never prepared for it created a vacuum, a space for things to get out of hand. People were thrust into a spotlight who weren't cut out to run multimillion-dollar empires and operations with hundreds of employees relying on them, and it all caught up with them. A major positive outcome of all this negative press is that it lit a fire—it was fucking time to get our act together as an industry. We need more women executive chefs and leaders in the industry. And we can no longer get by on burning people out, bootstrapping restaurants only to issue IOUs as paychecks. We can't get to the next level without strong leaders

who set examples, who have business competence as well as cooking chops. It's no longer an industry staffed by folks on the fringes of society who want to stay out all night, working hard and playing harder, abusing themselves and one another.

So much has been exposed in the last few years that has brought attention to a variety of extremely important issues. For me, there was another personally impactful revelation. I know now that I wasn't alone in experiencing depression and anxiety all those years. That the pressure, the stress both physically and mentally, the isolating hours that made it nearly impossible to maintain relationships with friends and family, the expectations that there was just no way to meet—they all took a toll on my colleagues, too. A number of chefs have given interviews in the last few years, being frank about their struggles with depression, anxiety, and other mental health strains that wreaked such havoc in their lives.

It would have done me a lot of good in my early days, I think, to know it wasn't just me. But no one was talking about things like that. Being "sad" was a sign of weakness. The message, if you weren't just straight-up mocked, was to man the fuck up and get back behind the stove.

Losing Anthony Bourdain in 2018 was was another massive wake-up call. Tony embodied everything about this business: the compassion and curiosity, the empathy that drives a cook to want to care for someone else. Through his writing, he was the first one to expose the world to what was going on in so many commercial kitchens. Then he connected us to the rest of the world throughout his career, telling these stories we could all relate to no matter where we were coming from. Maybe in his passing, he pointed out the most important thing we should be paying attention to: one another.

I'm encouraged now to see some of the changes in restaurants across the board. Chefs aren't staying out all night partying these days. Instead of meeting up for cocktails, they're getting together to train for marathons. Barroom parties have been swapped for trips to farmers' markets. Bottles of scotch for kale and spinach smoothies. Between shifts, dining rooms are converted to makeshift yoga studios where employees are invited to free classes, and restaurant groups are prioritizing health care packages. In general, there is finally a gentler, kinder idea of how to conduct a kitchen.

I take a lot of cues from this new generation of cooks. They're coming in with ideas about cool new dishes they've seen on TV or read about online, but they've also got great thoughts about a new restaurant culture, and how we can borrow ideas from other industries to create a sustainable future for our workers. I hope I have always provided a nurturing environment for my staff, one that my mom would be proud of, like the one she created for her own team. Because that's the soul and spirit of the hospitality industry. After all, how can we take care of our guests if we don't first take care of each other?

EPILOGUE

WHERE I COME FROM . . . AND WHERE I'M GOING

The slower pace of a Louisiana lifestyle has really agreed with me. Living here has been an opportunity to reflect, at a time in my life when I felt ready to take a step back and look at the bigger picture.

It's not that I slowed down personally, exactly. In fact, in some ways, I think I'm working now more than ever; it's just a different blend of activities. I'm shooting *MasterChef* and running the restaurant, plus traveling for events and endorsement gigs—all things that fill the hours when I can't spend time with my son. I'm still super busy, but my priorities have changed. Maybe part of that is being a father; something changes in you after you have a kid. You become more interested in helping others develop than chasing whatever new food trend is making waves.

I started understanding the idea of limitations and responsibilities later in my career. I have a better grasp now on what is possible for a chef, and what is possible for me. I also began really thinking about legacy, and what we all leave behind. As I've said, I believe a chef's responsibility is to leave the industry a little better than the way we found it. My mom's legacy is evident every time someone opens a new regional Mexican restaurant. So I had to make some decisions about the mark I wanted to make.

I hope my food makes an impression for my diners. I hope they leave my restaurants with a memory and a meaningful experience that sticks with them. But I realized what I really wanted to leave behind was not just an elevated understanding and value of Latin food, but a way to help further the lives and careers of the young Latino and Latina cooks who aspire to

be a part of this business, and who will continue to do the same in their own ways.

I was extremely fortunate that my mom was a chef and that I was initiated into the food world so early, and that someone like Chef Paul took me under his wing. I got to go to culinary school, and even though I didn't complete the program then, I know how valuable that education can be, especially as the industry becomes more competitive and discerning.

I've seen too many Latinos get stuck with shit jobs in the kitchen, when they could even get a gig at all. I have always done my best to make sure my hiring practices were inclusive of everyone, regardless of race, gender, background, or sexual orientation. Talent is talent. Skill is skill. Reliability is reliability. But the impact I can make with my own restaurants is limited, and I wanted to figure out how I could make a bigger one.

So in 2016, my team and I sat down to discuss my next big project: the Aarón Sánchez Scholarship Fund. The idea was to partner with the International Culinary Center in New York to arrange full rides for one recipient annually, selected from the Latino community. To date, we've had three awardees, and my only wish is that we could have sent all the kids who applied for a shot. I was astounded by the talent, the raw drive, and heart coming from these applicants. Choosing from this pool has been one of the hardest things I've ever had to do in my career.

I can't explain how rewarding it's been to prioritize the Aarón Sánchez Scholarship Fund (ASSF). It feels good to accomplish something, but there's nothing better than being able to help someone else, someone you believe in, and watch them succeed. The way I see it, if I'm not giving back in some way, then everything I'm doing with my life is for myself. I got into this business not just because I love to cook, but because I have always loved to take care of people. There's nothing more intimate than cooking for another person, than feeding them. That was what appealed to me when I was young and watched my mom making meals for family and friends, sharing food with truckers or New York City trendsetters. I wanted to find other ways to take care of my community. Teaching them directly, passing on the knowledge I've accumulated in my three decades of work, and helping them grow through this organized education felt like a new way for me to accomplish that goal.

Knowledge is power. I learned that in the days my mom took my brother and me to museums, or to outer-borough restaurants, to expand our palates and deepen our understanding of other cultures and the world around us. I knew it every time someone interviewing me for a job asked if I spoke Spanish. It was invaluable when it came time to cast a new TV show, and the host had to teach viewers something, whether culinary or cultural. I want to help a new generation understand that power, help them become armed and prepared for whatever the industry throws at them. Although none of us can possibly predict the challenges or opportunities ahead of us, what I do know is that skill, compassion, dedication, and education will always be valuable and will never go to waste.

* * *

These days, my life is still pretty hectic. But what I want for myself and my family is on a lot more even keel. I still daydream about restaurants I want to open, shows I want to create. I cook a lot, but a lot more at home, for my loved ones. I never expected to make this many grilled cheese sandwiches, but Yuma can't seem to get enough of them, and who am I to argue with an eight-year-old's palate?

I think a lot about how I can create a future for my family, and also for my team. I want them to feel cared for, to give them the employment experience that they deserve. One that makes them feel they have job security and benefits, and a chance to express themselves. I need them to be creatively satisfied, so they stay engaged and keep me on my toes, too. And I want to help them achieve their dreams. That means exploring new concepts and ways to partner with some of my younger cooks, to help them realize their own culinary voices and get their own ideas off the ground—while letting them teach me a thing or two in the process.

I still love to travel. I believe it's one of the most important ways to learn, grow, and connect with the world. I can't wait to take Yuma to Mexico and show him where his grandparents came from. But I have taken him to El Paso, and I let him know that Daddy's life started out there, too. I think a lot about my experience at Día de los Muertos all those years ago, especially

every November when Yuma and I put a photo of my dad on the *ofrenda*. In Mexican culture, we keep the spirits of our loved ones alive; as long as we remain in the memories of those we love and who love us, we will live on. A dish may be delicious, but what I have always hoped to leave behind me is an impression not only on people's palates, but in their hearts. This can't be done just by creating great food; it requires making human connections.

I still struggle with depression and anxiety. I know it's probably a life-long battle for me, but I manage it better than ever. I know my triggers and I have strategies that help me cope. I also know that I need to be aware of Yuma's experience, to watch him for any signs of his own struggle, to make sure that no matter what he goes through, no matter who he loves or what path he chooses to take, he will always be loved, cared for, and supported.

My biggest source of pain these days is the thought of how much I have to be away from him. I know it's never really enough time, even though I try to tell myself it is. His life has echoes of my own, having such limited time with my dad. So when we are together, I try to make up for it. I make sure I always show him affection. I hug him and kiss him (which he probably can't stand right now), and I hold his hand or put my hand on his back to let him know I'm always right there.

I try always to be teaching him something, too, but honestly a lot of the time I feel like I am maybe learning more from him. It's important to me that he stay connected to his heritage, that he learn Spanish, that he see Mexico. I tell him stories about his grandfather, and of course I always remind him what an amazing woman his grandmother is. I'll teach him to cook, if that's what he wants to learn. I'll make sure he knows how to treat women, and men, and people in general. How to do right by others and the importance of karma.

I want to make sure he has a relationship with his family and is always surrounded by people who show him the same kind of love, on both my and Ife's sides. I want him to feel safe, secure, and at home. I want him to know where he comes from, and that it doesn't have to be tied to Los Angeles or New Orleans, or anywhere else for that matter. That home is in the people around him, what he holds in his heart and how he carries himself, and how he treats others.

Because where I come from is not a place, it's an idea. It's family, it's a heritage rich in history and culture. It's a belief that being a good person, and looking out for others—really connecting with them—will always be the most rewarding, fulfilling, and soul-satisfying place to be.

I don't know exactly where I'm going next, but as long as I have that in mind, I know I'll always be right at home.

ACKNOWLEDGMENTS

In telling this story, my hope has always been to provide inspiration to others, to offer a light and a blueprint—a reason to believe that anything is possible.

This in turn wouldn't have been possible without everyone who has made an invaluable contribution to what has been an incredible journey. I want to express my deepest, most sincere gratitude to each and every one of them.

To my son, Yuma: You are my legacy, my heart, and the reason I try to better myself every day. You bring infectious joy to my world with your love for life itself. As a Buddhist, my responsibility is to make sure you surpass my own accomplishments. I have no doubt you will effortlessly achieve that.

To my dad, Adolfo: You were taken from us far too early, but you remain with me every day. I am the man I have become because you battled so much. You were a true trailblazer, a man who never complained and did what he knew needed to be done for his family. That's the example I aim to follow.

To my mother, Zarela: Thank you for making and providing such a beautiful life for our family. Your unrelenting pursuit of your own dreams has been an example I have always attempted to mirror. I have kept your journey in mind when it has come to my own, whether that means being the best chef, parent, or person I can be. You're my biggest fan and toughest critic, and I hope I have made you proud with this book.

To my twin, Rodrigo: You have been there throughout my life and never wavered in your love for me. I'm so proud of that the man and father you have become.

To my sister, Marissa: Thank you for your grace, laughter, and unparalleled love. The Paladar years will stay with me forever. Your amazing work was a magic ingredient that helped make that restaurant truly special.

To my older brother, Spanky, and his wife, Mary: for keeping El Paso—the place where we were born—a constant presence in my life, and for always sharing your family's love.

To Tio Mario: for always watching my back and helping me stay humble, for being there during some of the most difficult and beautiful parts of my life.

To Charity: for your constant support, for being there during this entire process, for always keeping a smile on my face. The meaning of your love is beyond words.

To Andrew and Danielle: for constantly watching my back. Working together over these last ten years has been so fruitful; you've allowed me to have a better quality of life, encouraged and supported me, and helped me find my full potential in so many ways. Thank you for listening, for sticking with me through different periods of my life, and for all the success.

To Cait Hoyt: for shepherding this book. To Michael Sand: for being a supportive, visionary editor who believed in the value of my story.

To Kate Floberg: for all you do, from the simplest things to the most important—your grace and spirit has added a special ingredient to the recipe of my life.

To Chef Paul Prudhomme: for teaching me what a mentor truly is. I don't believe I would have known how to assume that role myself without your generous heart, tough love, and thoughtful guidance when I needed it most. You taught me how to be a man at a young age, and your lessons saved my life.

To Chef Jonathan Waxman, my chef father: for always allowing me to laugh, for making sure that we don't take what we do too seriously and don't get overwhelmed, and for demonstrating that our job is about making others happy. You taught me to constantly look at life and the journey before us as an opportunity to grow and to always be better.

To Jimmy Bradley: for giving me an opportunity as a young kid who was way in over his head. You took a chance on me, and I will be eternally grateful for that recognition in an early part of my career.

To Chef Douglas Rodriguez: for teaching me the art, elegance, and sophistication of Latino cuisine, for elevating it from something cooked in the home to an art worthy of those three stars and then some. Your

inspiration, vision, and guidance gave me a true foundation in Latin flavors and techniques.

To Octavio Mantilla, my business partner: for teaching me so much and maintaining the business side of our restaurants so I could focus on the food. I'm deeply grateful for your friendship and our partnership.

To Chef Mark Miller: for making me a student of cuisine, helping me to understand its roots and cultural impact. I'll always be grateful to you for teaching me an academic approach to cooking, and how to truly taste food.

To Chef Emeril Lagasse: for your constant friendship and your larger-than-life personality. Your humbleness and unbelievable talent have been hugely inspiring to my life. You're truly a star.

To Chef Gordon Ramsay: for giving me great insight into my own value. You've made me understand that the impact we can have goes far beyond food. I've learned so much from you in our brief working and personal relationship, and I feel blessed to have you in my life.

To Ted Allen and my entire *Chopped* family (you know who you are): We've known each other for so many years, and I'm thrilled that we've been able to share in one another's successes. You've all impacted me in different ways both personally and professionally. I love my *Chopped* fam, and I hope I've made it clear how special you are and how dearly I hold all of you.

To Chef Miles Landrem: for your talent and your stewardship of our restaurant and ideas, for all our trips on the road together: Having you in my corner, as an ambassador of our vision, has been a blessing. I believe in you, and I know the future for our work together is a bright one.

To Rémy Robert: for your amazing work interpreting and re-creating the recipes in this book and capturing the essence of some of the most important times in my life.

To Stef Ferrari: Thank you for being my partner in crime in telling my story. Your unequaled professional approach and passion, and your talent in being able to extract so many poignant and intense moments, has made this an amazing process. I can't thank you enough for the star power you have brought to this project.